ETHOS AND EDUCATION IN GREEK MUSIC

ETHOS AND EDUCATION IN GREEK MUSIC

THE EVIDENCE OF POETRY AND PHILOSOPHY

Warren D. Anderson

HARVARD UNIVERSITY PRESS

CAMBRIDGE, MASSACHUSETTS

Second Printing, 1968

Distributed in Great Britain by Oxford University Press, London

Publication of this volume has been aided by a grant from the Ford Foundation.

Library of Congress Catalog Card Number 66-21328

Printed in the United States of America

PREFACE

In this book I have attempted to examine the thought of Greek poets and philosophers on the ethical and paideutic aspects of music. With one exception, my examination has been limited to writers of the Hellenic period. Concerning later developments beyond Philodemus I have not thought myself qualified to comment, though their importance for the shaping of Western musical thought might well merit separate treatment by a specialist. While I have drawn upon the work of musicologists, I cannot pretend that the present study makes any contribution to their field. It has been described as a chapter in the history of ideas: readers may be aided by bearing in mind this description and the limitations I have mentioned.

Among many debts which I gladly acknowledge here, the greatest is to Professor R. P. Winnington-Ingram, who commands a knowledge of Greek music possessed by no other scholar of our time. He kindly read an earlier version of the manuscript and also criticized the introductory chapter when it was nearing final form. The faults which remain are entirely my own responsibility; but I should be glad if this study proved to justify in some measure his continuing cordial interest, for which I am deeply grateful.

At various stages of the writing Professor Cedric H. Whitman gave his counsel with the greatest generosity and scholarly insight. I could not omit to note here, however inadequately, my appreciation of all his good offices. It is fitting also to recall with gratitude the helpful comments of the late Professor Werner W. Jaeger, master interpreter of paideia, who supervised the writing of this work in its very different original form as a doctoral thesis.

PREFACE

For permission to reproduce Figures 1-5 of *Das Musikleben der Griechen* (Berlin, 1949) my thanks to the author, Professor Max Wegner, and to the publishers, Walter de Gruyter & Co. The staff of the Andrews Memorial Library at the College of Wooster helped me secure many indispensable works on inter-library loan. The task of final revision was made possible chiefly through two research leaves granted in 1958-59 and 1963-64, when I had an opportunity to make extensive use of the general and music collections at the University of Michigan, Stanford University, and the University of London.

W.D.A.

Wooster, Ohio
August 1966

CONTENTS

ETHOS AND EDUCATION IN GREEK MUSIC

CHAPTER I

INTRODUCTION

Music was everywhere present in the Greek world. Schooling and religious ceremonial, public and private festivity constantly embodied it. The civic theaters were places not of the spoken word alone but of the word sung—of hymn, paean, and dithyramb given added dimension by sounding instruments and the movement of the dance.[1] All well-omened ritual, whether of the temple or of ordinary life, had its musical element. As the consort of poetry, music was at once the vehicle and the determinant of cultural patterns. Through it the Hellene encountered both tradition and innovation from childhood onward, for singing, dancing, and the use of strings or reed pipes gave much of Greek poetry its indispensable setting.

This setting demanded from performer and listener alike more profound responses than are known to Western man today, and the attempt to recreate any total experience from a reading of Greek literature is bound to fail. Moreover, we find ourselves frustrated for another reason. A vital part of the experience has become unavailable: Greek music is lost. A single specimen of text and notation, the papyrus fragment of a choral passage from Euripides' *Orestes*, may conceivably suggest musical practices during the Hellenic age; and at best this evidence reflects a specific period characterized by violent changes of style.[2] Only disconnected references to the subject occur earlier than about the year 388, when Plato wrote his *Republic*. Of the extant treatises on music, none antedates the close of the Hellenic period; most are much later. To add to the difficulty, the evidence we do possess often proves puzzling and continues to be interpreted in sharply varying ways.

The writers of Greece who represent Hellenic thought on music supposed that it could express, and even generate, qualities of good or evil: the present work deals with their beliefs concerning music's power. To this real or imagined power intellectuals of Socrates' generation gave the name ethos (our term is a transliteration with much the same meaning), and its close associations with modality thereupon came under objective analysis.[3] We shall be dealing also with the term paideia, another transliterated form. This designates the Greek cultural and ethical experience; it is not by any means limited to education in the formal sense. A study of the close connection between musical ethos and paideia, a relationship which prompted much speculation during antiquity, has seemed a promising approach. It will be convenient first to review the musical resources and practices of the Hellenic period, from the time of the pre-Socratic thinkers to Aristotle's death in 322.

Perhaps the first, and certainly the most basic, of all musical instruments is the human voice, consciously used to express patterns of sustained pitch and rhythm. Although the Greeks differed little from us in vocal range, their notation and modal systems cannot be explained on modern assumptions. The concept of high and low modality remained relative; the notational symbols give no such closed, precise scheme as the devices of staff, clef, middle C, and concert pitch provide for us.

Choral music was performed in unison. Of course a group which combined different ages or sexes necessarily sang in octaves, as a cathedral choir must today if it attempts a unison line, but apparently the rule was not further modified. What we understand by vocal harmony did not exist. One explanation for this lies in the fact that singers often had to be dancers as well. Only a stationary chorus can hope to establish vertical tone relationships securely. A dance group such as the citizen chorus of Attic drama, with every member moving his entire body in obedience to intricate patterns that required weeks of full-time training, will find it a sufficiently demanding task to execute a melodic line with precision.

Throughout most of the fifth century this line remained uncomplicated. If a later tradition is trustworthy, only one note might be sung to any given syllable. Yet the convention, real or supposed, came to be openly ignored during the century's closing decades: Aristophanes more than once attacks the flourishes and general extravagance of contemporary vocal performances. What lends credibility to the principle of one note to a syllable is the fact that musical settings previously had remained subordinate to the text. Their function had been to present it with enhanced clarity and effectiveness; any other contribution they might make could claim only secondary importance. No one before Aristotle is known to have formulated a distinctively aesthetic approach to music.

A further point concerns the rising and falling of the voice. Classical Greek had a system of tonic accent distinguished by actual variations in pitch. Among the symbols devised by Alexandrian scholars the acute accent mark indicates an original heightening, the grave accent a lowering, the circumflex a combined rise and fall. Such a language contains its own melody, the *logôdes melos* or "speech melody" attributed to Greek even as late as the time of Augustus. Pitch accent thus may have played some part in shaping melodic contour; and though a number of the extant examples of postclassical Greek music do show a notable degree of correspondence between the two, we cannot therefore suppose that any such strict correspondence existed during the classical period.[4]

The most familiar stringed instruments are those popularly referred to as lyres. For the time being it is necessary to delimit this term, recognizing the variety of names that describe the lyre family. One must make distinctions among the (true) lyre, kithara, kitharis, phorminx, and barbiton; in this task the following descriptions may be helpful (see Figs. 1-5).

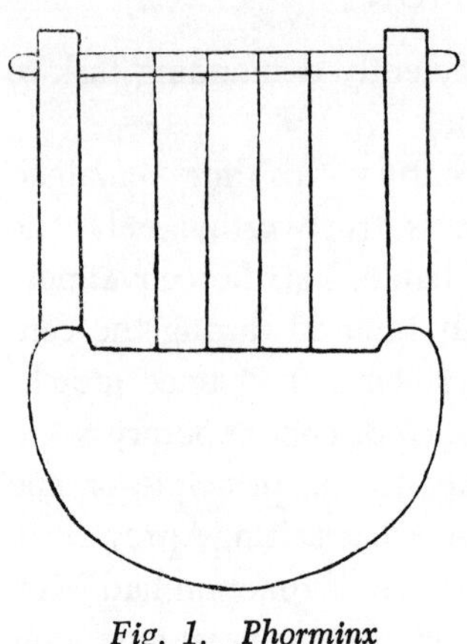

Fig. 1. Phorminx

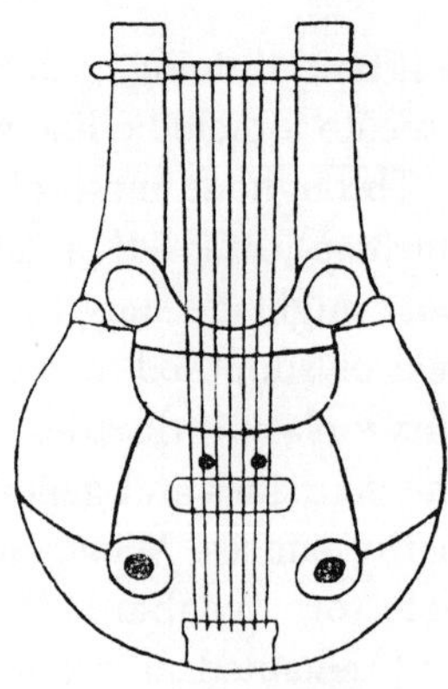

Fig. 2. Cradle Kithara

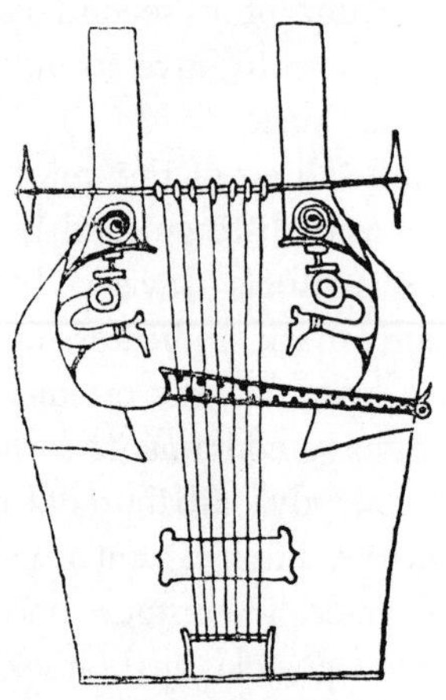

Fig. 3. Kithara

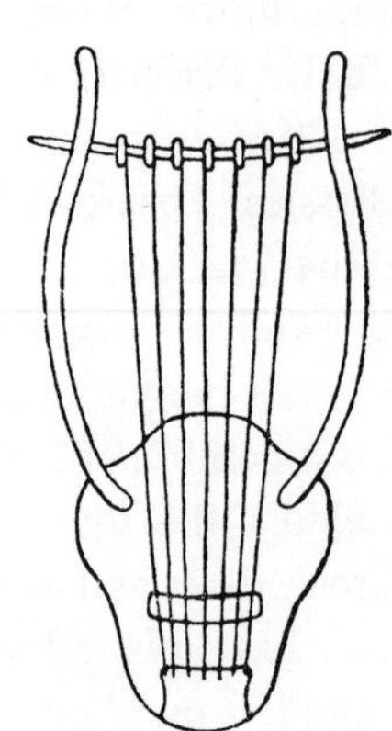

Fig. 4. Lyre

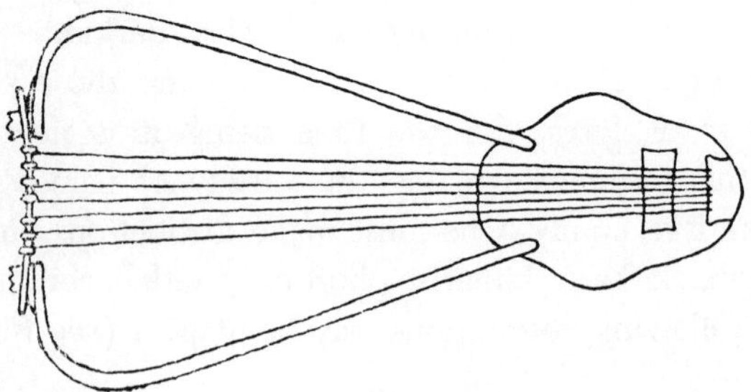

Fig. 5. Barbiton

The phorminx is Homer's instrument. At no time does he call it by any other name in the *Iliad,* and throughout the *Odyssey* he does so only once. Neither poem mentions kitharas or lyres. The term *kitharis* referring to an instrument occurs only in *Odyssey* 1.153, where it is synonymous with *phorminx;* elsewhere the word apparently refers to playing on the phorminx. The fragmentary evidence from Homer and the ampler testimony of eighth-century art show a U-shaped instrument with a large, semicircular sound chest. Its arms, at first straight and in most cases roughly parallel, came to be outcurving extensions of the sound chest. Between them, slightly below their tips, ran a horizontal rod. This was the yoke: it secured four strings (occasionally artists showed three or five), and possibly at some quite early date it came to be rotated with terminal grips as an ensemble tuning device.

The whole question of stringing and of tuning up or down remains a mystery. Homer (*Od.* 21.406-9) says that Odysseus strung his great bow as easily as a skilled musician fits a new string on a phorminx. This surely suggests a rapid, deft procedure. It does not accord with Eustathius' explanation in his commentary on the *Odyssey*: whereas Homer speaks only of looping the gut string at either end, the commentary mentions added fittings called *kollopes,* strips of cowhide or sheepskin with the fat left on the hide. They were wound onto the yoke with the strings and somehow held them fast. Nubian musicians still use this primitive, inefficient technique in playing the *kissar,* a lyre named for the kithara. The arrangement hardly seems adequate for the intense musical activity of fifth-century Greece; yet many vase paintings clearly show some kind of wrapping around the upper end of each kithara string. There existed also a type of yoke fitted with numerous studs for making fast the strings. Unfortunately no early evidence attests to its use, while pegs like those on modern stringed instruments were a Greco-Roman innovation. One would think it impossible, nevertheless, that any system involving so clumsy a device as the *kollopes* should have made available the exquisitely nuanced intervals described by later theorists.[5]

Apparently performers on the phorminx remained seated; the actual techniques employed are, for the most part, still under dispute. It was the prototype (perhaps in use rather than in actual development) of the professional's instrument; perhaps it was already professional. Among Homer's performers all but one or two of those who play the phorminx are bards, or at any rate public entertainers. The only notable exception is Achilles, and it is clear that the beautifully inlaid specimen which he has acquired from the spoils must once have been the treasured possession of some professional musician.

The rounded phorminx was replaced by the flat-bottomed instrument known to Greek literature after Homer by the name *kithara,* though poets were still using the old term *phorminx* in the later fifth century. Asiatic influence quite possibly accounted for the change of shape; details remain uncertain. The introduction of a seven-stringed Asiatic lyre by Terpander, a seventh-century poet from Lesbos, may have established the new squared shape along with the increased number of strings (which by a natural extension came to characterize the lyre as well). It may also have brought about a corollary development of the old Homeric phorminx into the round-bottomed instrument now known, from its shape, as the *Wiegenkithara* or "cradle kithara."

The squared-off concert kithara was new in other respects than mere outline. Its sound chest had become relatively larger, and the area of resonance now extended upward into the massive arms, which Cicero compares (somewhat unpoetically) to the nasal canals.[6] Throughout the classical period it had a normal complement of seven strings. The octave relationship which we make explicit in our scale therefore regularly remained implicit in kithara tunings. There is indeed reason to think that originally, and for some considerable time after its appearance in Pythagorean thought, the octave had importance only as it served to express the string-length ratio 2:1.[7] On the other hand, a feeling for the fundamental consonance of the octave—so the Greeks themselves described it—seems to be common to all peoples.

Unlike its Homeric predecessor, the concert kithara might be played either with the fingers alone or with a plectrum.[8] Works of art from the classical period usually show it in the hands of performers who are standing, not sitting; they support its weight by a leather band bracing the left arm.[9] Its widened compass and added refinements make the kithara relate to the earlier phorminx somewhat as the modern concert harp compares with the Anglo-Saxon *hearp.* Neither women nor children had access to it, so far as we can tell, though women used the cradle kithara.

In contrast, the lyre was light enough to be used by schoolboys for their music lessons, or by women who wished to entertain themselves. The form of its sound chest recalled its mythical origin, the carapace of a tortoise; its arms, unlike those of the kithara, were slender and added nothing to the resonance, which cannot have been great. Among the Greeks it bore the specific name of chelys, which means tortoise; German musicologists have named it the *Schildkrötenleier* or tortoise lyre. We may call it the true lyre, for Apollo regularly has this instrument when he is shown holding a lyre rather than a kithara.

Manifestly different from the Apolline lyre is the barbiton. Its sound chest, proportionately smaller, presented the same tortoise-shell outline. The real difference lies in the shape and length of the arms. These were bowed out wider than the body in long, graceful curves that turned suddenly toward the yoke, suggesting the profile of an inverted beaker. The vase painters showed Dionysus with the barbiton and frequently represented his ecstatic followers as playing or holding it; scholars have therefore termed it the Dionysiac lyre.[10] If we may judge from references in Anacreon, the gay Ionians favored it; certainly it was the instrument of Sappho and Alcaeus.

Other stringed instruments such as the trigonon and pektis belong to the harp family. Their sole importance for our inquiry lies in their extended compass and consequent capacity for modulation, features which made Plato account them a menace (*Rep.* 399c10-d1). On all other counts they are a part of the periphery of Greek music.

One need mention only a small group of wind instruments, dominated and all but overwhelmed by the aulos. The term "flute" is inadmissible: the aulos had a reed mouthpiece like that found on an oboe, not the right-angled aperture of a modern concert flute. Whereas kitharas and lyres seem always to have been of wooden construction, an aulos maker could also use cane (the normal material), ivory, metal, or bone. Choice of material altered the timbre somewhat, as did the various methods of trimming the reed. It does not appear, however, that tone was affected in any noticeable degree. Only professional soloists used a single pipe; the customary form was that of the double aulos, two separate tubes and reed mouthpieces. The function of the second pipe remains unknown. No direct evidence supports the conjecture that it accompanied the melody with a bourdon, or drone bass. Except for the *tibiae impares* of the so-called Phrygian aulos, the double aulos had pipes of the same length. The scale may have been divided between them; the compass must at any rate have been the same potentially, however it was employed in actual performance. While we do not know whether the pipes sounded together or separately, scholars have generally chosen one possibility or the other. Actually both techniques may have been used by the same performer on the same occasion: blocking the bore of a pipe with the tongue would not have been particularly difficult.

Even more than the barbiton, this double aulos was the instrument of Dionysus' followers and worshippers. The distinction between Apolline lyre or kithara (for both were in Apollo's province) and Dionysiac aulos has engaged men's thought since the Hellenic age. It has symbolized the conflict between indigenous and Oriental patterns of culture, between sobriety and ecstasy, reason and unreason. As a servant of Dionysus the aulete accompanied every performance of a tragedy, comedy, or satyr play with his double pipes.[11] At any well-omened sacrifice his presence was considered equally necessary; yet aulos music could be thoroughly secular, enlivening a supper party with the skill of girl performers.

Far different was the syrinx or shepherd's panpipe. The form which has pipes graduated according to length has a familiar place today among civilized Western peoples as well as among primitives. We are less well acquainted with the characteristic Greek type, in which the pipes measured the same overall but varied in their effective speaking length as wax stopped up a greater or smaller portion of the bore.[12] Unlike the aulos, syrinx pipes had no mouthpiece. This extremely ancient instrument, which has existed ever since the early Neolithic period, was not admitted to the dramatic or the purely musical competitions. Aeschylus and Euripides praise it, however, and Plato allowed its use in the pasturelands of his imagined city-state. The performer blew across the top of his reed tubes, producing notes almost devoid of overtones: it was a colorless, unexciting music that Plato presumably thought quite unlikely to cause any dangerous agitation within the soul. As the herdsman's instrument it had no associations with social occasions or religious ritual, whether orgiastic or tranquil. The modern conception of the pipes of Pan that could rouse man or beast to frenzy has no factual basis, though "panic" fear is in itself a well-attested ancient conception.

Other instruments require little comment. As actually used, the salpinx or trumpet was no more a musical instrument than were its descendants, the long banner-carrying trumpets of medieval Europe.[13] The crotala, cymbala, and tympanon were percussion devices, as they are now. Associated originally with orgiastic cult, particularly the rites of Dionysus, they became secularized as rhythmic dance accompaniments for light entertainment. Only the crotala or clappers appear to have been widely used. Finally, the flood of foreign instruments that entered Greece mainly during the postclassical period bore no positive relation either to ethical or to paideutic factors. The negative significance of two earlier importations, the trigonon and pektis, has already been mentioned.

Of the three chief instruments, neither the lyre nor the far more powerful kithara could project a melody incisively or with carrying power. The aulos, on the other hand, seems to have had a remarkably shrill tone in its upper register and a curiously penetrating one even in the lower, combining bagpipe and oboe sonorities. The notes of a kithara or lyre died away quickly yet were individually distinct, capable of punctuating a rhythm with precision. While an aulete could sustain his notes indefinitely if necessary,[14] he commanded no real staccato; during a performance of drama the chorus leader had to give the beat with a wooden clapper fixed to his sandal, since the singing and dancing choristers could not get it from the aulos accompaniment alone. Finally, the lyre held a place of high honor in elementary schooling, which consisted largely of learning to sing the cherished poetry of antiquity to one's own accompaniment. Since this ruled out any wind instrument, the aulos normally had no paideutic role. The Athenians did introduce it into the curriculum after the Persian Wars, but this innovation lasted only about twenty-five years. Broadly speaking, one may say that a freeborn man studied the lyre; any theory of modality which depends upon the aulos is suspect.

Rhythms used in singing and playing would require a separate study, and evidence bearing on rhythmic ethos is comparatively limited.[15] The rhythm of a sung text varied according to the duration of the various syllables which made up the words of that text. No musical "time" existed, as we understand that term; thus there were none of the false accents which so richly furnish forth our hymnals. By customary definition (though the etymology is disputed) rhythm is movement: the way a man moved seemed to the Greeks to be meaningfully related to his character. It is only natural that the various rhythms should have been described in terms of ethos. We shall be dealing with rhythmic ethos principally during the discussion of Plato's theories, where some attention to detail becomes necessary.

No aspect of Greek music is more puzzling than modality, nor has any occasioned greater disagreement. Comparative evidence enables us to assume with some confidence that two features, well attested in other cultures, characterized early Greece as well. First, each of the modes must originally have been a separate phenomenon, with no more than coincidental resemblances to any other mode. Moreover, each presumably originated through the association of those notes which characterized the singing of a particular group of persons. Perhaps the pattern originated unconsciously; sooner or later the singers became aware of it. This unknown, unknowable moment of realization marks the birth of the mode as a force in musical expression, and in ethical expression as well.

Concerning the earliest form of the tone relationships involved we know nothing; but they constitute only one part of modality. Among the other aspects, timbre and bodily movement have their own rightful claims to attention. The theorists of later times ignored both: it is unlikely that either would have seemed irrelevant to an educated Hellene.

The nature of the Greek modes during their first developed stages thus remains almost entirely outside the range of present-day knowledge. All that has come down from any really early period is a group of ethnic mode names: Dorian, Phrygian, Lydian. While these are taken as basic (the first two more clearly so than the third), still other names such as Aeolian had become well established before the fifth century. In the original group Phrygian and Lydian show the assimilation of foreign influences. Their accommodation to Greek ways of expression presupposes some scheme to which they were made to conform, becoming less distinctively Oriental. Tonality and scale structure assuredly cannot have provided more than a part of such a scheme. The reason for our speculating on these factors more than any others, here and elsewhere, is that the rest are so often irretrievably lost. From the theorists we have inherited a conception of modality as static: the great need is to bring this dead world to life.

Among primitive peoples vocal tone systems arise independently of instrumental tunings and differ markedly from them, using the pure fifth. M. Schneider points out that the vocal structure or scale pattern which emerges is very largely based on a series of such fifths. He goes on to draw a significant inference: "The fact that the keys formed from the series of fifths are so much closer than most of the primitive instrumental tunings to our European musical sense can probably be explained only by supposing that the vocal tone-system has been evolved in a natural and specifically musical fashion, whereas in the tuning of instruments (which are an artificial product) quite different principles were applied."[16]

There has been a tendency, even among specialists, to assume that in a preinstrumental culture the voice is not entirely equal to the task of grasping and accurately reproducing the patterns and intervals of the tone system. This belief may well be mistaken. While Greek musical culture is instrumental as far back as it can be traced, certain aboriginal peoples even today have not advanced beyond the possibilities of the voice; and the remarkably precise, systematic nature of what they have achieved at that level has only now begun to gain general attention.[17] What the history of Greek music does show is a series of situations which present the instrumental tradition as sharply differentiated from the vocal, or even contending with it. If we could command the facts necessary for a thorough study of this distinction, our knowledge of modality might be much less shadowy.

The early musical history of the Greek mainland may have seen the second of Schneider's patterns of development supplant the first. There can be no reasonable doubt, at any rate, that lyre and aulos brought increasing orderliness to musical practice. As the price of progress, the modes suffered a partial obscuring of those highly individual characteristics which they had once possessed as vocal patterns. On the other hand, the fact that they acquired new principles of individuation partially offset the loss. But we do not really know what the modes were like, either before or after their transformation had begun. Eventually, by a process which must have entailed striking alterations, the dimensions of their intervals taken as units or unit multiples admitted a common standard of measurement.

Scattered evidence suggests that this process was still going on as late as the first part of the fourth century. Nevertheless, the documented ages of Hellenic history provide no adequate documentation for modality. Detailed accounts become available no earlier than the Greco-Roman period, when a complex interlocking pattern had reached final form. No one supposes that the theorists' diagrams reproduce the modes known to Pindar or Aristophanes or even Plato; yet it is almost invariably to a late period that we must turn for data. This rule admits only one notable exception: Aristoxenus, who studied with Aristotle and whose *floruit* comes less than a generation after Plato's death in 347.

Aristoxenus based his presentation on a theoretical structure of quite recent origin, though presumably inherited. This was the so-called Greater Complete (or Perfect) System, a fifteen-note diatonic sequence of whole tones and semitones. The white keys from A to a′ on the piano will represent it well enough for purposes of rough illustration, but we must not think of the pattern as a double octave occupying a specific range of absolute pitch. Aristoxenus saw it in terms of tetrachordal groups composed of notes with entirely abstract pitch. The second through the eighth ascending degrees of this extended scale served as starting points for sequences named after one or another of the modes. But the old modal term Harmonia (a "fitting together" or "arrangement") no longer appears; Aristoxenus' sequences now bear the name of *eidê*, "species" of the octave. The accompanying diagram illustrates the grouping of tetrachords and gives the Greek names for the scale steps comprising them, with conventional approximations—actually about a minor third higher—to the notes of our scale.

The treatises tell also of a Lesser Complete System, composed of Proslambanomenos and tetrachords Hypaton and Meson plus a tetrachord called Synemmenon. The latter began conjunctly, on Mese; its components—Trite, Paranete, Nete—have the conventionalized note values of b flat, c, and d. Tetrachord Diezeugmenon by contrast begins disjunctly, on Paramese rather than Mese, and the note b which it includes is natural, not flatted. The two systems taken together form the Perfect Immutable (or Changeless) System, which did not figure in musical theory until long after the time of Aristoxenus.

Within the Greater Complete System the octave-species were

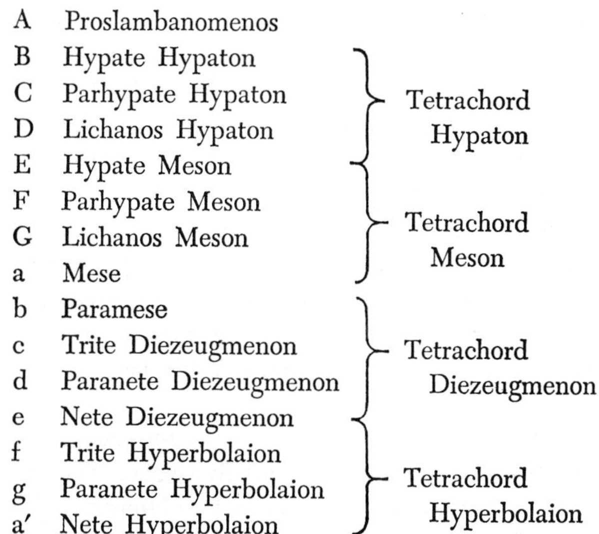

echeloned at whole-tone or semitone intervals as follows: Mixolydian, B—b; Lydian, C—c; Phrygian, D—d; Dorian, E—e; Hypolydian, F—f; Hypophrygian, G—g; Hypodorian, a—a′. Here the Greek scale steps are represented by notes of our scale according to the conventionally accepted pitch relationship, as in the preceding diagram. Sol-fa notation or perhaps an unequally barred staff would have been more accurate, but the correctness of the identifications has no great importance: they are only approximations in any case. One aspect of pitch, however, should be mentioned here. By the closing decades of the fourth century a system of Tonoi had come into use. Considered in its technical sense the word *tonos,* literally the "stretching" of a lyre string, has usually been thought to designate a pitch-key. According to this hypothesis the Perfect Immutable System was taken at varying levels of pitch, ranging through fifteen basic notes or Proslambanomenoi spaced a semitone apart. Aristoxenus refers to these tunings by modal names, actually the Harmoniai names which the octave-species had inherited. The sequence of Tonoi reversed the order of the octave-species in the three systems previously mentioned, presumably to make any desired scale pattern available in a gamut suiting the individual singer or the group. At the upper end of the sequence three of Aristoxenus' thirteen Tonoi were eventually renamed as Hyperphrygian, Hyperiastian, and Hyperdorian. Theorists later added two new pitch-keys, Hyperaeolian and Hyperlydian; the latter merely reduplicated Hypophrygian an octave higher. A gamut of over three octaves resulted, providing for the differing vocal compasses of men, women, and boys, and also for instruments which had an extensive range.

The final result was a tidy sequence of three groups arranged by semitones, each group containing five Tonoi. The old Harmoniai names were central: Dorian, Iastian (Ionian), Phrygian, Aeolian, and Lydian, beginning on b flat, b, c, c sharp, and d respectively. The same names in the same order, prefaced by "Hypo-" or "Hyper-," identified the groups placed at either end of the sequence. The former represented a semitone series of initial notes from F to a, the latter a series from e flat to g. From the tables of symbols provided by Alypius, a writer of the third or fourth century after Christ, we know that schemes of vocal and instrumental notation came to be based on this total gamut (F—g) with its succession of fifteen Tonoi, each reproducing the Perfect Immutable System and each taken in the various genera (see below).

Such is the generally accepted interpretation. Proponents of one important minority view deny that the Tonoi were pitch-keys and find fourth-century thought preserved in the modal complex of Ptolemy (Claudius Ptolemaeus, *floruit* A.D. 140 or 150), whose Tonoi clearly are not pitch-keys. Those who believe that Ptolemy correctly sets forth the Aristoxenian Tonoi must grant that Cleonides, writing in the same century, distorts their true nature. Here the experts cannot agree on what evidence should be admitted. Either interpretation involves vexing difficulties.

Without pretending to settle the question, we may cite two points which seem relevant. First, Ptolemy stresses the operation of the Tonoi inside a central octave, the range within which all the interval sequences can be found. Here the Tonoi which bear the names of the old octave-species (the *eidê* of the earlier Systems) display the intervals of those species and thus have a right to be named for them. It would appear that this amounts to something more than a mere use of pitch-keys. Possibly Ptolemy's abstract conception does help to clarify the use of Tonoi during the fourth century in one respect at least: the pitch-keys, it seems, often served not to afford variety of pitch as an end in itself, but to place a given octave-species within the central range of the normal male voice (E—e).

Moreover, we cannot equate the kind of pitch involved in the Systems and Tonoi with the kind presupposed by our own scale structure. There is no evidence for absolute pitch in Greek music, nor does it appear that such standardization could have been effective. The indispensable prerequisites are an efficient system of communications and a unit of tonal measurement. Ancient China had both; Imperial Rome had one but not the other; Greece had neither. Yet by the very fact of their existence the Systems bear witness to an eventual acceptance of set intervals, arranged in a chain of tetrachords. The feeling for these intervals insured that transposition was no random affair; whether it proceeded on a uniform basis of semitones in the Tonoi remains a matter of argument. As for the instruments, kitharas and lyres obviously did not embody fixed intervals, thereby differing somewhat from the aulos.

A final principle of differentiation is the distinction according to genus (*kata genos*), determined by the type of interval sequence within the fixed boundary notes of each tetrachord. While Aristoxenus lists a variety of diatonic and chromatic genera, we may disregard the nuanced varieties known as "shadings" (*chroai*) and cite the following sequences as fundamental: semitone, tone, tone for the diatonic; semitone, semitone, and sesquitone (tone plus semitone) for chromatic; and quarter tone, quarter tone, and ditone for enharmonic.[18] The tetrachord E F G A will represent these marked differences of genus, with E and A the "standing" or fixed boundary notes (*hestôtes*) and F and G the "movable" inner notes (*kinoumenoi*). Thus diatonic is E, F, G, A; chromatic is E, F, F sharp, A; enharmonic is E, E plus a quarter tone, F, A. To sum up: by the latter decades of the fourth century, if not earlier, a melody might require three categories of identification—by the Tonos, by the octave-species employed within the Tonos, and finally by the genus displayed in the tetrachords constituting the octave-species.

All this has a certain complex majesty, but it takes us into a realm of theoretical perfection which Harmoniai of the earlier Hellenic period can hardly have known. One must ask whether there is not some way of getting nearer to the origins. Surviving fragments of the music itself offer little help, and with a single exception the theorists can supply nothing but isolated conjectures or uncertain tradition. The exception is Aristides Quintilianus, a writer of the late Empire.[19] He presents the following six scales as the Harmoniai discussed in Plato's *Republic:*

	B	*B*	c	*c*	d	*d*	e	*e*	f	g	a	b	*b*	c′	*c′*	d′	*d′*	e′	*e′*
Lydian								*e*	f—	—	a	[b	*b*	c′—	—	—	—	e′]	*e′*
Dorian					d		[e	*e*	f—	—	a]	[b	*b*	c′—	—	—	—	e′]	
Phrygian					d		[e	*e*	f—	—	a]	[b	*b*	c′		d′]			
Ionian	[B	*B*	c—	—	—	—	e]			g	a								
Mixolydian	B	*B*	c		d		[e	*e*	f—	—	—	b](?)							
Syntonolydian	[B	*B*	c—	—	—	—	e]			g									

Here Ionian (Iastian) and Syntonolydian fall short of the octave; Dorian exceeds it by a tone. Moreover, Aristides' scales are not always complete within their actual ranges, as the tritone f—b in Mixolydian so strikingly illustrates. Rightly viewed, these peculiarities support the case for their genuineness; yet at the same time allowances must be made for an unknown but possibly extensive degree of alteration. That such alteration did occur becomes evident from a comparison of the bracketed sequences. Aristides has given every one of the scales in the enharmonic genus, and each contains at least one enharmonic tetrachord, though there is no strong indication here of scale building on a tetrachordal basis—a fact which may further support the claim of authenticity.

Whatever their other irregularities, scales so uniformly constructed cannot represent anything very much like the beginnings of Greek modality. One sees them as an intermediate step, probably rather a late one, in the process of systematization. It is not permissible, moreover, to speak of "scales" in the later sense. Possibly Bellermann saw the truth of the matter a century ago: Aristides, he suggested, took these sequences of notes from particular melodies which used only the notes given by him. Recently it has been suggested that Aristides simply copied out the material from some lost commentary on Plato. On this view, errors would have been only natural in the original information, supplied as it was by a literary scholar rather than a musicologist.[20] Nevertheless, modal schemes other than those of Aristoxenus presumably were current during the later fourth century. The period 390-385 may have seen such an early approach to the concept of octave-species as is suggested by the scales which Aristides cites. We ought not to dismiss out of hand his claim that they reflect the modes praised or condemned by Plato.

Whatever the assessment of Aristides' evidence, it remains true in any case that the theorists from Aristoxenus onward seem to know little or nothing about the actual nature and function of Harmoniai during the Hellenic period. They cannot tell us on what principles, or with what intervals and ratios, a modal tuning came into being. Most regrettable of all, we possess only a very little information on the functional importance and interrelation of individual scale steps. Aristoxenus himself laments the inability of notation to give a picture of the modes that would convey just such points.[21] We find Aristides stressing note selection, *petteia,* but we cannot say whether it is true that (as his translator and commentator Rudolf Schäfke maintains) he explained it as an ethically meaningful process, relevant to the gapped or overly full modes associated with the *Republic.*

A clear answer to questions of this kind would have considerable value, especially for the student of musical ethos. Such answers, unfortunately, are still to seek: thus Aristides may simply have failed to understand the proper meaning of *petteia* in his sources. To choose a more familiar example, some think the note Mese provided a focal point of melodic construction, but the musical facts involved are not available. Varying answers are still being given to the fundamental question of whether certain well-known references concern the fourth degree (Mese by position, *kata thesin*) of each octave-species in the Greater Complete System or instead designate the unchanging Dorian Mese (Mese by function, *kata dunamin*) at the center of the entire complex. The very possibility of a meaningful tension between the thetic and dynamic functions has occasioned much speculation. The earliest writer to mention this antithesis and thereby introduce a thetic nomenclature was Ptolemy.[22] Such a double system may conceivably have existed earlier than the second century after Christ—we have no true evidence that could either establish or refute the supposition; but the burden of proof rests upon those who have accepted it.

This unsatisfactory state of affairs has led various individuals during the past hundred years to seek a theory which would account for the existing evidence. The Victorian scholar Monro contended that modes differed in pitch alone, with the central Dorian Mese providing a tonic. His explanation seems to take the whole question back no farther than octave-species; yet Aristophanes and Plato both speak of Harmoniai that require individual lyre tunings, not mere transposition. Quite apart from this fact, we should have to reject Monro's theory as contradicting the known pattern of modal development established by comparative musicology. It will be evident, moreover, that a simple difference of pitch cannot account for the complex and subtle ethical qualities imputed to the modes.

At the turn of the century Macran, the editor of Aristoxenus, theorized that Mese *kata dunamin* not only served as a tonic for each mode but characterized the mode through its relative position. While his theory may well appear more promising than Monro's, it is open to several of the same objections and gains little support from the ancient evidence. In any case, the thetic-dynamic crux would have a direct bearing only on the last years of the Hellenic period, so far as one can tell—if indeed this concept can justly be taken farther back than the age of Greco-Roman theorizing. We need to know something, if possible, about the predecessors of the comparatively sophisticated octave-species; and we look for more adequate grounds upon which a theory of ethos might have been based.

During the productive years of musical scholarship after the First World War, attention shifted from disputes about pitch and abstract formulations to a study of the chief types of Greek musical instruments. The late Curt Sachs, whose memory is honored for his fundamental contributions to musicology, argued for a six-string pentatonic scale in two tunings: E—e minus F and c, and (alternatively) F—f minus B and e. The basic pattern involves only whole tones and ditones. Performers supposedly obtained the missing notes—those which would make available the semitone intervals, and those needed to express differences of genus—by stopping an open string with the index or middle finger.

This pentatonic hypothesis proves awkward on many counts. Without entering into technicalities, one may say that the most careful consideration has shown no way for such an arrangement to be realized effectively. By string stopping without a fingerboard (which admittedly is not unknown) the executant produces only muffled, characterless sounds; whether the results can be called tones is doubtful.[23] Distinct harmonics can of course be obtained: the literature of the classical guitar contains entire melodic sequences composed of harmonics. These sound most clearly at the midpoint of a string, which yields the sonorous octave harmonic, but they give no support to Sachs' theory. Admitting that a muffled quality would result, he sought to make it the source of ethos. If we are to achieve any realistic estimate of this attempt to salvage the hypothesis, we must bear in mind that Sachs was speaking of the inner notes of the tetrachord. These notes constituted the sole means of determining even identity according to genus, let alone ethos; and generic ethos seemed wholly real to musically sophisticated Greeks, although there were dissenting voices. Sachs' claim is not credible.

His younger contemporary, Otto Gombosi, realized that the pentatonic theory had not been justified in practical application. He sought therefore to establish it on new grounds. Citing a technique still used on the Japanese long zither or *koto,* he proposed that the Greek lyre player altered the pitch of a string momentarily by wedging his plectrum against it in the short nonspeaking length that stretched between bridge and crossbolt. Although this is not impossible, it has its own attendant difficulties in practice, and with one doubtful exception it receives no support from the extensive evidence of the vase paintings. To the objections previously raised must be added still another: the more nuanced types of genera would have required superhuman speed and exactness of pressure when plectrum leverage was applied. If the theorist finds cause for rejoicing in these two pentatonic hypotheses, anyone with practical knowledge of string playing has reason to approach them warily.

The performer on a wind instrument might well raise a quite different point: these attempts to establish lyre tunings fail to take into account the aulos. With Kathleen Schlesinger's exhaustive treatise *The Greek Aulos,* published in 1939, the balance swung toward the other extreme. This scholar, who was an authority on primitive reed pipes but had no adequate command of Greek, claimed to have found the key to modality. Her sovereign principle was the even spacing of finger holes on the aulos, an arrangement which characterizes the reed pipes of many non-Greek peoples. Such spacing according to aliquot parts of the total speaking length gives a set of Harmoniai with two characteristics: every degree of every modal pattern is at a different pitch from all other degrees, and the same intervals occur—echeloned in transposed sequence—throughout the various Harmoniai. The first of these points means that modulation is inconceivable when Harmoniai are taken from a common fundamental. The octave-species which the second point brings to mind became possible, according to this theory, when the characteristic ratios of Dorian were extended to form a system.

The individual Harmonia, as interpreted by Schlesinger, took its nature initially from the particular degree of the ascending harmonic series which represented its "Modal Determinant." The latter is the number of even parts into which one divided the total effective speaking length of the aulos to obtain the desired Harmonia. The harmonic series, taken downward from this degree, yields a sequence of scale steps, the last six or seven spaced at intervals of less than a whole tone. They all bear immutable harmonic relationships to the given degree: if the latter shows a sharpened or flattened tonic relationship, the scale steps must follow suit. This constitutes an important part of the physical ethos of a Harmonia; no less important was the relationship of tonic to (functional) Mese.

Although the theory seems uncommonly attractive on a number of counts, acceptance would involve many difficulties. It is sorely at variance with the theorists' accounts, and it has no unambiguous support from any written evidence. Moreover, competent scholars have seriously questioned the author's handling of texts. As one might have expected, the kithara receives comparatively little attention. The passages which deal with its development during the fifth century leave two crucial factors out of account: the consistently limited number of strings shown in vase paintings, and the double sense of *chordê* (either "string" or "note") which makes this term and its compounds so difficult to render in literary texts. One may grant that the aulos could have had, or even did at some point have, the equipartite borings and attendant modalities which Schlesinger champions at such length; but one must also point out what several critics have realized, namely, that this arrangement can only have characterized an archaic period in the development of Greek music. There is no room for the elaborateness and high degree of modal refinement that pose the real problem.[24]

Since 1939 the theory of equipartition has attracted only an occasional adherent; no champion has come forward to take up the cause. Had the author set forth her position with greater conciseness and clarity, the result might conceivably have been different. As it is, what she has written calls for assessment (as Professor Winnington-Ingram has pointed out) by a classically trained musicologist equipped with a specialized and profound knowledge of the reed pipe. It would appear that no such scholar is to be found; consequently the theory remains in limbo, rejected by most specialists and perhaps fully grasped by none. Those who have explored at least a part of its intricacies may have mixed feelings. At first sight some of the ancient mysteries do seem to have been solved, but the solutions manifest a suspicious degree of special pleading. Equipartition is a recognized phenomenon found in the musical cultures of certain non-Western peoples: one cannot dispute Schlesinger's claims on this score.[25] What remains without any convincing demonstration is the thesis that equipartite aulos modes account for the many intricacies of theory and performance which characterized the Hellenic musical scene.

Concentration on the theoretical is likely to obscure the fact that during the great period modality belonged first of all to the realm of actual performance. When Pindar and Aristophanes and Plato spoke of a Harmonia they meant something heard—an experience, not an abstraction diagramed in a treatise. The formidably difficult attempt to recapture their thought and feeling becomes a little easier if two points of usage are recalled. First, where we use only adjectives to refer to the modes, Greek writers often used adverbs. For example, English has "Dorian" but lacks a counterpart for *Dôristi:* this means literally "in the Dorian manner of speech" just as *Hellênisti* means "in Greek"; it was transferred to the idea of musical speech. Second, from at least as early as Pindar's time one of the ethnic modal adjectives—*Dôrios, Aioleus, Ludios*—might modify the term *tropos.* This term, which came to be used at times as a synonym for Tonos during the Greco-Roman period, originally and properly meant "manner" or "style." Taken together, these facts suggest that when a Hellene thought of what we would call modality, he had in mind not merely a particular scale pattern but also a distinctive musical idiom, as it were a dialect.[26] The general impression was far more diversified than we, with our compartmented musical experience, can well conceive. Repeated hearings of performances of the *ragas* by Indian musicians may suggest how much we shut out when we apply Western criteria.

The questions raised in the following chapters are so difficult, the answers hitherto proposed so various, that the writer may fairly declare himself on certain matters at the outset. The definitions and interpretive positions set forth below can serve as points of reference throughout the argument, testing it and likewise being tested by it. They should be regarded as working definitions and conjectural reconstructions, subject at all times to modification. As matters stand, the source of final authority here is the written word: the evidence of poet and philosopher remains sovereign, not to be coerced into agreement with any a priori assumption.

Recognizing the vulnerability of whatever statement may be attempted, we must posit first an introductory period of true modality in Greek music. This began in the seventh century, when the three basic Harmoniai and the two basic instruments gained general acceptance; it lasted until an unknown time within the limits of the fifth century. Circumscribed and weakened, beset by increasing pressures for one master scale pattern, pure modality survived into the earlier decades of the fourth century and perhaps even later. Its presence can be argued in Plato; one cannot with certainty exclude it from the thought of Aristotle. Post-Aristotelian practice and doctrine show no trace of it, unless there may be faint echoes in Ptolemy's treatise. Those precisely marked-out boundaries which afford such satisfaction to the scholar remain beyond the effective range of our inquiries. Ethnomusicological research warns us to expect to find not sequences of individual trends, each neatly compartmented, but instead (as the history of Javanese modality shows) a long history of overlapping and confusion.

We accepted earlier the hypothesis that mode originates in melody. Through frequent use a melodic pattern becomes associated with a group of persons. The group may be large or small; its basis of differentiation may be geographic or ethnic or occupational, with still other possibilities. When there comes into being an awareness of the particular melody as characteristic, modality makes its appearance; and a belief in ethos cannot be far behind.

What has been described here amounts more to a process than an entity. If the nucleus of mode is to be sought, we have no more likely source than the motif. A. Z. Idelsohn speaks of the mode in Jewish music as composed of a certain limited number of motifs contained within a given scale. These are traditional patterns: the executant works with them in accordance with a certain "mode," arranging and combining them. His creative freedom is essentially a freedom of modulation and ornamentation—though the second of these at least proves to have unexpected importance.[27]

We note that Idelsohn's analysis, which now represents the received interpretation, goes at once beyond the initial phenomenon to include its embodiment in a scale. This second step is, however, a distinctly separate one. After it has been taken—after the notes required for the motif pattern which determines melodic outline have been arranged according to their pitch sequence—the way then lies open to the dead abstractions of theory divorced from musical practice. The step is a necessary one if vocal patterns are to be transferred to instruments, but the initial stage must be recalled when one meets such a term as *tropos* in Hellenic literature. As long as modal structures retain some connection with actual performance they likewise retain an inner relationship with this prescalar period, though in themselves they are merely what a recent writer has termed "the skeleton that is left after all the practical reality has been stripped away."[28]

Among the ancient names used by Hellenic authors to describe these structures, the most prevalent was *harmonia.*

The term has no necessary connection with music, and it continued to designate nonmusical relationships at times during the whole of the central classical period. In every instance the root meaning of a fitting together remains evident.[29] The relevance of this idea to music, especially to modality, need not be labored. On the other hand, little notice has been taken of the fact that describing a mode by the term *harmonia* witnesses to a comparatively sophisticated stage, one of synthesis and abstraction. It is clearly postscalar, with a more pronounced technical ring than other early terms. One could wish, in fact, that the operative word were *tropos,* or the like. Nevertheless it is unquestionably *harmonia,* and we shall use this transliterated form interchangeably with "mode" strictly so called—referring to the various Hellenic scale patterns which in varying degrees maintained their individuality. The distinction thus obtains broadly between these "true modes" and the so-called octave-species, segments of a double-octave sequence of intervals.

Here closer distinctions become necessary, and much can be gained from the masterly summary of J. Chailley. After an initial contrast with prevalent misconceptions he proceeds to direct definition:

> The concept of mode is currently thought of as merely qualifying and supporting that of tonality: supposedly it fixes the intervals of the tonality, taken from tonic to tonic within the gamut of an octave. Apart from the notion of scale . . . analysis reveals five [modal] characteristics:
>
> [1] selection of an octave type, basis of unity;
> [2] identity of function on the part of the notes which reduplicate at any octave one of the notes of the octave type;
> [3] the fixing of a tonic, identified with the first note of the octave type;
> [4] establishing of a hierarchy among the other degrees of the scale through their relationship to the tonic or . . . to

the *finalis*, the function of the latter being more or less assimilated to that of a tonic;
[5] regarding the gamut as a matter of indifference.

Now, not a single one of these criteria has any value for ancient music. If one must speak of "modes," that term must be taken in the very different sense in which it is sometimes used, referring to certain clearly-defined melodic types (the *ragas* of Indian music, the Arab *maqam,* the Jewish "modes," and so forth) which have a characteristic scale defined in various ways—by its intervals, its *tessitura,* its timbre, its special formulas, the ethos which characterizes it, and by its structure within the framework of the system (the octave note not necessarily enjoying a favored role, the final note not necessarily the center of attraction, the intervals not necessarily occurring in the traditional order of the [genera] in use during the classical period).

Such were the *harmoniai* mentioned by Plato . . . and described by Aristides Quintilianus.[30]

The intervals of the Harmoniai have occasioned much speculation but little agreement. We cannot suppose that they were homogeneous: parallel evidence from the musical history of other developing cultures suggests quite the opposite. Recently a case has been made for the antiquity and central importance of the enharmonic genus,[31] but evidence for the genera is usually considered to be inconclusive, especially in view of the silence which fifth-century sources maintain on this subject.

One fact is beyond dispute: during the Hellenic period the old Harmoniai came to be rivaled and finally supplanted by the modal complex known as the Greater Complete System. The structure and operation of this complex have already been discussed: it will be recalled that instead of individual Harmoniai we now have segments of an extended Dorian scale pattern which begin on successive degrees of that scale. To call these segments modes and build a theory of modality on them, as has so often been done, is to make a strange use of language. Their Greek name is *eidos* (pl. *eidê;* the singular occurs only in late writers), meaning "kind" or "type" of scale segment—a Hellenistic sense of the term; the usual English rendering has been "octave-species" or simply "species." This is not entirely satisfactory, but we adopt it here as being the only familiar equivalent. The transliterated forms will also appear.

Neither the origin of the Greater Complete System nor its relationship to the Harmonia comes within our knowledge. Few scholars would now follow the conjecture of J. Curtis and date it back to Pythagoras; yet it cannot have sprung in full panoply from the brow of Aristoxenus.[32] There must have been experimental versions, and under one form or another the process may have been going on for a long time. To think of an inventor at all may be to fall into the error of so many late classical commentators: the fiction of a *prôtos heuretês,* or "first discoverer."

In some degree, relations between the Harmoniai and the System must have taken their color from a number of unknown or imperfectly known circumstances. It is possible to suggest some of the factors: the discrepancy between practice and theory; the shift of musical hegemony from Sparta to Athens; the interchange of ideas and discovery of similarities at the Panhellenic games; the strong local traditions such as the Theban school of aulos playing; and the theoretical interest in music evident among pre-Socratics and Sophists.[33] All these warn us that a simple answer to the problem of paralleling mode and modal complex should not be sought. Further consideration of the question directly involves Plato and will be reserved for later discussion.

It is necessary to mention the Tonoi once more. *Tonos* undoubtedly means "tuning," and "transposition scale" represents the accepted English rendering. The majority of continental scholars, and at least some of those in Britain as well, suppose the Tonoi to have been octave species taken at different pitches and echeloned within the central octave of vocal range.[34] Recently this interpretation, which we noted in another connection, has come under fire. Mrs. M. I. Henderson argues that the Tonoi were merely blackboard creations, quite without relation to pitch or any other aspect of actual performance.[35] This would mean that the theorist remained indifferent to pitch, while executants followed their own devices when faced with the problem. That they kept their own counsel on all such matters is only too evident: professional secrecy in antiquity accounts for no small part of our difficulties when we attempt to deal with Greek music.[36] While it is not yet clear that the majority opinion regarding the Tonoi is mistaken, "transposition scale" remains in any case a poor choice for *tonos*. The kind of process that may have been operating here offers only a specious analogy with transposition; "pitch-key" would be a better rendering.

Whether or not the Tonoi had a place in musical performance, there is no evidence for their use during the Hellenic period. *Tonos* as "pitch-key" appears only late: the infrequent Hellenic instances have other meanings. By the criterion of relevance to the true modes—the Harmoniai in the many aspects of their total being—Tonoi must be considered unimportant for our purposes.

It is with this more realistic attitude that one may best approach the question of ethos. Ethos cannot be confined to the purely ethical, nor can its manifestations ever be fully grasped in terms of scales alone. Wherever a musically advanced people or area of common culture has evolved a modal complex, as in India or the Arabic-speaking countries, men have given scale patterns and melodic archetypes associations with the phenomenal world, with unseen forces, and with man himself.[37] Despite the false predications to which this tendency has led, it represents a sound instinct. Mode expresses man's reaction to outward circumstance, and during the present century many experiments have shown the varied and profound effects of music on the human body.

A belief in modal ethos goes further than this, however. It supposes that the modes can qualify man's nature ethically, or at any rate express ethical states. The latter view is basic; the former tends to follow from it but appears less regularly. Observed physiological effects are seldom cited to support theories of ethos, though one might have expected their use. The Greeks, whose doctrines on ethos possess a maturity and philosophical interest beyond those of all other peoples, kept the supposed ethical properties of music largely distinct from the therapeutic. We shall mention therapy only incidentally; the main task will be to set forth the ethical doctrines as stated or implied in Hellenic poetry and philosophy.

The chapters which follow will show that many writers credited music with the double power of expressing and also of influencing our moral nature. This power constitutes the essential meaning of their term *êthos* (which cannot be rendered adequately by "character"), although they often discuss it when the term itself receives no mention whatsoever. To be sure, man's physical nature is also involved: a Greek would at once have understood Dryden's query, "What passions cannot music raise or quell?" We shall see, however, that the involvement was limited. One and only one concept is persistently associated with ethos: paideia, the Greek cultural experience of which formal education constituted only the beginning. The conjunction of these two ideas may prove to be significant.

The question we shall be asking is how the Greeks accounted for the real or supposed phenomenon of musical ethos. We shall seek to determine whether they explained it through ethnic character, by association with forms of literary composition, or in still other ways; whether religious considerations figured importantly, and whether notice was taken of the actual physical characteristics belonging to a given mode. No neat single solution is likely to dispatch this hydra of a problem, but we may perhaps clarify the difficulties that the struggle involves.

CHAPTER II

FROM PINDAR TO ARISTOPHANES

Pindar is the first Greek poet to present himself as a thoroughly professional musician. He has but a single direct reference to paideia;[1] it is not a lyric theme, and he scorns professional courses of training in music and literature. Nevertheless, his vehement theory of natural wisdom does not require a rejection of paideia. When his "wise citizens" gain stability through hearing the phorminx (*P.* 5.65-67), Pindar imagines them as listening not to an instrumental solo but to a kitharode's song of "the glorious deeds of heroes," such as Achilles sang when distressed. The epinician ode itself is a kindred work: if its immediate concern lies with contemporary victors and patrons, its distinctiveness involves much more than this occasional quality. Pindar's practice is not essentially different from what was later recommended by Plato, who in the *Laws* (801e1-802a5) sanctions encomia of distinguished citizens after their death; both writers are concerned with paideutic values.

For ethos the most important reference is *Fg.* 67 Schroeder (56 Bowra; Schol. *O.* 1.26): "With reference to the Dorian mode, Pindar says in the *Paeans* that the 'Dorian melody (*melos*)' is '(the?) most dignified.'" The scholiast's identification of Melos with Harmonia may seem surprising, since our musical theory regards melody and mode as quite distinct. No such division characterizes Greek music. While the original relationship between melody and mode has occasioned much speculation, R. P. Winnington-Ingram convincingly states the majority opinion:

> At least up to the fifth century B.C. (and probably the fourth) Greek music knew many styles of melodies differing in emotional character and named after Hellenic or barbarian tribes. The notes required for each constituted a *harmonia,* or tuning of the lyre. We have little evidence for the forms of these; but such as we have suggests considerable diversity, and it may not have been easy to combine them in a logical scale system, or possible without sacrifice of their individualities . . . Mode may be defined as the epitome of stylised song, of song stylised in a particular district or people or occupation.[2]

His analysis is borne out by the practice of musicologists under field conditions, when they attempt to establish a scale for some type of folk music never previously studied: it is of the greatest importance to determine which notes actually are used.[3]

At this point the term *tropos* enters the evidence. Commonly used as "manner," it had the basic meaning "turn." *Olympian* 14.17 speaks of the "Lydian Tropos," conceivably referring to the characteristic turning or contour of the melody when associated with the Lydian mode. If the definition will hold, Tropos can be largely identified with the kinetic aspect of Harmonia.[4] It thus parallels rhythm, dealing with vertical relationships of pitch between successive notes as rhythm does with horizontal relationships of time. It would be closest of all to Melos; the fragment last cited illustrates this relationship. Accordingly, when Pindar speaks of the Dorian Melos he may mean the melodic realization, with all its idiomatic developments (Tropos) of the Dorian Harmonia.

Support from the odes would be welcome for the suggestion that Pindar attributed an ethos of particular solemnity to the Dorian mode. It appears, however, that results can be obtained only by comparing Pindar's description of Dorian as "most dignified" with terms used by other writers. The fourth-century Academician known as Heraclides Ponticus (if it is he who speaks in Athenaeus, 624d) calls it "dour and vehement," a mode which exhibits "manliness" and "magnificence of bearing." If one tests the associations of Pindar's epithet with the rhythms discussed by other writers, further progress can be made. Aristotle calls the heroic hexameter "the most sedate and stately (or "weighty") of all meters." In the same way writers on rhythmic ethos, whose doctrines are particularly well illustrated by the odes of Aeschylus and Pindar, applied the term "solemn" to dactylic meters.[5]

When a fifth-century poet describes a particular Melos in the language of the later, fully developed theory of ethos, he may possibly be doing so without deliberate concern for the ethical factor attributed to music. Yet this is difficult to believe, and especially difficult in Pindar's case. *Pythian* 1 shows that he was eloquently aware of the power of music; other passages reflect his delight in musical innovations. If the arguments suggested here have any weight, Pindar probably was familiar with the practice of modal ethos. Whether his choice of modes was dictated by any conscious theory we cannot say.

With the all-important exception of Damon, pre-Socratic writers have little to say about music in the surviving fragments of their works. Whole treatises and even tetralogies on varying aspects of the subject have perished, leaving only titles. Democritus speaks directly of musical paideia (Diels 68B179): "If children are not allowed to work, they cannot learn letters or music or gymnastic, nor that which above all things embraces virtue, (namely) reverence. For it is precisely from these studies that reverence usually grows."[6] He is reported to have written extensively about music, but nothing further of importance on the subject has come down to us. Since he shows the greatest respect for music, poetry, and education alike, the loss is almost certainly a considerable one.

Excerpts have survived from the treatise on Pythagorean theory by Democritus' contemporary, Philolaus of Tarentum. One of these (44B11) shows with special clearness the importance of number theory in explaining music and all other activities: "Number, fitting all things into the soul through sense-perception, makes them recognisable and comparable with one another . . . You may see the nature of Number and its power at work not only in supernatural and divine existences but also in all human activities and words everywhere, both throughout all technical production and also in music." A later passage from the same excerpt opens the door, if only for a moment, to an ethical view of music: "The nature of Number and Harmony admits of no Falsehood; for this is unrelated to them . . . whereas Truth is related to and in close natural union with the race of Number."

The term *harmonia*, used by Homer (*Od.* 5.248) to mean a carpenter's clamp, now takes on a completely metaphorical and almost mystical sense. If Nicomachus (44B10) is relaying an accurate tradition, Philolaus defined it as a "union of things that are much mixed" or "of the heterogeneous" and also "agreement among those who have been at odds in their thinking." Here the "union (*henôsis*)" seems to some extent a musical reference; the "agreement" among dissident thinkers (*sumphronêsis*, "consensus" in the literal, etymological meaning of that term) clearly suggests the Pythagorean doctrine of "harmony" as a useful political watchword—a doctrine which is independently substantiated. The strong and purposeful conjunction of *mousikê* with polity in the *Republic* and *Laws* should not entirely surprise us, although Plato rejected the heterodox theory of the soul as a harmony. This may have originated with Philolaus, the teacher of Simmias and Cebes. Socrates' refutation of the doctrine has tended to obscure its importance, especially where music is concerned. "The starting-point of Greek musical theory," Egon Wellesz maintains,

> is the Pythagorean assertion that the soul is a kind of harmony . . . since harmony is "a blending and combining of opposites" (*krasis kai sunthesis enantiôn*). This blending is identical with *harmonia*, the fundamental principle in Greek musical theory. Here the term stands for the proper building up and arranging of the intervals constituting one of the musical modes. Since all the intervals of a mode had to be put together in an appropriate order, the term *harmonia* is also used for the mode itself. It is by the properly organized succession of intervals that the *êthos* . . . or character of a mode is defined.[7]

We shall see that the concluding sentence represents only a part of the truth. Taken as a whole, however, the statement provides a useful reminder of the background against which one must view the early development of doctrines on ethos.

Philolaus maintained, finally, that the basic principles of the cosmos, which underlie reality and enable us to apprehend it, have no meaningful interrelation through their own powers (44B6). This want, he says, is supplied by the cosmic force of *harmonia*, for "unlike and unrelated and unevenly ranked elements" must necessarily be brought into combination by the kind of *harmonia* that will enable them to be included in a cosmic order.[8] The phrase τῇ τοιαύτῃ ἁρμονίᾳ, "by such a harmony," offers added evidence of the multiple uses of this symbol by Pythagoras' followers.

These Pythagorean doctrines had already been disseminated for almost a hundred years when Philolaus collected and published them. Their importance for the development of a doctrine of musical ethos can hardly be overemphasized. Taken together with Damon's theory (no less Pythagorean)[9] of music producing motion in the soul, they constitute much of the foundation of Plato's systematic thought regarding the power of music—a foundation upon which he freely and powerfully builds.

For our purpose Damon of Athens is the most important

by far of all the pre-Socratics. A later chapter discusses Damonian theory, with special attention to the actual extent of its influence on Plato's musical-ethical thought. Also, Damon will be encountered again among Philodemus' opponents. Only a brief summary of his thought will be attempted here, through a listing of the Diels excerpts with added comment.

"Song and dance," according to Damon (37B6), "necessarily arise when the soul is in some way moved; liberal and beautiful songs and dances create a similar soul, and the reverse kind create a reverse kind of soul." The second of the two hypotheses contained here states the primary belief of all musical ethic; yet the first actually holds greater interest, for it shows an awareness that purposive action originates in the soul. Heraclitus had already said, "Character (*êthos*) for man is destiny." A century after Damon, Aristotle was to put the matter clearly: action develops the corresponding predisposition in a preexistent potential; it does so through habituation, which becomes our nature.[10]

Such is the process. Damon, as we have seen, declared its end to be the creation of a liberal and beautiful soul—or the reverse, should it so happen. If Aristides Quintilianus (p. 80.26-29 Winnington-Ingram, 95 Meibom; 37B7) is reporting an authentic tradition, this creative act was of a twofold nature which accords well with the remarks just made: "Through similarity, the notes even of continuous melody[11] create a character that did not exist in boys and in those more advanced in years, and also bring out the latent character. This was the doctrine of Damon's school also." The virtues of the liberal and beautiful soul are of course nothing other than the time-honored triad: according to Philodemus it was Damon's belief that "in singing and playing the lyre, a boy ought properly to reveal not only courage and moderation but also justice" (*Mus.* 3.77.13-17, p. 55 Kemke; 37B4).

It is important to take into account the significance of movement if we wish to understand how the Greeks could have attributed affective qualities to music, especially with regard to ethical behavior. In music, movement assumes a pattern and receives the name of rhythm, a name also given in Greek to any complex of metrical feet. Such matters naturally interested Damon; Socrates describes him as having assigned praise or blame "not only to the rhythms for moral quality, but also to the feet, or to both together" (Pl. *Rep.* 400c1-3; 37B9).[12]

Other details attributed to Damonian theorizing are less easily explained. Aristides continues the passage previously quoted with these words: "In the Harmoniai handed down by [Damon] it is possible to find in the sequence of notes that sometimes the female notes, sometimes the male, either predominate or diminish or are completely absent, obviously because a different Harmonia was serviceable according to the character (*êthos*) of each particular soul." The element of continuity appears to be intimately bound up with the fact of so-called male or female notes recurring frequently or seldom or not at all, and thus with the process of note selection (*petteia*) which Aristides mentions as an important technique of the Damonian school.

Past this point only conjecture is possible. It proves even more difficult, unfortunately, to deal with the notion of similarity as an effective means of building character through melody. While some connection with mimesis appears to be a certainty, there is good reason to treat similarity (*homoiotês*) as a Damonian principle originally quite separate from the Platonic mimesis which incorporated it.[13] Throughout much of the history of Greek philosophical thought, the topic of like and unlike was treated with a superstitious naiveté (as it seems to us) which embarrasses even in Plato at times. His conjectures on the mimetic origin of modes and rhythms, however, proceed realistically from a consideration of human physiology, while the pages of Aristides' treatise show what fantasies were associated with Damonian theory.

As for the question of male and female notes, Aristides does not say that this doctrine is Damonian. He merely claims to have seen Harmoniai associated with Damon's name in which certain notes recurred with striking frequency. These notes he differentiates according to male and female; he attributes their handling to a desire to meet the needs of "each particular soul" (this suggests late theory) by applying the right "arrangement" of them in a Harmonia. Since no primary source connects the male-female concept with Damon's school, this belief perhaps ought not to be ascribed to him personally.[14] On the other hand, Aristides shows a greater familiarity with Damonian theory than does any other ancient writer after the Hellenic period. The general context of the statement, furthermore, leaves little doubt that he believed he was presenting a part of that body of theory. If he was not mistaken, then clearly it represented a part which Plato chose to reject.

The final fragment (37B10; Pl. *Rep.* 424c5-6) sounds a note immediately familiar both to the Plato scholar and to the comparative musicologist: "Musical styles are nowhere altered without (changes in) the most important laws of the state."[15] This thesis, first propounded in the *Republic* and fundamental to the *Laws*, represents a belief which the Chinese emphasized to a remarkable degree. In Hellas, as elsewhere, it has usually issued from a conservative and even reactionary point of view. Toward all innovators, a Pindar as well as a Timotheus, it manifests the bitterest kind of opposition. Its connection with musical paideia was fully apparent to at least one school of thinkers; the task of working out its implications was undertaken by Plato and carried further by Aristotle.

Nothing certain is known about the antecedents of this strongly developed doctrine of musical ethos and paideia: it gives the impression of having entered the domain of Greek thought without warning and without credentials. We have reason to suppose, however, that the theory of ethos originated in the Orient. There and there alone can all its salient aspects be found even today, not merely in theory but in practice; the musical history of the West is devoid of all but a few analogies. That the Hellenic heritage was partly Oriental none will dispute, though various musicologists have made too much of this and not enough of the fact that much Near-Eastern theory actually derives from Arabic translations of Greco-Roman treatises on music.

The Hellenes themselves, normally so determined to show an autochthonous culture, proved excessively ready to ascribe Oriental origins to their instruments and musical forms.[16] It cannot be denied, nevertheless, that the historical period as well as the prehistoric shows the currents of musical influence running westward from Asia. For the most part the earlier history of ethos in Greece itself is an enigma, but we have found suggestions of the theory in fifth-century writers. Damon did not invent the theory of ethos; he did expand and codify it to a notable and perhaps an unparalleled degree.

The evidence of elegy and lyric begins with Tyrtaeus, the seventh-century elegiac poet. Sparta's rigorous system of upper-class education gave a prominent place to his works. Spartan youths learn by heart the battle songs he wrote, says Athenaeus (630f), and in war the adult Spartans deliver Tyrtaeus' poems from memory, moving in time to them.[17] Athenaeus' primary concern is with the pyrrhic dance, a war dance which he believes originated in Sparta.[18] Plato's pyrrhic dance appears to derive from this Spartan source. Tyrtaeus himself does not figure importantly here; what matters is the dance. Although Plato does not speak as if he proposed it should be sung, possibly it did feature singing in Tyrtaeus' day and even much later. The fact that Athenaeus speaks of Tyrtaeus to illustrate the nature of the war dance supports such a conclusion, and Sparta's conservative approach to such matters was notorious. Originally song and dance are inseparable, a fact which the war dance as a type illustrates particularly well.

The joint evidence of passages from the *Republic* (399a3-c4) and *Laws* (814d8-815b6) suggests that the pyrrhic dance is to be performed to an accompaniment in the Dorian mode. We may conjecture the use of Dorian by Tyrtaeus, whose martial songs mirror so strikingly its special ethos. Possibly he used Phrygian also, for Lucian describes a dance with two successive solo parts performed by a young man and woman: its details exactly portray the masculine and feminine characteristics distinguished by Plato in the passage from the *Laws.* Mode cannot have remained unaltered for the dance that Lucian knew, when mood changed so radically. If the accompanist used Phrygian, this Spartan version must have been marked above all by decorum, the womanly discretion which Plato regularly associates with Phrygian. The choice of modes in his *Republic* and *Laws* consequently becomes less perplexing.[19]

Two elegiac couplets by Ion of Chios deal explicitly with the modal resources of the lyre during the later fifth century: "Eleven-stringed(?) lyre, keeping an ordered array of ten steps / To the concordant meetings of the three roads of harmony, / In former time all the Greeks played you as seven-toned, through [groups of?] four [notes?], / Raising a scanty strain."[20] Whether the eleven *chordai* are strings or notes, this *lura* must presumably have given the three chief modes: Dorian, Phrygian, Lydian. The latter two would thus have been octave-species rather than true Harmoniai; Ion may have been speaking of a kind of Lesser Complete System which had a gamut of three conjunct tetrachords (*triodous dia tessara*) replacing the old heptatonic scale composed of two such tetrachords.

Whatever their loss in physical ethos, such modes would

remain distinct even as octave-species rather than true modes, if one could assume that each had the Dorian Mese (that is, Mese *kata dunamin*) as a pivot. The varying centers of gravity thus established would have given a characteristic placing of each mode. Actually this assumption is not justified by the evidence, which leaves it in the realm of conjecture while offering no disproof. We noted, also, that Ion may simply have been referring to an instrument on which eleven notes could be obtained. If this was his meaning, all the major terms of the problem are immediately scaled down: the lyre has seven strings, as it does in the overwhelming majority of the many vase paintings which show it, and the following reference is to the four-stringed phorminx with a compass of seven notes.[21] Yet Ion may have been proudly describing the unusual resources of an eleven-stringed instrument, one which would no more have resembled the ordinary lyre than a bass guitar resembles the normal six-stringed version.

By comparison with the elegists, lyric poets offer a reasonable amount of material which bears directly or indirectly on ethos. In the seventh century Terpander writes that he will "disdain four-voiced song and make new hymns resound on a phorminx of seven tones."[22] His words have been taken to imply the ancient enharmonic Dorian Harmonia with the upper octave note (Nete) added and the note just above Mese (Trite) removed. According to Schlesinger, the Elgin auloi in the British Museum, which date from about the year 500, embody the ratios of Terpander's libation scale. Its appearance may mark the climax of a long process which saw both kithara and aulos abandon an early tetrachordal compass—perhaps related to the main types of tonic accent—for a broader and more subtly expressive pattern of sound.

Since Terpander does not refer to *chordai,* it might be argued that his "phorminx of seven tones" is the familiar early version with four strings, given a wider compass through some system of stopping. Thus far, however, it has proved impossible to demonstrate a practicable stopping technique for the chief Greek stringed instruments of any period. This consideration alone would incline us to believe that Terpander refers to the four-stringed phorminx being superseded by the kithara of seven strings. Abundant evidence from vase paintings shows just such a change taking place around his time. It was decisive and permanent for the entire Hellenic period.

In two lines Terpander sketches the flourishing culture of Sparta when it was briefly free from the iron rule of "good order." He praises the vigor of "the warlike spirit of the young men, together with the clear-voiced Muse and Justice in the broad streets, helper in noble deeds." Alcman, who lived perhaps a generation later, reveals even more clearly the honored place of music at Sparta: "For rivaling the use of the arms / Is excellence in playing upon the lyre."[23] This perfectly expresses an advanced culture which still is virile, still in balance. It recalls the claim that Pericles makes for Athens in the Funeral Oration, and it is the paideia to which Plato looks back.

One of the most surprising statements concerned with Greek music is Alcman's declaration that Apollo himself played the aulos. The Athenian tradition which makes him cherish the lyre and hate the aulos is a familiar one; Alcman's words show how different an attitude prevailed at Sparta, then far more receptive to musical ideas from across the Aegean. It would seem that here an attribute of Dionysus was actually transferred to Apollo. Plato links the two when he claims that musical consciousness is a gift from "the Muses, Apollo, and Dionysus."[24] During Alcman's time, three centuries before the age of Plato, the aulos was still at an early stage of development. At Sparta its use must have been marked, according to the occasion, by a tranquil ethos equally as well as a frenzied one.[25]

Possible support for this conclusion comes from a somewhat later source. The Sicilian poet Stesichorus, whose *floruit* we may place provisionally at the beginning of the sixth century, has left one line with which any inquiry into modal ethos must attempt to deal. To sing of the fair-tressed Graces at the coming of spring, he says, we shall have to "find out a gentle Phrygian tune." Literally he speaks of "delicately finding out a Phrygian melody." The language suggests that Stesichorus may be indicating a new development. At any rate, the ethos of Phrygian here is indisputably tranquil, delicate, and joyous. Another line, apparently part of the same poem, exquisitely sets its tone: ". . . when in the season of spring the swallow sounds her note."[26] Since the Greeks closely associated Phrygian modality with the aulos throughout the classical period, Stesichorus' words may have some bearing on Alcman's description of Apollo as an aulete. Technical considerations do not seem to be relevant: here, as in the following excerpt, the poet is concerned about broad characterization through such aspects as contour and tone color.

Lasus of Hermione speaks in the late sixth century of "voicing a hymn in the Aeolian mode / On the deep-sounding (*barubromon*) Harmonia."[27] When he discusses the Aeolian character Athenaeus notes that "Heraclides Ponticus" identifies the ancient Aeolian mode with Hypodorian. Dorian Mese is the initial note of the Hypodorian octave-species, a fact which might in itself suggest a low *tessitura* centering about thetic Mese; but until the addition of the "Hyper-" scales Hypodorian had relatively the highest compass of any octave-species. We cannot of course suppose that a sixth-century poet referred to the species as such; nor can we say with any confidence what qualities of a given Harmonia were carried over into the matching octave-species. It does seem reasonable to grant that Lasus was trying to describe accurately the pitch and timbre of his mode, its physical ethos. The explanation may be simply that he associated the Aeolian style—for in this period the Harmonia must not be understood as essentially a scale pattern—with the distinctive instrument of the Aeolic poets, the barbiton that was "deep-sounding" because of its unusually long strings.

Pratinas of Phlius, Aeschylus' older contemporary, is represented by a half-dozen fragments, and most of these have value for anyone interested in modality. Athenaeus interprets his well-known hyporcheme as a protest against the reversal of tradition which altered choric song, turning it into an excuse for virtuoso displays on the aulos. The opening lines may be rendered as follows: "What is this uproar? What mean these choral dances? What outrage comes against the altar of Dionysus, beset with tumult?"[28] The meter emerges in the next line as anapestic, but these two lines use a torrent of short syllables to give the impression of metrical chaos.[29] It is a parody of the kind of "libretto writing" that Timotheus, a century later, would offer the public in all seriousness.

Since Pratinas claims (line 18) to be writing a "Dorian choric song," his opening may be directed against an abuse of the text by unrestrained development of aulos melodies in Phrygian, the mode closely associated with the earlier dithyramb.[30] Yet one must not assume that the ethos of Phrygian so used would have been wild and ecstatic, for the music of Dionysiac ritual at Athens early lost its original intensity.[31] What Pratinas criticizes is rather the violation of rhythmic and melodic propriety (14); besides this, he objects to the dominating role of the aulos. "It is song," he says (6-8), "which the Muse of Pieria has made queen. The aulos must come second in the dance, as befits a servant."[32] At the beginning of the fifth century the ills of which he complains were not epidemic, even in lyric poetry; Pindar and Aeschylus give proof enough of that. They were present, nonetheless, and another hundred years would see them become irresistible.

Varying meanings have been assigned to the following lines from another poem by this same writer: "Pursue neither tense (*suntonon*) music / Nor yet the relaxed (*aneimenan*) Iastian, but plow the middle / Furrow and compose your song in the Aeolian mode . . . / Well suited, indeed, to all braggarts in song / Is the Aeolian Harmonia."[33] As the mode name Aeolian was replaced by the species name Hypodorian, so Iastian gave way to Hypophrygian. The "tense" music, however, seemingly could be any one of a number of modes. It may well be Mixolydian, which Plato and Aristotle contrast with "relaxed" modes or octave-species; Plato calls its ethos threnodic.

This point probably must remain obscure. A clearer statement is possible on one other matter: Aeolian, which Pratinas describes as a mean, cannot be so in any technical sense known to us. Within the Greater Complete System its successor Hypodorian is an extreme, the most "relaxed" octave-species of all as related to dynamic Mese.[34] It would seem therefore that Pratinas speaks not of the physical character of Aeolian, though this is a real and important type of ethos, but of the supposed mimesis of character traits through attitudes and actions.[35] Only on such terms does Aeolian become understandable as a mean. Avoiding the anguished intensity of Mixolydian,[36] avoiding equally the serene and easygoing temper assigned to Hypophrygian, it was thought to express the blithe, free-spoken nature of the Aeolian peoples. If the interpretation proposed here is accepted, Pratinas' concluding remark that the Aeolian Harmonia is a fitting one for "braggarts in song" takes on relevance to what has preceded it. Together with the introductory statement by Athenaeus that "he is more explicit in what follows," it shows that the first four lines are far from being general advice. They do not single out the best mode of any; they are specific advice for a particular situation, and very probably their tone is a scolding one, as in the hyporcheme fragment.

Another attack upon the new dithyrambists comes from a far more famous composer-poet of the conservative school. In the *Clouds* Aristophanes makes Socrates condemn certain unspecified persons as Sophists and "song twisters (*âismatokamptas*)" of the cyclic choruses. The scholiast claims that Aristophanes refers to dithyrambic poets like Cinesias and Philoxenus, who trained such choruses, and that they too are held to be Sophists. The epithet itself is not precisely defined, since the scholiast cannot decide whether the "twists (*kampai*)" involved are abrupt modulations or artificial metrical systems. Either, or both together, may have been meant by Aristophanes.[37] Very possibly his reference corroborates what is known from other sources concerning the modality of the late-fifth-century dithyramb, namely that it was no longer contained within the limits of Phrygian. Its ethos, then, was not single and thus intelligible, but multiple and thus a puzzling confusion. Aristophanes thought the old-fashioned dithyramb paideutic; according to the conservative view its association with paideia had been almost wholly lost by the closing decades of the fifth century. One of Plato's aims in the *Laws* is to reestablish this earlier relationship.

Telestes of Selinus, a Spartan poet active during the years immediately following the Peloponnesian War, appears to have been a vigorous defender of the aulos. Unlike Pratinas he champions its right to serve Dionysus, and he speaks of "a Phrygian king of holy . . . auloi, who first put together the Lydian pattern of melody (*nomon*) in answer to the Dorian Muse." The reference is clearly to Olympus, and the contrast of Lydian with Dorian, which accords with the whole classical view of Lydian, constitutes one of several indications that the eulogy of this mode in Aristotle's *Politics* comes from the hand of a late interpolator. Elsewhere Telestes speaks of the high pitch of instruments accompanying the "Lydian hymn."[38] This might have resulted naturally from a high center of gravity in the Lydian octave-species, where dynamic Mese comes on the sixth ascending degree; but it cannot be assumed that Spartan conservatism would have allowed a system of species.[39]

Timotheus of Miletus, contemporary and associate of Euripides, claimed to champion the "old music" against those who would debauch it. The known evidence scarcely bears this out, and Timotheus elsewhere contradicts his own claim.[40] We shall attempt to determine what his innovations may have been and what new evidence they may offer with regard to modal ethos.

The treatise *On Music* formerly ascribed to Plutarch quotes from Pherecrates' *Chiron* the celebrated speech by Music herself. She complains that Timotheus has utterly undone her with his "erratic, extra-modal ant tracks," and mentions his use of eleven strings or notes to accompany solo singing. Since Pherecrates first won a prize for his comedies in 438, this estimate of Timotheus' handling of the modes is contemporary and therefore unusually valuable. The noun used means properly an ant's nest; the figurative plural here refers to the antlike scurryings this way and that of a melody which is forever changing direction—*ektrapelous,* "erratic," is literally "turned out of the regular course." That these changes of direction were modulations follows from Pherecrates' description of them as "extra-modal" or "inharmonious."[41] The word *exarmonios* occurs earlier in Mistress Musica's lament: the "extra-modal twistings (*kampas*)" which Cinesias makes in his strophes[42] have, it seems, so radically confused his dithyrambs that one part cannot be distinguished from another. Apparently both nouns refer to the same thing, a sudden change melodically or metrically or in both respects. Pherecrates at once makes his reference precise: what Timotheus did was to introduce "impious uses of the uppermost tetrachord and shrill squealings."[43]

So far as kithara modality is concerned, all this suggests an instrument of at least seven basic strings, with added stringing or some unknown device to permit the use of Hypodorian, Hypophrygian, and Hypolydian species. Timotheus appears to have had just such an instrument, for he speaks expressly of "making the lyre spring to life again with meters and rhythms" of eleven strings or notes.[44] The total compass of these three species can take the singer up into the extreme limit of high tenor range, and Pherecrates presumably means that Timotheus' vocal writing emphasized high notes. Such a melodic line may have been sensational; considered simply as sound, it cannot have been unpleasant when executed by a trained singer in a monody.

Pherecrates' concluding lines, however, show that his criticisms apply not to monodic art song but to accompanied choral singing and dancing. The central (Dorian) octave of the Greek male voice is thought to have extended from about F below middle c to the f above, and it must have been extremely difficult to find choruses capable of producing good unison tones at levels as much as a fourth above the normal upper limit.[45]

Timotheus' compositions for accompanied chorus, being instrumentally conceived, were not sympathetic to the voice. Their demands proved to be excessive in a stage of monophonic musical culture, when the idea of a professional chorus had not yet been conceived. Within the accustomed Hellenic frame of reference such writing is soloistic, implying a trained individual. Whether by design or by accident, it works to render the citizen chorus obsolete. This end was achieved: the words of one of the pseudo-Aristotelian *Problems,* "In the old days choruses were made up of the freeborn citizens themselves," form the epitaph of the Hellenic dithyrambic chorus.

The same source, which considers why nomes were not composed antistrophically, emphasizes two other factors, modulation and mimesis:

The nomes were performed by professional artists who

> were capable of sustained mimetic presentation to begin with. As a result, what they sang came to be long and varying in shape; the melody, just like the words, would follow the lead of the mimesis, changing continually. (It is more needful that the melody be imitative than that the words should be so.)
>
> The same explanation applies to the dithyrambs, which are no longer, as formerly, antistrophic, now that they have become mimetic . . . In the old days choruses were made up of the freeborn citizens themselves. Since it was difficult for a sizable group to sing as a professional soloist would, they sang melodies which stayed in a single mode (*enarmonia*—the mode normally being Phrygian); for frequent modulation is easier for a single individual than for a group, and easier for the trained soloist than for persons who maintain their own character (*êthos*) and present no other . . . The dramatic actor is a professional mimic; the chorus, however, is less imitative.[46]

Of Timotheus' dithyrambs we have but a few words from the *Scylla.* Much material from his nomes has been preserved, however, especially the more than 250 lines of his *Persae.* This evidence indicates sufficiently well the degeneration of the text, which at times lacks any perceptible metrical shape and obviously has been made secondary to some other factor.[47] The solution that words and melody alike have become nothing but mimetic vehicles overlooks the subordination of text to music which is involved, the rise of the libretto concept. During the course of such a process the music comes to display that "embroidery" which Plato so detested. It modulates and shifts rhythms incessantly; in the Platonic dialogues this marks a depraved type of vocal composition (*lexis,* musical "speech"). The citizen nonprofessional cannot readily be trained to follow its florid, amorphous line through extended phrasing, particularly when there is no stable basis of modality. He finds it utterly impossible to express through the dance, moreover, since it possesses neither strophic arrangement nor metrical stability. As we have seen, it does away with the civic chorus, which the *Laws* presents as the supreme embodiment and medium of civic paideia.[48]

Throughout the ancient period dithyrambs kept to one mode. Until the fifth century this mode seems to have been an individual Harmonia, distinguished from all other Harmoniai by the sequence and dimension of its degrees as well as by certain other characteristics less easily defined. From a purely musical point of view at least, such a mode clearly had an *êthos* or "character" of its own; and this remains true, no matter how conclusively one may show that modal ethos, taken in its active aspect, was based on association. The dubious achievement of Timotheus and his fellow innovators was to destroy modal individuality in melopoeia.[49] Incessant modulation prevented the realization of any firmly established ethos, so far as mode might contribute to this. It must be concluded that if the Platonic view is one's point of departure, the works of Timotheus had nothing to do with paideutic ethos.

According to the source previously quoted, a person could not "keep his own ethos" when performing this composer's dithyrambs. While the *Problems* modify Aristotle's doctrines at times, he himself strongly condemned the importation of virtuoso kithara and aulos techniques from the theater into the classroom.[50] He shared Plato's concern over the fact that actual training in music, as seen at first hand, often employed random materials which any thoughtful assessment would condemn as unwholesome. In short, systematic Greek thought on paideutic ethos during the late Hellenic period weighed the innovations of Timotheus and utterly rejected them.[51]

Except for the lament of Mistress Musica from Pherecrates' *Chiron,* the older comic poets other than Aristophanes can tell us little or nothing that has relevance to the present inquiry. Plato Comicus (*Fg.* 69 Kock) mentions a banquet singer who performs "a kind of Ionic melody (*melos Iônikon ti*)" to the accompaniment of her trigonon. This raises the question of the ethos of that mode known as Iastian or Ionian. The earliest and most celebrated description is that given by the anonymous Academician whom we call Heraclides Ponticus (*ap.* Athen. 625b-c): "The kind of music known as the Ionian mode is neither bright nor cheerful, but austere and hard, having a seriousness which is not ignoble; and so their mode is well adapted to tragedy. But the character of the Ionians today is more voluptuous, and the character of their mode is much altered."

The voluptuous nature of Ionian music at the end of the fifth century, shortly before Heraclides' time, can be illustrated from the comic poets already cited and from Aristophanes as well. In the *Ecclesiazusae,* for example, one of the lecherous old women proposes to sing "a little song, one of the Ionian sort" (883, cf. 918). Two points of evidence seem to be set against this interpretation: the first of these is a line from a chorus of Aeschylus' *Supplices* (69), "I, fond of sorrowing in Ionian patterns of melody"; the second is an anonymous saying, "He pipes on Mariandynian auloi, playing in the Iastian mode," which the scholiast cites on line 939 of Aeschylus' *Persae.*[52] Both of these apparently contradict the usual identification of Iastian with Hypophrygian.

When it has a musical reference, however, *nomos* most often is not a mode but a melodic archetype or "pattern of melody," as in the translation given above. There must have been many such Ionian patterns of song; Aeschylus' generalized reference proves nothing about the ethos of Iastian-Hypophrygian. As for the scholiast's quotation, if it makes straightforward sense this mode must have been threnodic at times. The final clause may just possibly be adversative, with an unexpected twist at the close: "Piping on Mariandynian (threnodic) auloi, he plays in—Iastian," a metaphor of feigned grief. One cannot be sure, however, that the scholiast has quoted a *sententia.*

There remains Heraclides' contention that the Ionian spirit and musical ethos had both suffered a certain dissolution. On such matters he is a poor source—one would like to know when the Ionians had ever shown themselves austere, hard, and serious. Yet it is at least credible that the fifth-century musical scene was changing not only in the mainland city-states but eastward. The great technical change to octave-species had already begun, though evidently this did not concern Heraclides. He took the new interrelated scales for granted: his interest was directed rather to musical and ethical generalities, and any value his remarks may have is probably accidental.

One further portion of Mistress Musica's lament requires examination: her complaint that the dithyrambist Melanippides made her "more slack (*chalarôteran*)" by means of nine *chordai.*[53] Melanippides was court musician to King Perdiccas of Macedonia during most of the second half of the fifth century. *Chalaros* had a well-attested musical sense, although its status as part of an actual mode name or species name is disputed. Here one finds an ambiguous use of the epithet more than a generation before Plato wrote the *Republic.* If any serious ethical discrimination is meant to be conveyed here, it does not rest on any discernible technical grounds. This leaves the possibility of an adventitious ethos, reflecting the morality of the texts which were employed.[54]

Despite inadequate recognition by musicologists, Aristophanes more than any other poet has afforded us a view of Hellenic music as a working reality. In this aspect his contribution rivals even that of Plato, perhaps outweighing it and certainly forming an invaluable supplement.

Aristophanes' musical thought gives a place of some importance to the *nomos* or nome, a term referring to any traditionally established melodic pattern.[55] Most celebrated of all was the high-pitched (*orthios*) nome, mentioned as universally familiar (*Eq.* 1278-79) and sometimes designated by the adjective alone (*Ach.* 16). By the closing years of the fifth century this had become a set piece, or well-defined type; usage seems to have been far less fixed when Aeschylus wrote. Tradition ascribed the "invention" of nomes to Terpander, who was said to have used them as settings for epic poetry. It might be argued that what he actually did was to employ extant melodies in a new way. Conceivably this is the fact behind the statement that he combined Homer's words with the music of Orpheus.[56]

The important thing is that at an early date Greek thought came to associate the nome with a sung text. As the rule of "one syllable, one note" began to be disregarded, the likelihood increased that a singer would be influenced by figurations hitherto peculiar to the aulos or kithara. Aristophanes' disapproval of such developments was only to be expected: he strongly condemned the mixing of two idioms regarded as properly separate, the instrumental and the vocal.[57] In this respect his position was Plato's also, despite his vigorous indictment of Socrates' onslaughts (*Ran.* 1493-95).

During the course of Western musical history such confusion of idiom has at times been the symptom, not of decay, but of a decidedly healthy transition from one predominant style to another; the confusion was part of a defining process.[58] Thus an early sixteenth-century score might be prefaced with the words "apt for voices or viols." It is a debated question whether Plato and Aristophanes were simply reactionaries, resisting the natural course of development, or whether they justly diagnosed pathological symptoms. Musicologists tend to take the former view and philologists the latter, as might have been predicted.

Aristophanic comedy seldom deals directly with the modes, but such few passages as we do have are forthright. In fact, they are so circumstantial as to remain an intriguing puzzle.

A burlesqued Agathon proclaims his use of the "Phrygian foot" for choric song (*Thesm.* 121); this phrase, deliberately and maliciously high-flown, may indicate a Hypophrygian mode or species fitted to the meter. Again, the expansion of *Dôristi* into *Dôrodokisti* (*Eq.* 989-96) involves an interesting technical point. The case is posited of a boy's unwillingness to learn any lyre tuning for frequent use other than that of the Dorian mode.

Very probably this last reference looks back to a time at least as early as the middle of the fifth century. The developed kithara of wide compass can hardly be referred to, therefore, nor the concomitant use of octave-species. What is significant here is the indication that at least a few of the modes were still taught in earlier and more distinctive forms, at a time when Greek music had already advanced so far. However mistaken the imputation of ethos may have been, it gained considerable plausibility through being associated with a strong underlying difference in modal patterns which, taken as a group, seemed broadly homogeneous.

One other passage deals strikingly with the modes. Describing the hapless state of Cratinus, Aristophanes (*Eq.* 531-33) pictures this once popular poet "in his dotage, with the electrum pegs falling out, the tuning no longer present, and the modes showing yawning holes." Here the Greek definite articles could be translated as possessives, for it seems clear enough that Aristophanes' intended meaning applies not to Cratinus' musical technique but to the man himself. He is an old, battered lyre that will no longer stay in tune; his pegs have come loose and are slipping from their sockets; as a result, string tension or tuning cannot be maintained and the intervals of the mode, relaxed beyond proper bounds, "gape open." It is a typically Aristophanic treatment of the Pythagorean doctrine which views the soul as a Harmonia, to be slackened or tightened by musical paideia.[59]

The eleven surviving comedies also reflect radical changes of musical fashion during the fifth century's final decades, with the attendant upheaval. By now the lyre ranks low in popular esteem. To play it is "old-fashioned," though the very admission of inability to do so witnesses to an earlier period when lyre lessons were a standard part of education. Aristophanes' remark that the effeminate Agathon ought not to handle the lyre, a man's instrument, shows the attitude of the poet himself. Witness also the unsympathetic picture of a dainty amateur of music, so worn out with playing the lyre and aulos that he cannot dream of undertaking manual labor.[60] All this jesting hides real concern over a tendency increasingly apparent among amateurs and professionals alike, the willingness to exploit music for purposes of meaningless exhibitionism and thus divorce it from reality.

Nowhere were the discouraging symptoms more clearly visible than in the drama, and no area of music comes under attack by Aristophanes more frequently. By the closing decades of the fifth century, unscrupulous advocates of mere sensationalism in music had dissolved the old partnership between text and setting as dominant and subordinate elements. At its worst this meant the sort of banal and even absurd mimesis (*Eq.* 522-23) which later alarmed Plato as well, and which has proved distasteful to cultivated persons in every age.

Euripides does not seem to have been guilty of such absurdities, but he was open to attack on other and similar grounds: thus Aristophanes parodies his practice of setting a word to more than one note (*Ran.* 1314, 1348). The course of Western music has so accustomed us to this license that we find it difficult to understand the poet's concern; and yet a papal *motu proprio* on music, issued within the memory of living men, represents a very similar reaction. The basic fact is that any breakdown of the "one word, one note" convention makes the text less clear, and this convention happened to be one of long and hallowed standing.

According to Dionysius of Halicarnassus (*De Comp. Verb.* 11), Euripides further abused his texts by ignoring the patterns of tonic word accent when he was composing his melodies.[61] Aristophanes says nothing about this, and it is very doubtful whether Dionysius' supposed evidence is actually as old as the later fifth century. Aristophanes' comments on musical borrowings, however, deserve mention. Euripides is charged with "compiling Cretan monodies" and with getting help in this from Cephisophon; his lyric dramatic choruses are said to derive from kitharodic nomes and indeed from all kinds of improbable and improper sources. By contrast, the Aristophanic Aeschylus says that he made a deliberate effort not to use Phrynichus' material, taken supposedly from religious nomes. On several occasions, moreover, his excellence as a composer of lyric choruses is emphasized.[62] He represents the old order, the early fifth century when the tragic poet was *poiêtês,* "maker," not only of the text but of most or all of its musical setting as well.

The age in which Aristophanes wrote had already seen musical practices change greatly. Kitharodes were celebrated to a degree never before known. Like the theoreticians, they had followings and could exert a marked influence for good or (as was the case with Phrynis and his school, *Nub.* 970) for evil. If Euripides did make use of nomes designed for the kithara—and Aristophanes certainly is explicit here—pitch conflicts of the kind criticized by Dionysius may indeed have arisen. The kitharodic nome was loosely constructed like a dithyramb, lacking strophic correspondence; thus the phrasing of its text could not be transferred to the strophe and antistrophe of dramatic choral lyric. Neither could its melody, if any parallelism was sought between accentual pitch and melodic pitch. It is uncertain how far Phrynis had compromised the principle; we do know with reasonable certainty that Euripides sometimes did not hesitate simply to abandon it.[63]

Aristophanes' specific treatment of paideia greatly helps us to understand musical education in the middle years of the fifth century. "The old-fashioned training" (*Nub.* 961-71), meaning the paideia given by a kithara teacher, proves to be a strict regime with compulsory attendance and a curriculum which consisted of memorizing patriotic songs. A special ban is laid against any attempt at vocal ornamentation with such trills and roulades as Phrynis or Euripides liked to use. Clearly the latter cannot have been absolute innovators if, decades earlier, schoolboys had risked a beating by the same practices.

In the old days, Aristophanes notes, pupils would "keep intact" the mode handed down from their father's time.[64] It may be that he uses this typically oblique and figurative approach to suggest by his image a contrast with the contemporary musical scene, which was already featuring modes such as the "slack" Lydian and Iastian. The reference itself is not necessarily to any single mode, as one might at first suppose: we have seen that the old paideia included mastery of a number of distinct Harmoniai.[65]

There can be no doubt that Aristophanes thought of the traditional education in music as character training. His aristocratic Athenians, whom he sees the state casting aside for worthless rascals, are men "brought up in a discipline of wrestling and choral song and music" (*Ran.* 729). To this extent his conservative views accord fully with those of Plato; the paideia of the *Laws* rests on essentially the same triad. Further one may not go. A great gulf divides Aristophanes from Damon, Socrates, and Plato, and the extent of this difference in the approach to music may not have been fully realized.[66] It comes down to whether or not one is willing to regard the theoretical philosophical nature as important.

The next chapter will treat the question of Plato's precise attitude toward Damonian theory: for the present, we may state that the *Republic* treats Damon's views with some respect. Wholly another position underlies the attempt of the Aristophanic Socrates to persuade Strepsiades that he ought to become familiar with the rhythms (*Nub.* 647-51).[67] Asked what practical good this will do, Socrates replies that the ability to tell an enoplius from a dactylic line is one of the social graces. Aristophanes himself speaks through both masks. His criterion is indeed practical benefit, and by this criterion the technicalities of Damon could not seem to him anything more than trifles for the dilettanti. If this was not the whole truth, nonetheless it seemed to him to be essentially true.

A further ground for supposing disagreement may be found in that rejection of tragic drama which one normally associates with Plato, especially with the positions taken up most clearly during his later period. Actually Aristophanes' vigorous attack (*Ran.* 1491-99) shows that it was proposed by Socrates. Such a doctrine amounts to the death warrant of all drama, comic as well as tragic, and no Athenian dramatist of the first rank could have met it with anything but extreme hostility and dismay. The only surprising thing is that Aristophanes attacks it so briefly. Perhaps he considered the threat unreal, as in fact it was.

The byplay of the *Frogs* proves that its author's estimate of Aeschylus was not uncritical. Some have gone on from this to conclude that it was insincere; the fact is that both the style and the content of Aeschylean tragedy call forth explicit admiration. Such tribute was intended to apply importantly to the writer's skill as a musician. His handling of lyric choruses, in particular, receives the praise of an expert (*Ran.* 1251-60). A more general estimate informs the poet's cry (1500-3): "Come quickly then, Aeschylus! Hasten, and save our city by your good counsels; teach those—and they are many—who lack understanding." This is one of the few things in Aristophanes which may truly be called pathetic and moving. With his earthy sureness of instinct he grasped, almost unconsciously, what eluded the mystic inward gaze of Socrates and Plato: that the free creative thought of genius, if it is guided by a civic conscience, magnificently embodies paideia. To attack freedom of creativity was to attempt a substitution of synthetic dogma for the genuine expression of moral experience, significant not merely at the personal level but in terms of the *polis* as well.

Taken all together, the evidence reveals Aristophanes as a conservative in music.[68] He dissented from the radical paideutic theories of Damon which he had seen Socrates adopt, and which he was to see partially taken up by Plato. There is neither any indication of countering views systematically presented nor any likelihood that Aristophanes actually proposed them. Dislike of the theoretical forms one of his main characteristics as a satirist, and if there existed at this time any organized opposition to the Damonian school we do not know of it. His attitude toward modality seems to resemble that of the other comic poets: though aware of the modes as distinct in their broad aspects and effects, he considered them vehicles essentially of enjoyment rather than paideia.

Perhaps it is by attempting to suggest the musical scene of the middle and later fifth century that we can best see Aristophanes in a final perspective. During this period the individual character of the various modes appears to have been widely felt. The feeling must have been partly associative, based on tradition or fancy. In some degree, however, it traces back to the real and perceptible differences between one true Harmonia and another, differences not yet wholly obscured by the increasingly prevalent use of octave-species. If no formal canons of usage existed, neither was there anything resembling the casualness which marks key selection today. Belief in the paideutic value of *mousikê* was real, without resting on any patterned conception of ethos.

The emergence of a new and dogmatic philosophy, that of the Damonian school, disturbed this easygoing approach; yet the theories of Damon did not find universal acceptance among Athenians, despite a measure of endorsement from Socrates and others. Poet-composers fought these doctrines, inevitably, and Aristophanes is their spokesman. What he says has importance: it must have been akin to the average cultured point of view toward musical ethos and paideia. This should be remembered when we listen to the voice of Plato.

CHAPTER III

PLATO

Like other writers, Plato regards the aulos and kithara as the only important instruments, and in his eyes the aulos was important for evil rather than good. Its strangely penetrating tone had a compelling power—he says it could fill the listener's whole consciousness;[1] but Plato's belief that the aulos has the greatest compass of any instrument is what makes him ban it from Kallipolis, the imagined city-state of his *Republic.* The other "panharmonic" instruments, he declares, only imitate it (*Rep.* 399d4-5).[2]

Here a distinction must be noted. Stringed instruments like the trigonon and pektis (*Rep.* 399c10-d1) suffer no such innate handicap of construction as does the aulos. Theoretically one could go on adding to their compass until several times the original number of strings was obtained. A reed pipe, on the other hand, cannot extend its range unless the effective speaking length is increased. Furthermore, its powers of modulation are limited to a very few modes at best, as long as it is fitted with a single row of four to six finger holes; and Greek artists regularly portrayed just this type of aulos, normally in pairs. The limitation remains even if one supposes that the second pipe of the double aulos was used to make available an added portion of the modal gamut, rather than to produce a drone bass.

Plato, however, declares that the vulgarly florid and imitative type of speaker requires all the available modes to accompany his recitation fittingly (*Rep.* 397c3-6, cf. a1-c2). The "panharmonic" aulos which would meet the special needs of such a man was everywhere available when Plato wrote. While the details of its boring and fittings can only be conjectured, very probably it showed a profusion of finger holes spaced in staggered rows and also devices for opening or closing them, such as appear on many of the auloi surviving from later periods.[3] Plato's attacks on the harmonic empiricists indicate that the old modes, inextricably bound up with "the classics" and traditional paideia, were by that time all but overwhelmed by a system empirically produced and based on an elusive minimal interval known, in later times at least, as the diesis. No one knows when the change took place: probably it began after the Archidamian War, during that period when so much of the traditional was challenged or actually discarded; probably, too, the beginning of the fourth century saw it well established. Thus the type of aulos Plato banned from Kallipolis likely was designed to modulate within a "tempered" scale compass. The essential point is that it had a capacity for extensive modulation; and this sufficed to banish it.

A celebrated passage from the *Laws* (790d1-e4) tells how mothers rock their babies and sing to them when they wish to put them to sleep, "practically lulling them as it were with aulos music"; just so the Bacchantes, in their cures for frenzy, make use of this combination of dance(?) and music.[4] Plato continues with an explanation of the way Corybantism is cured by the use of external motion to quiet violent internal motion, sometimes lulling the Corybants to rest and at other times rousing them so that they dance to the aulos. The purpose in either case is to produce "rational attitudes instead of frenzied states of mind" (*Laws* 790e8-791b1).

While the therapy of Bacchic and Corybantic seizures does not clearly come under the heading of paideia, it is impossible to grasp the significance of the aulos for actual tragic paideia without taking this therapy momentarily into account. The sound of the piper would be stilled in Kallipolis' streets and theater (*Rep.* 399d3-4); the city's choristers would of necessity sing to the kithara. As Socrates points out, the aulos is the instrument of Marsyas, and we must follow the Muses in preferring Apollo's instruments (*ibid.*, e1-3). All this nonetheless is only wishful thinking on Plato's part. In reality an aulete normally provided the musical accompaniment for drama. Moreover, as Plato recognized again and again, chorus training constituted the highest and most painstaking education that the state could offer an ordinary citizen.

Kithara and lyre are to be allowed in the ideal city (*ibid.*, d7-8); as we have seen, they are the instruments of Apollo. The significance of their being approved while the aulos suffers banishment is that Plato, in the *Republic* and especially in the *Laws,* wishes to make music wholly hieratic. The halls of Olympus never echoed to the aulos,[5] nor were the Olympians worshiped to its sound on earth: these proposals aim at eradicating an essentially alien, though powerful, element in Greek religion. Other instruments receive little attention. The syrinx and salpinx are noted; herdsmen may have "some sort of syrinx," though the many-stringed trigonon and pektis are banished because of their excessive capacities (*Rep.* 397a4-7, 399d8-9, c10-d1). Plato surely has such instruments in mind when he makes Laches speak of those which exist to give pleasure (*Lach.* 188d4); the syrinx has a place in paideia, where they have none.

It would appear that techniques of performance,[6] which require dexterity alone, interested Plato no more than technical cant;[7] nor does he represent himself as familiar with technical theory.[8] The *Philebus,* however, speaks in quite an unusual way of making clashing elements "commensurable and harmonious by introducing the principle of number" (25d11-e2). Had Plato been more specific here, our understanding of the modes might now be very much greater. His estimate of the value of harmonic science is a high one: he notes approvingly the Pythagorean contention that harmonics and celestial mechanics are sister sciences (*Rep.* 530d7-9).[9]

As reverence for the principles of measure and number undergirds the whole structure of Platonic aesthetic, so outrage at their nonobservance lends direction to the attacks on contemporary music. The *Philebus* (55e1-56a3) states the argument clearly: once any art is deprived of number, measurement, and weighing, what is left will be at bottom mere guessing and empirical concern with the senses; music furnishes a prime example of this, being (as he claims) full of such shortcomings. As always, the empirical harmonicists feel the main force of Plato's anger; yet in the same breath with another such attack he criticizes his friends the Pythagoreans. They display, he says, an exclusive preoccupation with the numerical properties of consonances, considered apart from other characteristics (*Rep.* 531b7-c4).[10]

The effects of music always had more significance for him than did its theoretical structure. Marsyas charmed men with his melodies, says Alcibiades (*Symp.* 215c1-6), and they still possess incomparable power. Whether the trained musician or a mediocre girl performer plays them, they alone grip the soul and "show the wants of those who have need of gods and mysteries," for they are inspired. Alcibiades goes on to declare that Socrates can achieve all this using only his voice, without any instrument. The scholiast quite rightly emphasizes the point that in the case of Marsyas' nomes it is their own nature, not the aulete's performance, which gives them such expressive force. We thus are dealing here with an ethos essentially melodic, independent of technical nuances. Alcibiades speaks as if these wild Phrygian aulos tunes were the only ones with penetrating ethical power; but he has arrived at that stage of drunkenness known as the verbose, and Plato characterizes his condition by the intensity of expression and exaggeration attendant upon it. The "gods and mysteries," we note, are not those of the state religion; clearly Plato takes a different view.[11]

Aulos music of this sort has an exciting, orgiastic effect; there is no place for it in Kallipolis, where worship remains forever ordered and stately—all such worship, that is, which the state recognizes. Schlesinger speaks of plucked stringed instruments as "honoured by all nations as the favourites of the gods . . . inspiring and exalting the soul of man," while reed-blown pipes lead to "a more intimate musical experience which may become devotional or Dionysiac, according to the individual."[12] (The closing antithesis is debatable.) Such individualism was precisely what Plato did not want.

Socrates' own concern with the power of music does not tend toward mystery religions. Education in poetry and music is crucially important, he tells Glaucon, because "rhythm and harmony sink deep into the recesses of the soul and take the strongest hold there, bringing that grace of body and mind which is only to be found in one who is brought up in the right way" (*Rep.* 401d5-e1, tr. Cornford). How much of this is intended as physiology and how much as sheer metaphor, no one can say. In the preceding text the metaphorical verbs have been taken from the language of the dyer's trade. One can be sure only that Plato is describing the efficient aspect of that mimetic process whereby a man's habits become his nature, manifested as ethos.[13]

The *Timaeus,* which deals so notably with the soul's motion, holds (47c7-e2) that

> music too, in so far as it uses audible sound, was bestowed upon us for the sake of harmony. And harmony, which has motions akin to the revolutions of the soul within us, was given by the Muses to him who makes intelligent use of the Muses, not as an aid to irrational pleasure (as is now supposed), but as an auxiliary to the inner revolution of the soul, when it has lost its harmony, to assist in restoring it to order and concord with itself. And because of the unmodu-

> lated condition, deficient in grace, which exists in most of us, rhythm also was bestowed upon us (tr. Bury).

Without a doubt this states Plato's main belief, as other passages will show. Unfortunately we are never told precisely how the soul is, or could be, affected by external patterns of motion having harmonic kinship with it. A baffling silence on this point characterizes Aristotle's far more analytical treatment of the problems of sensation, notably in *De Anima* and *De Sensu;* but where the lucidity of Aristotle becomes silence, Plato instead veils his meaning in metaphor and myth. His obscurity regarding the present matter may seem pardonable when we recall the intricate and esoteric nature of Pythagorean theories of harmonic number, to which he often committed himself. There is also the fundamental difficulty involved in saying how the eternal and nonmaterial can partake of change or be influenced toward it by what is temporal and material.

Philosophy and musical-literary training serve, then, to "provide the soul with motion," as the *Timaeus* later explicitly states (88c4-5). One learns, moreover, that the criterion of concord is the regularity of this motion set up within us; discordant (literally, "unharmonized") sounds are due to a want of evenness (80a3-6). When all has been properly regularized, high and low sounds blend into a single experience which gives pleasure even to the unintelligent, while for the trained intelligence this provides "that intellectual delight . . . caused by the imitation of the divine harmony revealed in mortal motions" (80b4-8). In this connection we may note that pleasure, whether unreflective or intellectual, is not to be taken as a constituent of musical ethos in Plato's reasoning. According to the *Laws* a man enjoys the music to which he has become accustomed: considered on its own merits, that music may be sober and ordered or vulgar and cloying. So far as pleasure is concerned, says Plato, there is thus no advantage on either side; but the former type of music makes men better, the other makes them worse (*Laws* 802c6-d6). Imperceptibly, gradually, with cumulative force, the ethical power of the Harmonia works upon the soul.

It is no doubt natural for us to regard modality and rhythm as purely musical characteristics. While the greater number of Plato's comments on them might confirm our way of thinking, certain passages remind us of the close connection in Greek thought between these factors and the spoken word. The *Gorgias* (502c5-7), for example, declares them to be all that differentiates poetry from prose; and according to the *Republic* (601a7-b2, cf. 600e4-6) meter, rhythm, and mode have such inherent charm as to make a discourse on any technical subject whatsoever seem excellent, though the poet actually knows nothing more than how to represent appearances as against reality. This is the secret of music's power; this is what makes music so invaluable an aid in the process of paideia. When Plato in the *Laws* (659e1-2) proposes to achieve his paideutic ideal by "chants" which will have the power to "enchant," he fully realizes that all music enchants, except as one may have been conditioned against it or not conditioned to understand it. He gives warning, accordingly, that rhythms and modes must be subordinate to the text if they are to observe their rightful place (*Rep.* 398d8-9). It has been well said that Plato sometimes was as near to magic as he was to metaphysics.[14]

The *Laws* (673c9-d5) ascribes the origin of choric song, where the dance joins with singing, to the natural tendency of all creatures toward swiftness of movement. This appears to provide indirectly an origin for rhythm, which together with mode is one of the two essential divisions of choric song (*ibid.*, 664e8-665a3); thus the *Philebus* (17d4-6) calls the rhythms refinements of the innate impulses which appear in bodily movements.

Modal genesis on the lyre of course forms a central topic in the argument between Simmias and Socrates that takes up one portion of the *Phaedo;* but for present purposes this material is unhelpful. The same passage from the *Philebus* (17c11-d3) contains a simple analysis of mode: distinct gradations of pitch exist; these have certain limits; out of them have been compounded systems, traditionally known as Harmoniai. The limits are Nete, Hypate, and Mese, characterized as such in the *Republic* (443d6-7). One notes that *sustêma,* so familiar from Aristoxenus onward, has come to be the accepted term. This suggests that Plato assumed octave-species to be the normal type of modality in his day, and such limited evidence as we possess would seem to confirm the assumption. If ethos had been closely connected with individual modal characteristics that were lost when the old Harmoniai were brought into conformity with a scheme of interlocking octave-species, we should have expected an indication of this at some point in the dialogues; there is none. On the other hand, it is not likely that Plato would have had any vivid impression of modes as they had been before the period of systematization—such modes as Aristophanes still seems to remember as a part of paideia during the earlier fifth century. Plato's own training in *mousikê* was obtained after the Archidamian War, and the scales which Aristides Quintilianus presents as those of the *Republic* suggest some approximation to a Complete System. The available evidence is slight, however, and will hardly support absolute conclusions.

All these considerations, especially the last, make it difficult to credit Chailley's claim that Plato clearly distinguished between Harmoniai and octave-species (*eidê*), imputing ethical values only to the former.[15] According to this theory, the scales cited by Aristides Quintilianus represent a mediate form. That is, they do suggest a prototype of the System; yet various nonstructural aspects persist, giving them genuine individuality. It would seem that if one accepts a distinction between Harmoniai and species in Plato one ought properly to reject a set of scale patterns which blur the differences between the two—and evidence is very much needed for the distinction itself. Also, Aristides' scales may come from one of the lost portions of Aristoxenus' works. So far as this remains a possibility, it militates against Chailley's explanation; for a prize pupil of Aristotle who was a master theorist (and the son of a professional musician as well) ought to have been accurately informed on the way in which Aristotle's teacher understood modality. He, of all men, should have had the facts at his command.[16] If Plato was indeed thinking in terms of the System, we must view his statements differently.

Plato very often speaks of music and refers not infrequently to Harmonia as a concept or factor, but he seldom mentions modes by name. It is possible that his approach betrays a deliberate touch of that chauvinism, based on distinctions of ethnic character, which "Heraclides Ponticus" shows when he contrasts Aeolian and Ionian (Iastian) with Dorian.[17] Laches, the bluff warrior, accordingly is made to assume that the man who has achieved personal harmoniousness has harmonized word and action, employing not the Iastian mode "nor yet, I take it, . . . the Phrygian or Lydian" but Dorian, "the only truly Hellenic mode."[18] Of course this must not be taken too seriously; Plato's own views on modality are perceptibly more tolerant.

Besides naming the chief modes Plato singles out a number of subordinate ones, invariably for censure and rejection. He divides them into two classes, the threnodic ("Mixolydian, Syntono-Lydian, and those of that sort") and the soft or convivial (the "slack" Lydian and Iastian modes) (*Rep.* 398e1-2, 9-10).[19] None but Dorian and Phrygian are approved, the former to imitate the tones and accents of a brave man under extreme stress, the latter to portray temperance in prosperity (*Rep.* 399a3-c4). That is, they severally express manly courage and discretion, the elements of Plato's concept of musical-literary training. This may explain why Laches chooses Dorian for the inner "harmony," rejecting all the rest.

The fact that Plato does admit Phrygian along with Dorian into his ideal civic scheme has always troubled commentators. The soul-searching begins with Aristotle, who felt that his teacher had formed a mistaken notion of the ethos of Phrygian. This difficulty will be taken up in a later portion of the present chapter, but we may note one point here. Just before he passes judgment on the modes Plato declares that, as regards musically accompanied speech, the man who speaks rightly can dispense with all but slight changes in the accompanying rhythm and mode (*ibid.*, 397b6-c1). This means that a certain minimum of modulation is indispensable; and therefore Plato approves the use of Phrygian to express moral excellence made manifest in tranquillity, choosing the mode which, in spite of its different associations, is proportionally the next related to Dorian. A city-state dedicated essentially to the life of peace rather than war would find such provision altogether necessary. It is true that Eunomia, "the good life under law," was interpreted at Sparta as meaning whatever those in power wanted it to mean; nevertheless, Eunomia as an ideal represents the goal of Plato's political thinking both in the *Republic* and in the *Laws*. The latter work, however, is neither so specific nor so harsh when it deals with modality. Several passages (notably 670a6-671a1) can hardly be explained unless we suppose that Eunomopolis (as we shall term it), the city of Eunomia, will permit a variety of modes.[20]

The connection of the Harmonia with "rightness" may be seen from Plato's insistence in the *Laws* (670a6-b6) that the choristers of his city have a knowledge of modality, since this alone—accompanied, of course, by a grasp of the rhythms—will enable them to determine the "rightness" of a melody. Its implicit connection with bravery in Laches' words has been noted; it lies behind the rejection of all modes other than

Dorian and Phrygian. To speak at length here of musical ethos or mimesis would be premature; but the implications of these two concepts, rightness and bravery, lead one to question whether Plato ever realized the ambiguity of his views on paideutic ethos in the modes of Greek music. *Laws* 669b5-670a3, of which the following is a condensed version, will illustrate the difficulty:

> Music, the most celebrated of all forms of imitation (literally, "images"), is the most dangerous as well. A mistake in handling it may cause untold harm, for one may become receptive to evil habits. Remember that poets, who do not have the Muses' skill, sometimes wrongly separate or combine words, melodies, dance figures, and rhythms. Where only melody and rhythm combine, as in the use of solo kithara or aulos, it is extremely difficult to recognize any meaning or the imitation of any worthy object in the rhythm and mode. The rapidity, glibness, and animal imitations characteristic of such playing are utterly boorish; solo instrumental performances display every sort of crudity (literally, "unmusicalness" in the Hellenic sense) and trickery.

We know as well as Plato did that music can seem unutterably vulgar and stupid, but we question the possibility of actual evil being impressed upon the hearer. Though the hypotheses involved in Plato's conception of mode are both arresting and productive, they hardly appear here. To raise questions of technique, furthermore, is irrelevant to the real issue.[21] Elsewhere Plato, with greater consistency, holds that technical finish has secondary importance (*Laws* 654b8-d7). Broadly viewed, his stand on this matter seems an aggregate of attitudes and theories which never became properly integrated into any kind of philosophical Harmonia.

Readers of the *Republic* will recall that when the Platonic Socrates deals with the ethical and paideutic effects of modes and rhythms, he clearly acknowledges his indebtedness to Damon, the most famous musical authority of the Periclean

Age. It has generally been supposed that Plato draws directly upon Damonian theory for his own views on musical ethos, making no attempt to be original. One must readily admit that Damon's influence was real and important, up to a certain point. There are nevertheless good reasons for crediting Plato with vigorous independence in several prominent aspects of his musical-ethical thinking.[22]

At first glance Plato's references to Damon seem highly complimentary. The *Laches* provides several examples. Nicias calls him thoroughly versatile and accomplished, entirely fit to associate with young men. Socrates credits Nicias' own skill (*sophia*) at arguing the nature of courage to "my friend Damon," a close associate of Prodicus, who ranks above all the other Sophists as an expert in terminology. Later Laches while conversing with Nicias refers somewhat sarcastically to "the wisdom you got from Damon." Again, in the *Republic* Socrates proposes that Damon's expert advice be sought on Glaucon's questions regarding rhythmic ethos; and he touches with studied vagueness upon certain elementary examples of Damonian metrical theory, for all the world as if they were Eleusinian mysteries. Finally, Socrates states his agreement with Damon's thesis that "musical modes (*tropoi*) are nowhere altered without changes in the most important laws of the state."[23]

On second reading these passages give a decidedly mixed impression. Versatility did not commend itself to Plato: instead, it annoyed him sufficiently to make him attack it again and again. Furthermore, he credited technical proficiency with minor importance at best, as we have seen. His apparent reluctance to deal with details of the Damonian theory of rhythmic ethos cannot be due to genuine ignorance. Either he is pretending simply as a joke not to know what he in fact knows very well, or he has some motive for avoiding the appearance of having a specialized knowledge of musical theory and is willing even to indulge in gentle parody. No doubt the first alternative is possible, but the natural reason for such a show of diffidence seems rather to be Plato's unceasing distrust of professionalism. His political planning centers around the musically educated amateur, whose talents will be exercised within a restricted field of technique; the great majority of modal and rhythmic *metabolai* will have been abolished. Such a man is not to specialize: to do so would be to forget that the proper function of musical training is educative (*Prot.* 312b2-4). Plato's paideia rejects equally the extremes of versatility, represented most obviously by the Sophist Hippias of Elis, and specialization, perhaps as seen in the Sophist Prodicus of Ceos; and certainly none can state with assurance that Damon's activities confined themselves to the mean which Plato thought proper.

As for the question of whether Damon was a Sophist (so Isocr. 15.235, Plut. *Per.* 4), his connections speak for themselves. Like Euripides he attached himself closely to Prodicus, as we noted, and the Platonic Protagoras called his music teacher Agathocles a mighty Sophist in disguise. His skill at subtle definition has already been mentioned: he taught *sophia,* skill applied not to playing the aulos or lyre but to making distinctions (*diairein*) among terms as an eristic technique. He was no mere elementary teacher, no *kitharistês,* but a professor of musical theory and ethic (*mousikos*) and evidently of "logic" and political science as well.[24] From Plato's point of view these subjects should reveal their interconnection through a unity of purpose and deportment. This evidently was true of Damon's pronouncements, for we cannot think that Plato would have misquoted him. If the historical evidence can be believed, however, his political counseling had no essential relationship to his musical theorizing. That it was formidable may be inferred from the fact of his eventual banishment; Plutarch refers to Damon's *deinotês* and to his uncommon powers of political thought.[25] In short, his activities would seem to illustrate Prodicus' contention (84B6 Diels) that Sophists were partly philosophers and partly statesmen, combining the best qualities of both.

The problem remains of Damon's statement, cited and endorsed by Socrates, that musical innovation always is attended by radical change in the laws of the state. We can hardly be in doubt about Socrates' personal attitude; yet these words, once they are removed from the Platonic context, do not necessarily indict musical change. Perhaps Damon really was the champion of conservatism a few scholars have made him out to be (it would appear that they are untroubled by the well-attested fact of his intimacy with Pericles); yet the pseudo-Plutarchian *De Musica* (16, p. 118.17-18 Lasserre, p. 13.10-14 Ziegler) certainly states that he "is said to have discovered the relaxed Lydian, a mode opposite to Mixolydian but much like Ionian." If this represents an authentic tradition, then Plato (*Rep.* 398e9-399a3) indirectly banned from Kallipolis a discovery of Damon's. Even if the ascription is erroneous, which seems very possible, one would not have expected a specific instance of modal innovation to be assigned to an improbable candidate.

The view proposed here is that Plato regarded Damon as an ally, but a dangerous one. Damon had brilliantly grasped the basic principles (as Plato saw them) of paideutic ethos in music and had expanded his researches well beyond anything achieved by his predecessors. He had already said a number of the things about music's meaning that Plato felt needed saying; thus on the one hand his work could not be overlooked while on the other it could be used most conveniently. Nevertheless he was not a man after the model of the *Republic* and *Laws*. More than half in love with Sophism, he did not tune his heart to his music: there was not within him that "finest of all Harmoniai" which Laches praises so eloquently (*Lach.* 188c6-d8). Apparently Damon was a research scholar whose practical, active side found creative expression mainly through the political intrigues of Periclean Athens; as a scholar he enjoyed technicalities and categories, though he did not abandon himself to them (37B1 Diels = Cic. *De Or.* 3.33.132). The musical paideia of Plato's state planning, however, is deliberately kept simple. In Kallipolis the welter of modes and rhythms which Plato saw about him would exist no longer, though the *Laws* (cf. 670a6-671a1) does perhaps allow them back to some extent.

One might object here that if Damon had been such a person as these arguments contend, Plato would never have called him an eminently fit associate for young men (*Lach.* 180d3). To suppose this is to forget that not every pronouncement in the dialogues comes ex cathedra. Plato met the demands of dramatic realism with a varying, but generally high, level of success: this means that any statement must be interpreted within its context, especially when the speaker is someone other than Socrates. It is thus of some interest to note that the tribute to Damon which we are now considering was delivered by Nicias. To the fourth-century Athenian, to any Greek with the slightest knowledge of main strategy during the Peloponnesian War, Nicias was the man whose deference to superstition deprived Athens of her last chance to escape disaster. This one impression must have overridden all others. What Nicias actually or reportedly said about anyone would inevitably have been discounted in Plato's day.

A number of points have now emerged on which there was a marked lack of accord between Plato and Damon. The most telling difference of all is that which characterizes their attitudes toward musical innovation. For Plato perfection was necessarily static, and his educational program represented perfection. Such evidence as we possess regarding Damon points to a different view. He was a great figure in his own right, and what he had achieved as a musicologist won a tribute from Plato; nonetheless, the alliance between these brilliant thinkers was never anything but uneasy.

The most direct single clash occurred over the possibility of an ethos of justice. Philodemus of Gadara quotes Damon as holding that "in singing and playing the lyre a boy ought properly to reveal not only courage and moderation but also justice" (*Mus.* 3.77.13-17, p. 55 Kemke; 37B4 Diels). His own criticisms are found in a later passage (*Mus.* 4.24.9-36, pp. 92-93 Kemke) which recurs to this doctrine. It is absurd, he counters, to connect justice with music. Had Plato claimed that music conduces to justness we should ask for proof; but in fact he speaks differently, holding that the just has analogies with the musical. He claims neither that the musical man is just nor that the just man is musical, nor yet that either aspect assists the other as regards the two special fields of knowledge.

These two fields discussed by Philodemus come closest to an explicit interconnection when the *Laws* (700d4-5) states that poets have shown themselves ignorant regarding what is equitable in their province, *to dikaion tês Mousês.* An analogy of justice with the Harmonia may be found in the *Republic* (443c9-e2, esp. d5-7). Except for the instance from the *Laws,* when Plato connects justice with music he introduces the latter merely to illustrate the former. Thus he does use analogy, but without making explicit any bond of inner relation. One may ask, however, whether he does not of necessity presuppose the bond, for example when in the *Republic* he attributes political decay to the neglect of *mousikê.* In such decay injustice plays a prominent part. The point can be more clearly illustrated from the *Laws* (701a5-7): Plato contends that musical license offers a foothold for a universal pretension to expertise in all fields, for lawlessness, and for license generally—qualities which, as he goes on to show, have proved the ruin of the whole state.

There would nevertheless seem to be some base for Philodemus' objection, since Platonic discussions of the qualities which are portrayed musically and through the dance regularly omit justice from consideration. Both the *Republic* and the *Laws* speak consistently of courage and moderation, associating them respectively with the manly and womanly natures and the Dorian and Phrygian modes. Justice never receives a like category. The omission can be explained: to permit only two Harmoniai creates an embarrassing problem for the introduction of a third cardinal virtue, and there is the further point that Plato's best-known later conception of justice presents it as subsuming the main virtues, not as merely coordinate with them. What should be noticed, however, is that Platonic theory shows complete independence here. Very possibly Plato builds on Damon's foundation, but the end toward which he builds is an original achievement.

Aristides Quintilianus' *De Musica* briefly presents certain doctrines of ethos which show a strong cosmological basis.[26] They thus run directly counter to Plato's approach; and if we could assume with confidence that they did form part of Damon's teaching, we should find ourselves equipped with an excellent added supply of specific proofs. The assumption cannot safely be made. Recent scholarship has tended to show that the view of Aristides as a continuator of Damonian theory—a view set forth by Deiters in 1870 and strongly urged by Schäfke in 1937—requires a much more rigorous examination than its proponents have ever undertaken. On the other hand, it does not seem to be altogether without foundation. One may perhaps say that the references to Damon in Aristides should neither be accepted uncritically nor simply ignored.

To sum up the whole matter, it appears reasonable to believe that Plato used Damonian theories for his own independently established ends, adopting some points and discarding many others, doubtless with compromises not now perceptible. Most important of all, the dialogues nowhere mention certain main beliefs held by Damon, while the most striking Platonic speculations, such as his admirable explanation of the origin of modes and rhythms in speech and gesture respectively, owe little or nothing to Damon. It is time to discard the old idea of Plato as an unoriginal musical theorist, a mere Damonian echo. Where predecessors had laid a secure foundation, he built on the past; but he built powerfully, daringly, and above all with individualism. We have granted Plato much where other realms of *sophia* are concerned; by taking thought, we may add a cubit to his stature in musical theory as well.[27]

The connection between music and legislation is established almost entirely in the *Laws*.[28] At the same time, what Plato says embodies the careful thought of many years, so that now and again the earlier works reveal foreshadowings. Whereas paideutic ethos in music is the province of the *Republic,* the *Laws* presents with a special degree of concreteness its author's views on paideia generally and particularly musical paideia.[29] One will search in vain for sourness or shortsightedness here: musical-literary training is treated most realistically; both its realism and its tolerance set the *Laws* ahead of the *Republic.*

Egypt, Crete, Sparta, and finally Athens as it once had been: these are Plato's models. He admires the absolute conservatism of Egyptian art and music,[30] and also the fact that it had been proved possible to legislate those melodies which possess "rightness" naturally; he cannot imagine a better example to follow.[31] Cleinias remarks that, so far as he knows, only Sparta and Crete have actually enforced musical propriety; elsewhere men obey the dictates of a disorganized set of pleasures which utterly lack the consistency of those canons by which the Egyptians regulate such matters. Another passage (805e7-806a2) notes that Spartan girls are taught gymnastic and "music"; similarly, equal education for both sexes will be a feature of the state planning of Eunomopolis (804d6-e1). The disorderly present-day performances were matched (we are told) by the disorderliness of the audience; yet even at Athens this state of affairs had not always prevailed. Once, says Plato, musical exhibitions were judged worthy of prize or penalty by means other than the whistling, clapping, and rude noises of the contemporary theater-going rabble. The officials concerned with instruction had a rule that the audience should remain quiet throughout the whole performance; among boys and their tutors, and throughout most of the crowd, order was kept with a rod (700c1-7).

For Plato the "truest tragedy" is a mimesis of the noblest and best kind of life, and he takes the polity of Eunomopolis to be just such an imitation. This noblest of dramas, as he calls it, can be realized in everyday life by true law and by nothing else (817b1-8). Vulgarity and blaspheming which employ the medium of music are intolerable: such abuses we must legislate out of existence.[32] It is to be remembered above all that our songs are our laws—a paradoxical assumption, but one which we should accept (799e10-11).[33]

The parallel is particularly suggestive as it involves the broad concept of preluding. All discourses (so runs the argument) and everything in which sound plays a deliberate part have preludes and, so to speak, overtures characterized by a kind of technical beginning useful for what will subsequently be performed. This is particularly true of the so-called kitharodic nomes. The political nomes, however, those *nomoi* which are the laws of the state, have never been given preludes. In this case such preludes will consist of exhortation (722d3-723b2).[34] It is worth noting that Plato never intended any laws actually to be sung. Rejecting popular etymology, he held that the legal sense of the term *nomos* came first. He directly develops the paradox "our songs are our laws" to reveal his political emphasis. Music, it seems, must be under state jurisdiction so as to conform to civic ideals (political "rightness") under pain of punishment, with the use of actual force if necessary. The corollary, that legislation must borrow from music the technique of preluding, is by contrast essentially a *jeu d'esprit.*[35]

Practical discussions of music as a part of public life must deal with the poet: Plato does so in detail. Poets and prose writers too compete with lawgivers for public attention. A choice must be made; and Plato unhesitatingly, if regretfully, subordinates creative ability to legislative. The lawgiver must be the one to advise the people about what is good and just; if he counsels toward wrong ends he is no better than Homer or Tyrtaeus, who give bad advice as poets (858c6-e4). Poets and prose writers are here said to have set down their "notes on life," a forcefully contemptuous phrase. Plato refuses to recognize these literary works as serious observations because they deal not with the Forms, which alone are real, but merely with the phenomenal world, which is image and illusion. The lawgiver approaches much nearer to reality; his place here seems to be almost that of the philosopher-king.

Poets as a class are not entirely capable of recognizing good and evil, Plato tells us. Out of this confusion an error "in words or even in melody" may result, making our citizens supplicate the gods in an incorrect manner. Few errors could be more serious (801b10-c5). The poet, after all, does not have to know whether his imitations are good or the reverse, though technical fundamentals must be at his disposal. One has only to look (Plato notes) at what happened in Athens and other cities where poets gradually introduced the rule of uncultured lawlessness. They were of a genuinely poetic nature, but ignorant concerning what was right and sanctioned by musical and literary tradition; thus they gave way to frenzy and were immoderately swayed by pleasure. Though they did not mean to do what they did, because of their lack of knowledge they spread the false doctrine that rightness is not in any degree whatsoever a characteristic of music, and they claimed that it is most correctly judged according to the pleasure of the person enjoying it, whether he is good or bad (700d2-e4).

The *Ion* offers a specific example of poetic ecstasy. Lyric poets, Plato says, compose in a divine frenzy. Whenever they embark upon modes and rhythms they rave, gripped by ecstasy, like the Bacchantes who can perform miracles when they are rapt, and then only. It is not by art that the poet sings, but by divine power; for if the poet had learned one theme through art he would be master of all other themes as well. God therefore takes away the poet's mind and uses him as a minister of the divine.[36] The *Republic,* however, sees the poet as one who "knows nothing more than how to represent the things that seem to be."[37]

Plato's opinions regarding poetic talent cannot be said to form any consistent broad pattern. They suggest that he was thinking at one time about the heights of a Homer or a Pindar, at another about the depths of a Cinesias or a Timotheus. He most emphatically did not believe, as Cinesias believed, that in matters of artistic judgment the voice of the people is the voice of heaven; yet there could hardly be any clearer affirmation of the belief that the poet actually does speak with the voice of heaven. The strange thing is that, as we shall see, he regarded the divine inspiration of poetry with undisguised alarm. Viewing these opposed reactions, one seems to discern that combination of fighting against the pull of the irrational and surrendering to it which Euripides embodied in Pentheus' fatal cravings and fears.

The poet, then, is dangerous, and the *Laws* imposes on him restrictions which the *Republic* already had foreshadowed. Poets who train choruses will not be allowed free choice of rhythms, melodies, or texts; compositions which reveal no concern with possible ethical effects will be banned (656c1-7). There must be a law that no poet shall produce anything contrary to those standards of excellence which have traditionally obtained in the state; nor may he make his work available to any private citizen before it has been reviewed and deemed acceptable by the duly appointed judges and guardians of the law (801c8-d4). The corollary is that no one when singing or dancing may exceed the bounds of what is publicly ordained (800a4-7).

The content of this musical-literary ideal is not merely negatively defined. Poets will have to say that virtue is happiness and that its opposite spells unhappiness, regardless of all other circumstances (660e2-6); and they must accompany such sentiments with appropriate rhythms and modes, so that they may educate the young (661c5-8). This is closely related to an ordinance in the *Republic* (379a7-b1) that all poets shall always describe the divine nature as it is, namely good.

Shortly after laying down these regulations, Plato suddenly seems almost ready to grant that the righteous man is not necessarily happier than the unrighteous; yet "if one were actually to venture to tell a falsehood to the young, what could be more profitable than this one, or more potent in implanting virtue without the use of compulsion?" The fable of the dragon's teeth proves that the immature mind will believe anything. The only problem, therefore, is to determine what belief will do the city-state the greatest good, and how the entire community may come to voice always one and the same sentiment in song, story, and speech (663d8-664a7). This new instance of "fiction on the grand scale" might incline one to conjecture that the official theory of divine goodness ought to be suspect as well. To Plato the good was single and unambiguous in its essence; the divine was not, and its seemingly complex nature troubled him. Such matters aside, we need not hesitate to say that his main concern is over the question of what practical means of employing paideutic ethos will best lead to the ideal end of uniform excellence. Indeed, his whole attitude towards the paideutic ethos of music can properly be grasped only in terms of a practical approach, one which did not include a bent for theorizing and was impatient even of theoretical technicalities. There could be no more profound error than to conceive of Plato as a research scholar.[38]

If we remember this we cannot be overly surprised at Plato's description of the civic poet and his theme. His function will be that of a more restricted Pindar: he will celebrate victorious citizens in epinician odes. He must be elderly, and a citizen of proven distinction. If he happens to lack poetic and musical talent, no matter; the important thing is that he should be known as a man of conspicuously noble deeds. To him, and to him alone, will be granted freedom of expression (829c6-d7).[39]

Anyone who knows the *Republic* and *Laws* will at first find it odd that there should be such an absence of restraint on the activities of a person whose contribution to paideia is obviously an important one; and it calls for no special knowledge of the dialogues to feel surprise at the fact that a reasonable level of skill in composition would not be required. From Plato's point of view neither circumstance is strange. The civic poet will be a man precisely like Laches' exemplar, for he and his words will show a "mutual fitness and harmoniousness," and he will be in the truest sense musical. Inner excellence must be present first: the problem of how it will find expression is secondary. On the one hand, a mere lack of technical proficiency cannot keep virtue silent. On the other, the actual process of expression requires no surveillance by the state, being already a perfect expression of the civic ideal.

It is the lawgiver who dominates all public speech. He, and not the poet, speaks with the voice of ultimate authority (858c6-e4). Yet even the lawgiver is subject to the demands of changeless civic perfection: once he has consecrated the dancing and other aspects of "music" suitable for the various religious festivals, he must never thereafter make any change (816c5-7). The concept of a single lawgiver occurs throughout Greek political thought, as a part of its mythology. He is lost in the dim beginnings of the city-state; often he seems indistinct and rather unreal. While the hierarchy of officials in the *Laws* comes much nearer reality, Plato has not ignored the philosophical basis: according to the *Republic* (395b8-c1), the Guards were to act as "skilled craftsmen of the freeborn life." Neither is the actual past forgotten: Plato's account of the origin of lawlessness in theatrical license (700a3-701b8) looks back to a past era when the supervisors of education curbed the theater-going public with a firm hand.

The hierarchy itself is minutely described in the *Laws* (764c5-765c1); only relevant points will be mentioned here. In the musical contests judging is to be the task of chosen elders working in two groups, one for the solo singing and imitative music—such as that of rhapsodes, kitharodes, and auletes—and the other for the choral singing. Two or three individuals will work directly with the various performers, and everything that has to do with music will be supervised by a special official. One learns elsewhere (670a6-b6) that the elders must have a good command of rhythms and modes and be able to distinguish them; otherwise they could not judge the "rightness" of a melody, for example, in the Dorian mode.[40] The stability of advancing age is highly valued: we must take as notably correct the judgment of elderly men, those who when judging a mixed contest (one in which rhapsodes competed) would award the prize to recitations of Homer or Hesiod (658d6-e3). The double criterion deserves notice. Hesiod's plebeian ethic ranks with the feudal, heroic standards of the *Iliad* and *Odyssey,* though his consciously didactic method contrasts sharply with Homer's narrative. Plato thus has taken thought for the common man as well as for the uncommon.

Passing to a discussion of the hedonistic evaluation of music, Plato at the outset suggests that qualified agreement be given to the popular notion that one should judge music according to the pleasure it gives. This judgment, however, cannot be haphazard: the music must be of the finest kind, notably such as delights one who excels in nobility of character and paideia. It is this sort of man, equipped with courage and sound judgment, who is to give the verdict. He will not seek instruction from the theater; he will not be swayed by the crowd's clamor, nor yet by his own lack of training.[41] He sits in judgment not as a learner but as a teacher (658e6-659b3).

Such passages underscore the fact that any notion of music as having ethos in itself was completely foreign to Platonic thought. For Plato, and for Aristotle as well, music can never be anything more than a vehicle of ethos through mimesis; good music must be that which is concordant with the excellence of a good man. One notes here, incidentally, an essential opposition to the cosmological theory of musical ethos, which assigns distinct powers and values to the individual notes.

As this same passage goes on to show, the desirable pleasure is that which ought to be desired; the fact that a pleasure actually is desired has no necessary relevance. Plato thus avoided that fatal confusion of "desirable" with "desired" which, twenty-two centuries later, compromised John Stuart

Mill's theory of hedonistic utilitarianism. Both Plato and Aristotle, however, run a risk almost equally great (one which Mill also incurs), since they make the ultimate criterion of pleasure subjective, as the opinion of the "expert" (cf. 657d8-e6). Aristotle was far more inclined to trust the voice of the people; Plato's profound distrust of mass opinion kept him from ever entertaining such a point of view. Thus he will not tolerate selection of the winning contestants by audience vote, a method formerly practiced by the Greeks and known in Sicily and Italy. This custom, he believes, has proved to be the ruin of the poets, who write to please the groundlings rather than to educate the audience as a whole (659b5-c5).

Plato proposes to make the fullest possible use of tradition. The details of his planning, however, show that an uncritical acceptance of the past had no place in his thought. There are many fine musical and choreographic compositions, he says, which have been handed down to us from antiquity. No objection can be made to choosing from these materials what is becoming and harmonious, and the choice should be left to men who are fifty years old or more. They will admit such traditional music as they consider adequate; if anything is deficient or wholly superfluous, they will either reject it or give it a new musical setting.[42] While they will draw upon the creative powers of literary and musical experts, they will not cater to any but a few of the pleasures and desires. Their duty will be to make clear to these experts the goals aimed at by the lawgiver, and to achieve their intent as regards the dance, vocal music, and the whole of choric song. What must be heard are the approved compositions assigned to the gods, and also the laudatory or censorious works of poets who are good men. The prescribed noble sentiments to be embodied in such works will be varied constantly, however, so that no one has a chance to become bored with them.[43]

The purpose of this paideia is uniformity, considered as a means to civic virtue. The basic truth or falsehood of its content matters less to Plato than being certain that "the whole community may come to voice always one and the same sentiment in song, story, and speech" (664a4-7). He has two related ideals for the citizen: first, from the *Republic*, that in private life "every individual does one thing," this one thing being whatever is peculiarly appropriate to his craft or general status; second, from the *Laws*, that civically "every individual does the same thing." If the balance of diversity and uniformity is endangered from either direction, the state cannot stand. It is for this reason that musical training must be as nearly universal as possible.[44]

Of the many controls over music which are imposed upon the people of Eunomopolis, perhaps the most important is the requirement that every adult and child, slave or free, male or female, must endlessly chorus these prescribed sentiments with which we have been dealing.[45] As in Egypt, a calendar will specify musical selections for each holy day, and no deviation from this schedule can be countenanced; the prescribed bounds of song and dance are no more to be violated than the laws of the state. One must distinguish between the types of songs suitable for men and those suitable for women, and modes and rhythms must be fitted to them; for a mode or rhythm may be completely off when the melody is not suitably matched. Division must be made according to the characteristics of the sexes: what is grand and conduces to bravery necessarily characterizes the male, we may say; again, what tends to orderliness and discreetness will be more like the character of womankind. Both the law and the usages of ordinary conversation will maintain this division.[46]

It seems clear that Dorian embodies the male characteristics, Phrygian the female. A theory current in Aristotle's day counted these the only two main modes; many instances from the dialogues suggest the same presupposition, especially the critical review of modal types in the *Republic* (see especially 399a3-c4). Bravery and discretion are there the principal traits of a brave man, such as the Guard must be (*Rep.* 410d3-411a1), and so constitute the main ethical goals of Platonic paideia—a training which we remember is to be given to both sexes. It might appear reasonable to conjecture that Plato's division of music according to the sexes relates somehow to the tradition of actual "male" and "female" notes in the modal sequences handed down, according to Aristides Quintilianus, by Damon.[47] One might, for example, guess at a parallel between male-female and the "fixed" (outer) and "movable" (inner) notes of the tetrachord. We have already contended that such a direction of thought would be wrong. Actually it is difficult to tell what factors may be involved—perhaps the contrast of "gapped" and continuous modes. The clues unfortunately are too indefinite to yield solid results.

Some attempt to define Platonic paideia is necessary here. In a sense this is not possible, since the text of Plato offers many definitions (all but one from the *Laws*) which view paideia from a variety of aspects, all legitimate and none self-sufficient. As opposed to actual composition, it is the proper use of melodies and meters originated by someone else (*Symp.* 187c8-d3). In the training of youth it is represented by a consistent habit of mind revealed through fondness for, or aversion from, the proper objects.[48] From a civic point of view paideia is having received a good chorus training, which means having been trained to sing and dance well.[49] The word "well" here refers to dexterity, not to moral excellence, since education is in itself neither good nor bad, but only a means of conveying good or bad ethical attitudes. Plato therefore adds almost at once that right education is loving good and hating evil, technical proficiency being comparatively unimportant.[50] It produces an inclination toward excellence: men of distinguished moral excellence and paideia will enjoy only the finest kind of music. For Plato education is not a matter of cultivating individual tastes, nor yet of developing mass tastes without guidance. When poets write merely to gratify the coarsest element in their audience the immediate result (he maintains) is that the audience educates itself, while eventually the poet, his listeners, and the theater as an institution all come to ruin. The spectator ought properly to be elevating his conception of pleasure by constantly hearing about what is superior to his own ethical code. For Plato, education which does not uplift men is not education; to uplift oneself he considers an impossibility.[51]

It would appear that the dialogues present two main senses of paideia. It is first of all a technical term which refers to the systematic training of children in liberal subjects, and then an idea rapidly extending to every aspect of intellectual and ethical experience, including maturity no less than childhood. On one occasion Plato calls it the drawing and leading of youth toward "right reason" as set forth in the law and as judged truly good by the experience of the best of our elders. He then ordains that childhood and age alike should revere the law. Now, since a child's mind cannot handle serious material, the precepts of the law will be conveyed to him through terms he understands, namely those of play and song.[52] In this way, through modal and rhythmic training, he will come to welcome and love the good and to turn away from what is bad even during his childhood, before he is capable of being reasoned with. When reason does come, it will find the most cordial welcome from the kind of man who can recognize it by the instinct of relationship, having received this type of education. His conscious grasp of the connection between paideia and play (*paidia*), puts Plato far ahead of his contemporaries generally and of Aristotle in particular.[53]

A close kinship exists between *paideia,* "education," and *paideusis,* "educating." Plato declares the latter to be co-extensive with choric song, a combination of vocal rhythms and modes with rhythm in bodily movement. While vocal rhythms constitute a common factor of movement, they are realized in melody: that is, vocal "gesture" does not exist, gesture being a separate category that belongs to the body. We call *mousikê* "that function of the voice which reaches the soul to achieve moral excellence in education" (672e5-673a5). It may be inferred that for Plato paideia is vocal, a view which his great pupil attempts to counter. The next chapter will discuss factors entering into this problem with regard to both Aristotle and Plato.

Later Plato startles the reader of the *Laws* with his contention that man is made to be "the plaything of God."[54] This, he continues, actually is the best thing about us; hence we should live accordingly, devoting ourselves to "the noblest of pastimes," which is to live the life of peace as best one may. If it should be asked what is correct (literally, what "rightness" is) here, the answer will be: the pastimes of sacrificing and singing and dancing.[55] While this passage is designed to explain and justify the root notion of childish play in lesser *pai-* words as applied to mature activities, it also throws light on Platonic paideia.[56] Worship of the gods is the focal point of Plato's educational system, as always in the *Republic* and *Laws;* and here the contrast with Aristotle has a special force, since the music of Aristotelian paideia is flatly secular. We note also that Plato fails to mention instrumental music when he names the constituents of "rightness" in "the life of peace." But this does not mean its total exclusion: we should, with Plato, suppose its presence under the form of accompaniment. It is solo instrumental music that he bans, as having no ethos or at best an undefinable one.

Socrates names the principal elements of paideia when he

asks in the *Theaetetus* whether a certain person has learned celestial mechanics, computation, "music," and "whatever else belongs to paideia," meaning of course gymnastic. While the latter two usually appear together in the dialogues, their separate occurrences are sufficiently important or even problematical to merit some attention. The *locus classicus* is *Republic* 401d5-8: music has decisive importance for paideia because rhythmic and harmonic elements permanently grip the soul's innermost recesses. Later Plato characteristically attempts to limit musical paideia to a function of the voice. This proposal gains a truer perspective from his frequent references to the music masters and their teaching; nevertheless the appropriate function of the kithara, according to Platonic doctrine, is accompaniment and nothing else.[57]

Gymnastic receives less attention. Not increased physical strength but stimulation of the "spirited" element within one's soul constitutes the proper end of such exercise, says Socrates in the *Republic*. The *Laws* merely ordains that boys and girls should learn dancing and gymnastic; under the latter heading is included every sort of military exercise.[58] These two categories, so often closely allied, seem to be kept separate here. One would like to think, however, that these lines represent a passing oversight with no power to contradict Plato's earlier statement. The latter (795d6-e1) is as follows: first, the subjects of learning comprise gymnastic, which has to do most immediately with bodily excellence, and "music," which aims at the improvement of the soul; second, gymnastic divides into wrestling and dancing.

The passage just cited contains a contradiction. By associating gymnastic first of all with bodily excellence, Plato largely cancels his earlier claim that it aims chiefly at the soul's improvement. Here can be seen one out of many indications that his treatment of music suffered from a failure to bring together its two apparent forms of ethos, the rhythmic-melodic element and the element mimetic of human attitudes. The *Republic* at any rate continues consistently: the Guard's nature must represent a harmonious blend of "music" and gymnastic, to insure that he will prove both wise and courageous. The balance must be correct, for too great a preoccupation with either will make one's nature extreme—brutally hard, or effeminately soft and weak. Finally, the established system of "music" and gymnastic will tolerate no innovations. Presumably Plato means the system which will be ordained from the beginning in Kallipolis. At all events, the *Laws* contains a disparaging reference to those members of the citizen body "who have been drilled into singing and moving rhythmically" and so do not stop to realize their ignorance of the details involved.[59]

That Plato paid extensive attention to the methods and aims of paideia is both obvious and well known; the background of contemporary thought on such matters tends to be ignored. At least one passage in the dialogues, however, suggests this background and thereby enables us to see the Platonic position more clearly: it is *Protagoras* 325d7-e1. The great Sophist, apparently unconvinced of the theoretical necessity for music as a part of education, says that during a boy's early schooling seemly behavior is the practical result actually sought for, rather than a skilled command of letters or of playing the kithara. This he presents as the view of the ordinary Athenian. He then notes with approval that the music teachers do in fact obtain such a result. These remarks, which the standard discussions of Greek music notice only cursorily, have considerable importance for paideutic ethos: they presumably represent not Platonic but Sophistic doctrine. If this is so—if Plato permits Protagoras to speak for himself here, as Gomperz supposed—there is a strong indication that the more lasting significance of childhood training in rhythms and modes was widely realized.

Plato himself always treats paideia as a lifelong activity which includes everything that has cultural significance, whether religious or secular. Nowhere does he propose to limit its effective sphere to childhood: he realized no less fully than Protagoras that the results of elementary education extend even into old age.[60] The word nevertheless was traditionally associated with this elementary education, and Plato thinks often of the pedagogic aspect of paideia, making many provisions for it. Thus there are to be gymnasiums and public schools in the middle of the city, where foreigners will teach military science (largely if not wholly gymnastic) and music. Attendance will be compulsory, even if the child's father does not wish him to go to school. Instruction will be coeducational, uniform, and as far as possible universal, on the principle that the pupil belongs to the state first and to his parents second. Three years of compulsory lyre study begin when the child is thirteen.[61]

The *Protagoras* gives an excellent description of the system Aristophanes looked back on fondly as the "old-fashioned" paideia (*Prot.* 326a4-b6). Plato himself, writing as it were personally in the *Laws*, discusses the type of instruction to be found three quarters of a century later. He plainly seeks to correct abuses—as he saw them—which had crept into the system. A summary of the passage (812d1-e6) follows.

For the sake of good melodic mimesis, meaning representation of the soul of a good man under the stress of events, the lyre must be so used that its notes will be clear. Teacher and pupil must make their instruments sound in unison with the voice, using no heterophony[62] or ornamentation. The accompaniment cannot include melodies which differ from those of the composer when he created the vocal line or indeed any use, whether simultaneous or antiphonal,[63] of close spacing of the notes contrasted with wide, of fast tempo with slow, or of high range with low. Neither should any and every kind of rhythmic ornamentation be fitted onto the notes of the lyre. All that sort of thing is unsuitable for those who have to acquire a rapid practical knowledge of music, since (as Jowett translates it) "opposite principles are confusing, and create a difficulty in learning."

Years earlier, Plato had attacked the empirical harmonicists and their preoccupation with microtones.[64] Though the details of instrumental technique cannot be paralleled from the dialogues, his strictures upon rhythmic ornamentation accord perfectly with what he says in the *Republic* (397b6-c6) concerning the two types of musically accompanied speech and the demands made by each on rhythm and mode. A practical grasp of music as the goal of paideia is consonant with Plato's whole doctrine. As for his objection to complicated "opposite principles," we recall the explicit civic ideal of having always one and the same sentiment in song, story, and speech (*Laws* 664a4-7).

Neither of these points startles the reader. There is, however, another which has great significance, namely the insistence upon note for note unison. Such unison had been the rule in accompanied singing until the time of Archilochus, if we may believe pseudo-Plutarch. Plato here proposes nothing short of a reversion to the musical standards of the period before Archilochus' innovation—an age almost as dim, in the fourth century, as the age of Homer and Hesiod.[65] The matter should not be thought trifling. On the contrary: it would be one of the most essential features of Platonic paideia, contributing greatly to that singleness of form which his planning so ruthlessly pursues.

The remaining references which deal with the methods and aims of paideia cannot be understood according to any narrowed meaning of the word, even when children alone are referred to. It becomes clear that the school program of musical and literary training not only could but did include the works of contemporary composers, and that this was so much taken for granted as to make Plato think in the same terms, for all the fierceness of his censorship. The brief and scattered notices available to us will not yield a clear picture, but one may conjecture that the program proceeded by chronological order. This would almost automatically produce the proper gradation of technical difficulty.[66]

One thing at any rate is certain: Plato wishes every effort directed toward the end that the youth of Eunomopolis may neither be eager for new and different imitations in singing and dancing, nor be persuaded by anyone who proposes to furnish them with every variety of pleasure. As Plato became an old man his instinctive aristocrat's distaste for novelty grew to be almost an obsession; yet when it deals with music the *Laws* generally shows a surprising degree of realism. It seems in some respects to have more marked affinities with the *Politics* of Aristotle than with the writer's own *Republic*. This realistic attitude becomes especially prominent when Plato considers what ought actually to be done. He sees that the curriculum can draw upon a great many poets, both tragic and comic, whose works almost everyone considers to be the necessary basis of a proper education; he sees also that "they all have some good in them, and some bad, too." As for the procedure to be followed, the Athenian Stranger believes their present discourse will provide an excellent pattern. Considerably less tolerance marks the earlier *Gorgias,* which undertakes an ethical evaluation of contemporary music. Its conclusions prove to be unfavorable: solo kithara playing at the competitions and aulos playing in general seek only to provide the listener with pleasure; choral productions and dithyrambic writing are no different. Broadly speaking, all professional singing to the kithara, together with dithyramb writing, was contrived for the sake of pleasure. Even tragic poetry, "stately and wonderful though it is," aims primarily at pleasing and gratifying the audience. All such activity is "nothing but flattery."[67]

Although the so-called healthy city-state in the *Republic* (373b2-7) has no tragic poets or actors, it is foreseen that tragic poets will seek permission to enter the deme and city of Eunomopolis, bringing their compositions with them. They will be told, says Plato, that the citizens are themselves writers "according to their powers" of the truest and noblest and best type of tragedy. This is nothing more nor less than imitating, under the rule of true law, the noblest and best kind of life in every aspect of government. "So then," he goes on, "children of the tender (almost, "effeminate") Muses, let your composition first be exhibited before our magistrates side by side with our own compositions. If they are the same or better, we will give you a chorus; but if not, then . . . we could not do so, now or ever."[68] The phrase "our own compositions" goes unexplained, but it seems likely that the reference is to the *nomoi,* the laws, which harmonize the civic life of the projected community. "Our songs are our laws": Plato recognizes the claim as a paradox, and recommends its acceptance. Very possibly the present passage sets forth the other aspect of this relationship: "our laws are our songs." The conception has a poetic grandeur which makes it entirely worthy of Plato, who has Socrates recall the old Pythagorean view of philosophy as the supreme "music" and say that hitherto he had always supposed it to be the truth of the matter.[69]

In the *Laws* two passages specify the permissible types of song as hymns, prayers, and encomiums. First Plato speaks of the "song of praise," together with all other songs on that theme.[70] A second musical law or type (Nomos) is embodied in the kind of supplication used at sacrifices. Plato's third Nomos somewhat disconcertingly proves to be an ethical restriction on poets and not a type at all. The second of these passages indicates that the encomium may be thought of; but here the direction of approach has altered yet once again, so that this third Nomos now appears as the assigning of hymns, prayers, and encomiums to their proper objects. A review of this whole treatment shows that Plato has shuffled the two senses of Nomos in such a way as to lose, or greatly complicate, his original sequence of thought.

The public performance of these types through the medium of choric song was for Plato a vital element of paideia.[71] He declares that by choosing modes and rhythms which suit their age and position, the civic chorus members will innocently divert themselves and also furnish examples of profitable ways (his term is *êthos*) to the young. This can be called "a better education than the ordinary man gets, better even than that of the poets themselves." It is indeed doubly paideutic, since the choristers strengthen their own education by active use, while they educate the listening youth by example. Plato never doubts the value of such training of others through the example one sets, though we shall find Aristotle holding that ethos is formed by a person's own repeated activity; and the *Laws* later states that the melodies to be taught by the chorus trainers will provide "a beneficial pleasure." So important is this goal that Plato does not hesitate to make the poets of his imaginary city-state affirm the happiness of the good man and the wretchedness of the unjust, no matter how humble the one or how prosperous the other. The poets will also have to choose modes and rhythms appropriate to accompany such sentiments, as a means to the goal of rightly educating the young.[72]

Deeply involved in all musical paideia is mimesis, which for the Hellene seems to have been much more a literal re-creating than a matter of mimicry. Plato's doctrine of habituation teaches that mimetic practices eventually grow into habits and become second nature; this will apply both physically and intellectually, if the mimesis begins at an early age (*Rep.* 395d1-3). Such habits can serve paideutically in choric song to set a good example for the young, as was just shown. The choristers of the *Laws* are to select modes and rhythms which suit their age and position. Actually the fundamental criterion, mentioned earlier and simply taken for granted here, is based on two assumptions which Plato specifies. First, there are separate dance figures and melodies of the brave and again of the cowardly person. Second, those which directly or even indirectly express excellence in the body or the soul are without exception good, while the converse applies to vice (*Laws* 655a4-b6).

It would be worth a great deal to have Plato's detailed description of just how this direct and indirect mimesis is worked out.[73] The dance poses no serious problem, since it gave such importance to miming;[74] what we need is an explicit theory of melodic mimesis, and this Plato never provides. He does at least contribute an eminently helpful, if rather idealistic, description of the two varieties of that dance which is associated with the finer bodily types and which aims at dignity. Each class divides into two subclasses, and here we are immediately reminded of the characterizations of Dorian and Phrygian in the *Republic;* for one class is concerned with war and the strenuous exertions of fine bodies and manly souls, while the other expresses the activities of a discreet spirit enjoying prosperity among pleasures which maintain due proportion. This, Plato suggests, might be called the "dance of peace," and the warlike kind the "pyrrhic." The latter imitates the defensive and offensive postures of warriors, and may be judged correct in proportion as the dancer's limbs are straight and well extended and his joints move easily.[75] The dance of peace is to be judged according to the degree to which it imitates the manner of law-abiding men—men who live under Eunomia (814d8-815b6).

The pyrrhic dance will be especially suited to a direct expression of physical excellence. It is possible, moreover, that such dances of this type as embody military exercises might represent physical excellence through images—for example, the imagery of shield movement. This dance is concerned also with the strenuous exertions of manly souls, since its goal is courage; yet Plato proposes that it be judged on grounds of purely physical harmony. The dance of peace, in contrast, will be judged on ethical grounds. Moreover, when one compares its description with that of the constituents and purposes of paideia and with the definitions of Dorian and Phrygian ethos (*Rep.* 410b10-411a1, 399a5-c4), it proves to have strong affinities with "music," though itself a subdivision of gymnastic. It could surely present likenesses of the measured and deliberate manner which characterizes men living under Eunomia.[76] Direct representation of the soul's excellence, however, seems out of the question.

Plato presumably would not have said anything more on this point, since he professes ignorance of the details of rhythmic ethos and refers the whole matter to Damon when technical questions arise in the *Republic*. The *Laws* holds that a man may do himself untold harm by handling music wrongly, since he embraces bad habits. The remarks that follow strongly suggest one great source of potential error to be the use of solo kithara and aulos. Much of this concern is understandable: the presence of a text makes ethical criticism comparatively easy; its absence turns the same task into a formidable, if not impossible, matter in which one does not know where to begin. We note that Plato does not flatly reject the possibility of meaning in solo instrumental playing. Instead he says it is extremely difficult to recognize what its modes and rhythms mean, or to see that they imitate any "worthy object." Aristotle fails to summon up more than an empirical proof for his countering view that a sung text is not essential for ethos; and while we may accept this view (taking the term ethos to mean a lasting mood) we may yet feel that in the matter of ethical judgment Plato's agnosticism, at a short remove from disbelief, represents a more reasoned approach. He sums up the whole matter by saying, "The elements of the rhythms and music as a whole are imitations of the characters possessed by the better and the worse sort of man."[77]

Since music is mimetic we must, Plato says, be particularly careful to judge it not by pleasure but by another criterion altogether. We should, moreover, seek out such music as bears a likeness to the imitation of the good, taking rightness rather than pleasure to be our standard, since the success of mimesis depends on its rightness.[78] Good music accordingly represents the soul of a good man under external influences. Rhythms as well as modes express these mimetic qualities, and they will of necessity take their pattern from the natural rhythm of a good man's life.[79] Similarly, Plato might have been expected to say that the modes should be those which express the inner Harmonia or Harmoniai of a good man. The words which he puts into Laches' mouth do imply such an approach. But what actually happens proves to be quite different: in the *Republic* the tones and accents of brave and temperate men are to serve as models. The idea of speech has a central place, for in his summary Plato speaks simply of the tones (φθόγγοι) of both classes of good men (*Rep.* 399c1-4).[80] At no point does he suggest any analogy with an inner Harmonia. It is natural to ask why he deliberately avoided what appears to be a feasible line of argument.

The parallel case of rhythmic ethos indicates what may have determined his procedure. Rhythms permissible in music will be based on observed reality—the physical manifestations, real or supposed, of rhythmic excellence in the life of a good man. Plato was by no means the first to realize the importance of properly regulating the rhythm of one's activities: fifth-century Sophism knew the principle, if the Platonic Protagoras speaks with his own voice when he says that the whole of man's life should be rhythmic and harmonious (*Prot.* 326b5-6). Plato's hesitant remarks on rhythmic ethos in the *Republic* (400b1-c3) do not contain a great deal of information; we recall that Socrates feels detailed inquiries should be directed to Damon, the expert.[81]

Although ancient critics of the later period discussed rhythmic ethos at length, their analysis turns out to be fundamentally mathematical; it is as if Socrates' words had been seized upon and enormously expanded. What we want to know are the characteristics of movement on which to base a theory of ethos, and in this matter we are fortunate to possess even as much as Socrates' assumption (*Rep.* 400c7-9) that "grace or again awkwardness accompanies a good or a bad rhythm"—a highly realistic criterion. His following remarks show the point of this parallel. He assumes, again as an obvious fact, that good and bad rhythm and modality result from a good or a bad style, if it be agreed that the music must suit itself to the words and not vice versa. The kind of style and the substance of what is expressed are governed by the soul's moral condition, but "everything else is determined by the style."

That is, a study of rhythm led Plato to physical movement in normal life, its only possible origin.[82] If rhythm necessarily imitated certain activities of man, then presumably mode did too. A sounder musicologist than he knew, Plato here traces the beginnings of music back to man's natural impulses. Elsewhere he states that all animals naturally tend to move swiftly, and that in man this impulse is the origin of the dance, of choric song, and of play.[83] Later, unhappily, this brilliant conjecture is replaced by the proposal that imitation of words by gestures has created the whole art of the dance. The shift of position betrays, as do other signs, the fundamental uncertainty which marks Plato's views on musical ethos.

If one looks again at the supposed connection between mode and speech, several points become clear. First, the mention of "tones and accents" witnesses to the markedly tonic quality of Hellenic Greek. In such circumstances battle cry and battle song, for example, are merely earlier and later stages of the same process. Second, the connection does much to explain Plato's contention, so sharply challenged by Aristotle, that melody includes words as well as mode and rhythm.[84] Aristotle sees no necessary connection at all between the modes and the human voice, and partly for this reason he does not hesitate to ascribe modal ethos to instrumental music not associated with singing. Plato regards such ethos with extreme skepticism; it may be only his belief in the mimetic nature of the Harmonia generally which prevents him from rejecting outright the possibility of its existence. The three criteria proposed by Plato for judging any work of art are its nature, its rightness, and its excellence; this (?) applies to words, melodies, and rhythms.[85] He objects to solo instrumental music because the first and last of these canons are almost impossible to apply, and because the last, when it can be applied to contemporary music, shows an unmistakable lack of excellence in such works.

A more sweeping judgment delivered by Plato proves to be unjustifiable because it is inconsistent. Examining Greek poetry from Homer onwards, he pronounces it mere mimesis, with no grasp of truth; when he refers later to other examples of mimetic art such as painting and music he calls them "forms of amusement which do not partake of the nature of truth to any great extent, but give rise to mere kindred images" of real things.[86] There seems no denying that he puts far too low a value on music here; elsewhere he unfailingly assigns it a place of utmost paideutic importance and kinship with eternal truth. On this particular occasion, apparently, Plato felt Pythagorean hypotheses to be irreconcilable with his own doctrine of appearance and reality.[87]

A passage from the *Republic* (522a3-8) defines the limits of musical paideia: it educates through the influence of habit, imparting through its two main elements a rhythmic and harmonious nature but not true knowledge. Likewise, through the literary content (whether true or fictional) it forms certain other traits of character different from the foregoing but akin to them. We recall that true knowledge can be attained only through dialectic, the coping stone of Platonic paideia. Since mode and rhythm are nonrational, while musical texts are not dialectical, it is evident that musical and literary training will never yield true knowledge. The "images" with which the arts deal stand far removed from reality. Furthermore, poets are morally irresponsible, though they may be well meaning and genuinely filled with divine inspiration. All these points involve the fundamental difficulty which regularly complicates an understanding of Plato's paideia: his tendency to combine ethical and nonethical factors. His strange distrust of the poets has already been noted; we may say here merely that the real grounds for objection probably can be found in the belief that God takes away the poet's mind to use him as his minister (*Ion* 534c7-8). This suspicious attitude toward the irrational, even when unreason expresses divinity, may partly explain why Plato banned the solo kithara and aulos: from a musical and ethical point of view they speak incoherently, yet they possess a profound affective force.[88]

The *Republic*, as we have seen, says of literary paideia merely that it produces certain traits of character which differ from the habits implanted by mode and rhythm but are nearly related to them. This near relationship certainly does not at once appear. The character traits of literary training are ethical attitudes: they imply rational acceptance of the conclusion that a given action or attitude is good or bad, to be entered upon or shunned accordingly. Mode and rhythm, however, involve neither the "is" of ethical predication nor the "ought" of ethical command. They are, quite simply, facts of existence—not immutable, to be sure, but forever outside the rightful province of moral qualification. No mode or rhythm can be good or bad in itself, and Plato always recognizes this. He does, however, link the two provinces by association.

The dialogues always discuss modal ethos empirically, defining it by some type of association. Thus Dorian and Phrygian are based on the "tones and accents" of good men undergoing violent stress or enjoying quiet well-being. Although one can understand the point of view, these assignments seem highly artificial,[89] since the actions which each mode supposedly represents are given in such detail. The fact that Plato chose Phrygian at all has always been perplexing, since references usually cited for the mode, beginning with Euripides (*Bacch.* 159), stress its association with religious frenzy. With avowed hesitation, Abert in his famous study of Greek musical-ethical theory analyzes Plato's very different attitude as follows: (1) wishing to distinguish clearly between the two chief Hellenic modes, he made Phrygian stand for passivity, for the inner life of man; (2) this is why its special characteristics are not stressed; (3) by thus generalizing wrongly, Plato omitted the distinctive element of divine infilling (*enthousiasmos*). Abert concludes that Plato's remarks reflect his own thinking, not the general view of his age, and that they gained no later supporters because they were merely one individual's arbitrary compilation. Other commentators have had approximately the same thing to say: Plato was perverse or at best inconsistent, distorting the facts so that they would fit into his system.[90] The association of Phrygian with discretion one would gather to be just another "large-scale fiction."

We must seriously question whether this is so. As a matter of fact, we must ask whether any such view would have arisen at all if the nature of Dionysiac worship at Athens during the late Hellenic period had been carefully considered. Concerning the situation at the close of the fifth century Winnington-Ingram writes:

> Nowhere, it seems, had the ecstatic tradition more completely disappeared. Once Attica too had had its wild women, as the very name of the Lenaean festival testifies; but in historical times, apart from a mission of Attic Thyiades sent regularly to assist in the Delphic rite, ecstasy had disappeared from the Athenian cult of Dionysus; his festivals were either rude and grotesque or sober and magnificent; the women of Athens carried baskets not thyrsi in his service.[91]

Such were the impressions made upon Plato's mind by the liturgy of Dionysus as he saw it actually performed. One exciting influence was obvious, namely, the aulos. This, as Aristotle notes (*Pol.* 1342b1-3), had close associations with the Phrygian mode, as did the kithara with Dorian. Plato, however, banishes the aulos altogether from his state and thereby makes Phrygian a kithara mode. This, he thought (and it was reasonable to think so), would enrich civic religious life. Considerations of religion were as vital to Plato's thinking as they were unimportant to Aristotle's.

The religious nature of Phrygian was widely recognized;[92] very possibly what Plato proposed was to adapt this nature to his concept of the state by eliminating the disquieting, irrational influence of the aulos. Also banished was the dithyramb, normally set to Phrygian (Arist. *Pol.* 1342b7); nevertheless it is clear that the worship of Dionysus will continue and will have importance in Eunomopolis. The *Republic* simply leaves religious legislation to the Delphic oracle; as a matter of historical fact the Dionysiac cult was established at Delphi by the fifth century, and its priestesses were civic officials controlled by the oracle.[93] Aristotle, who bars the aulos (and the kithara as well, rather surprisingly) from education only, is naturally impressed by the "ecstatic" and "enthusiastic" powers of Phrygian; he flatly disagrees with his teacher's analysis of its ethos. Plato, however, has taken actual experience, and not theory, as his point of departure. The empirical procedure of Aristotle is quite another matter. It is based largely on association, whereas Plato's choice of Phrygian surprises us most of all by its implication that he ignored associative factors here, as having no absolute power to determine ethos. The preceding explanation is offered as a conjecture, not as a demonstration of fact; but it does seem that the accepted criticism of Plato on this matter proves to be somewhat beside the point.[94]

A number of other serious charges remain. Plato's estimate of music's practical worth contradicts his condemnation of the arts as twice removed from reality. He applies ethical terms to the modes themselves;[95] he intellectualizes the origins of music against his own better judgment. He views the pleasure-giving function of music without Aristotle's reasonableness and breadth of outlook; unlike Aristotle, he seems never to have become aware of the importance of tension and release in musical experience. One can understand his various refusals to deal with details of musical doctrine, since he claims—or at any rate makes Socrates claim—neither to possess specialized knowledge nor to desire it. Yet when he does come to grips with some point of musical paideia the result is often vague, incomplete, and partly contradictory. It would not be just to speak sweepingly of contradiction, since the dialogues treat musical matters without any serious internal inconsistency; the differences which do appear are those between the *Republic* and the *Laws*. Undoubtedly Plato's thought changed in his old age, and his views on music are not likely to have been an exception to this broad rule. What surprises the reader of the *Laws* is to find, at many points, a position of slightly greater tolerance.

When everything possible has been said by way of criticism, Plato's theory of paideutic ethos remains fundamentally unassailable provided we accept his assumptions. His scheme of paideia well suits the *polis* and the political life for which it was designed, though by any normal criterion the pattern has a repellent rigidity. It shows a heritage of thought from Pythagorean, Sophistic, and Damonian sources; and even as it has itself drawn upon other minds, so also it contributes to the thought of the future. It is preeminently the basis upon which Aristotle builds his own structure; in a larger context, it remains the archetype for all considerations of modal ethos.

CHAPTER IV

ARISTOTLE

For Aristotle the factors of agent and patient in perception are generically alike but specifically unlike. This characteristic places them among the contrary qualities, which "suffer action and change reciprocally." Coming to be is a process by which a thing changes into its contrary; thus the patient, or sense organ, must necessarily change into the agent, or object of sense perception—the hand becomes hot, the eye colored, and so on. In perceiving we acquire the form but not the matter of an object, and our actual awareness of the fact of perceiving comes not from any one specific sense but from undifferentiated perception. The forms thus acquired are mental images, for "the soul never thinks without an image." A thing may become, or become like, its contrary; but it cannot become what it is not. Using this hypothesis Aristotle treats the subjective aspect of sense perception positively, as a developing of potential into actual.[1] Accordingly, the attitudes which constitute a person's individual ethos have existed in his nature as potentials from the beginning. The role of music thus is not to implant but to evoke.

On sound as a medium, Aristotle has little to say that would be helpful here. The *De Anima* distinguishes precisely between sound and voice in two passages: "Voice is a kind of sound characteristic of what has soul in it; nothing that is without soul utters voice. It is only by a metaphor that we speak of the voice of the aulos or the lyre . . . Not every sound made by an animal is voice . . . What produces the impact must have soul in it and must be accompanied by an act of imagination, for voice is sound with a meaning."[2]

On the further question of interplay between body and soul this same treatise takes a clear position: "All the affections of soul involve the body—passion, gentleness, fear, pity, courage, joy, loving, hating; in all these there is a concurrent affection of the body." A subsequent passage makes the point more strongly, holding that these affections are "inseparable from the material substratum of animal life." They cannot be termed causes of the soul's movement, for it moves without being moved. The *De Motu Animalium* gives an account of how the soul initiates action. In conduct, says Aristotle, it is the object of desire or of the intellect which calls movement into being. The motive is a relative good rather than the good as a whole, and may sometimes be spurious. True beauty and goodness, however, cannot be relative; and so the prime mover moves but is not moved, while desire and its faculty are moved and so move.[3]

These arguments still do not seem to account completely for sensation and reaction. One feels the lack, for example, of any detailed account of the active reason and its role in this reciprocal process. Yet Aristotle has made clear the major outlines of his theory, and it should now be possible to examine intelligently his views on the formation of ethical attitudes. The *Nicomachean Ethics* emphasizes these attitudes; the *Metaphysics* defines an attitude as a disposition for evil or good, whether absolute or relative. Elsewhere Aristotle speaks more precisely, holding that an attitude implies relative permanence. This distinction between attitudes and dispositions will appear again.[4] While he recognizes the attitudes as differentiae of a movement or activity, this recognition is after all implicit in the definition cited above from the *Metaphysics.* What we really require is an account of virtue and vice as attitudes translated into actions. For this we must go to the second book of the *Nicomachean Ethics,* which will lead to a passage in the *Physics.* The relevant conclusions of this part of the *Ethics* (1103a14-1106a24) may be summarized as follows.

Of the two types of virtue or excellence, intellectual virtue comes for the most part from instruction, while moral virtue is a result of habit. None of the moral virtues is engendered naturally within us, but we are naturally receptive of them and habit perfects us.[5] The same circumstances and actions both give rise to and destroy every virtue, but men differ according to good or bad as a result of acting well or badly; otherwise instruction on ethical matters would be unnecessary. "In short," Aristotle sums up, "like attitudes arise from like activities. This is why we must let our activities be seen as having certain characteristics rather than others; for it is in accordance with the ethical distinctions thus embodied that our attitudes ensue. And so it makes no small difference whether a man is habituated, from young manhood on, in the way of good or in the way of evil; actually it makes . . . all the difference."[6]

Virtues such as have been discussed are destroyed by excess or its opposite, whereas the observance of due measure creates and preserves and increases them. This is the principle of the mean. It is by abstaining from pleasures that we become temperate-minded, and once we have become so we are best able to practice this abstinence. Plato therefore is quite right when he says that we must be trained from young manhood onward so that we always feel pleasure and pain correctly; proper education is nothing other than this. Yet how can it be said that we become just or wise by acting justly or wisely? Must our natures not already contain these qualities? The analogy of the arts shows us that such is not the case. Rather, the opposite holds true; for one may act thus accidentally, or at another's suggestion. An action has meaning only when it is an expression of the agent's inward nature.[7]

Here we note that an action originating under the former circumstances will be "just" in an equivocal sense. Not until it is fully an expression of the agent will it be just in the strict sense. The virtue must preexist potentially, but only something already actually existing can actualize it. Chance behavior does not come within the scope of ethical analysis; acting at another's suggestion is on the other hand really important, being from one point of view the very essence of paideia.[8] Burnet, *ad loc.*, remarks that when a man acts at another's suggestion "he is realizing the *logos* or form which exists in that other's soul." Both the opportunity and the danger as regards paideia lie just here; for the soul's original capacity for moral development, though preconditioned somewhat by heredity, is largely open to impressions from without. Now during their period of study with the music teacher, which is to say during early adolescence, boys are hardly accountable. Their incapacity for direct ethical training was recognized by Plato. Aristotle, holding that "the possession of understanding and true knowledge is produced by the soul's settling down out of the restlessness natural to it," says that while learning and forming judgments based on sense perception "children are inferior to adults because of the great amount of restlessness and motion in their souls."[9] During later life a man does become accountable, and yet he does not cease to form attitudes. The classroom of the music master was the first training ground of paideia; the theater was the second, and the Greeks took this so much for granted that Aristophanes could speak quite naturally of Aeschylus as a teacher of his people. We have seen Plato's great concern for the moral standards, purposes, and effects of drama and of agonistic music—the display pieces heard at the major musical competitions.

Aristotle goes on to point out a vital difference between the arts and the virtues. A fine work of art, he says, has its excellences within itself; their presence suffices. A just or wise act, on the other hand, is further judged according to whether the agent acted deliberately, choosing means to a good end simply because it was good, and out of a constant and unchangeable disposition. The last two requirements are all-important with regard to the virtues, for it is the force of repetition which calls them into actualized being.[10]

What then is virtue? It must be either a feeling, a capacity, or an attitude of the soul. Many considerations make the first two categories unsuitable; and so we must conclude that virtue, together with the individual virtues, belongs generically to the attitudes. The next question is, what sort of attitude? Let it be said, then, that every virtue or excellence brings to perfection both the condition and the special function of that of which it is a part. Thus the virtue or excellence of a man must be that attitude which causes him to become a good man and to perform his special function well.[11] (After a reference to his earlier introduction of the doctrine of the mean, Aristotle proceeds to demonstrate it at length from natural grounds.)

It remains to consider the nature of alteration, definitively treated in the *Physics*. The following excerpts are relevant:

> Everything . . . that undergoes alteration is altered by sensible causes, and there is alteration only in things that are said to be essentially affected by sensible things . . . Acquired states, whether of the body or of the soul, are not alterations. For some are excellences and others are defects, and neither excellence nor defect is an alteration: excellence is a perfection . . . while defect is a perishing of or departure from this condition . . . Neither states nor the processes of losing and acquiring states are alterations . . . (This is true of the states of the soul no less than of the bodily states), though their becoming is necessarily the result of an alteration of the sensitive part of the soul, and this is altered by sensible objects; for all moral excellence is concerned with bodily pleasures and pains . . .[12]

Such is the background of the theory of sense perception and ethical behavior against which Aristotle's views on music must be seen, and upon which the interpretation of these views depends.

We have noticed that Plato often uses figuratively such musical terms as Harmonia; they especially characterize the dialogues of his earlier and middle periods. Aristotle on the other hand shuns musical symbolism, partly no doubt because his distinctive theory of the mean originated in medicine, as did the terms for "attitude" and "disposition." Mainly, however, his avoidance results from a reasoned impatience with Pythagorean number theories and their popular distortions. He explains the origin of all this numerology by saying that the Pythagoreans, having noted that the modifications and the ratios of the Harmoniai were capable of being expressed numerically, "supposed the whole heaven to be a Harmonia and a number." No student of the *Republic* needs to be told of the "harmony of the spheres"; Aristotle very briefly explains it in his *De Caelo*, having already branded it as untrue, though original and charming. That the supposed interplanetary distances really do embody proportionate ratios he does not doubt. What he deplores is the fact that Pythagoras' followers, perceiving so many attributes of number in sensible bodies, supposed real things to be numbers—"not separable numbers, however, but numbers of which real things consist."[13]

This, Aristotle believes, is the *ignis fatuus* that led his great teacher astray. Concerning the doctrines of Plato's lecture "On Philosophy," he says: "The numbers are expressly identified by him with the Forms themselves or principles." It will not help the present inquiry to continue the controversy over Aristotle's trustworthiness on such points. We report his words here because they suggest a certain attitude and pattern of thought. At any rate, his account in the *Metaphysics* of popular numerological delusions should convince critics, in view of the statements made by Philodemus and the author of the Hibeh musical papyrus. The portions which most concern us read as follows:

> Some say . . . that the middle strings (of the lyre) are represented by 9 and 8, and that the epic line has 17 syllables, which is equal in number to the two strings, and that the scansion is, in the right (i.e., first) half of the line 9 syllables, and in the left 8. They say also that (the number of letters in the alphabet) equals that from the lowest note of the aulos to the highest, and that the number of this aulos equals that of the whole choir of heaven.[14]

Aristotle goes on to say that when one looks at these contentions critically they seem to vanish away. Actually they embody fact along with fancy; what is distressing is the irresponsible thinking which so unjustifiably related unrelated facts involving number. This section of the *Metaphysics* leaves the impression that, by the later fourth century at least, number theory was no longer an exercise worthy of serious minds.

Aristotle regularly treats the Harmonia itself as fact rather than symbol. He does use it to illustrate the point that "even inanimate things contain a ruling principle"; but the *Topics* says it consists of notes and nothing else. Furthermore, it must not be applied to the soul; in this connection Aristotle defines it with a preciseness that merits quotation:

> In using the word "harmony" we have one or the other of two cases in our mind: the most proper sense is in relation to spatial magnitudes which have motion and position, where harmony means the disposition and cohesion of their parts in such a manner as to prevent the introduction into the whole of anything not homogeneous with it. The secondary sense, derived from the former, is that in which it means the ratio between the constituents so blended. In neither of these senses is it plausible to predicate it of soul.[15]

Aristotle's references seem to presuppose the interchangeable and, so to speak, tempered modal complex which replaced the original modes, and which was to achieve theoretical perfection through Ptolemy's elaborate systematization. The relevant passages are discussed in an appendix. Like Plato, Aristotle never directly discusses this question and seldom even notices it. There is no indication that it seemed important to either thinker. This does not mean, however, that the old Harmoniai underwent no serious changes while they were becoming octave-species. By the later fourth century the species very likely dominated completely both theory and practice, at least in cultured circles; there would thus have been no standard of comparison.

Dealing with specifics, Aristotle singles out Dorian and Phrygian as the modes which some consider the chief modal categories, so that the other scales bear one or the other of these two names. Aeolian and Iastian did come under these categories, perhaps as soon as a modal complex began to take definite shape, and it is clear that much or all of the Lydian system was in disfavor, at least with theoreticians, because of its threnodic associations.[16] Although Aristotle differed with Plato over the ethos of Phrygian, he himself did think, for other reasons, that Dorian and Phrygian had central importance.

On many occasions Aristotle emphasizes the role of music as a main constituent of paideia. It will be remembered that Aristotle agrees with Plato's definition of correct education as being trained to experience pleasure or pain properly. These, he says, are the determining factors in moral excellence, since pleasure impels us to bad acts while pain keeps us back from noble ones. Aristotle does not mean that evil must always be pleasant, and good unpleasant, but that correct paideia should see to it no such attitude has a chance to become ingrained. Guidance towards "rightness" will produce, through proper habituation, that moral excellence which the *Politics* defines as "feeling enjoyment and liking and disliking, all in the proper way"—an attitude of distaste for what is evil and fondness for what is noble and good. Our natures have a capacity for growth in either direction; systematic training is needed to develop them for good and not for evil. This will produce an "ascetic" in the finest possible sense of the term.[17]

The same point characterizes another passage which possibly has significance for the study of musical ethos. Here the contention is that the activity of a happy and good man is in itself pleasant, since the good man *qua* good enjoys actions which accord with virtue and is displeased by those which manifest vice. Just so, says Aristotle, the man who is musical enjoys good melodies but is pained at bad ones.[18] The point at issue here is whether he means to speak of ethically good and bad melodies. Since the choice of epithets reveals nothing,[19] one must decide how far the contrast extends beyond the good man and the man who is musical. Obviously actions and melodies are included, but to assume an extension to the terms which describe them is not justified without proof. A passage mentioned earlier, *E.N.* 1105a27-33, provides such proof: it states that the excellences of a work of art are self-contained and have merely to be present, whereas the actions of men must possess other qualifications in order to lay claim to moral excellence. Aristotle's whole intention is, as he avows, to show that virtues are not comparable with skills; and as one of two examples singled out to illustrate skills he names music, using a neuter plural for which our English derivative is a close equivalent. The present passage thus must make a distinction between the quite separate categories of ethically good or bad human actions and technically excellent or poor compositions.

One regrets the necessity of deciding against an apparent testimony to the reality and power of musical ethos. The type of individual mentioned here, far from being an average person, is a specialist with an expert knowledge of all that comes within the province of music as an art. Aristotle nowhere shows particular interest in musicology; the field that concerns him is the much wider one of musical and literary training, the essential constituent of all organized Greek education. Looking at music from an educator's point of view, he saw that its influence proved to be at one time beneficial and at another detrimental, according to the particular attitude it tended to establish. He did not, however, confound his own principles by applying the language of ethical valuation to the experiencing of music, which is not an attitude but only an affection (*pathos*).

Some have thought that the last chapter of the *Nicomachean Ethics* (10.9, 1179a33-1181b23) does not really belong with what has gone before, and that it introduces the subject of the *Politics*. For present purposes, at all events, it forms a convenient bridge. Its main thesis is that men become good by nature, by habit, or by instruction. Natural endowment is a thing outside one's personal control. Again, reason and instruction are not universally effective: the hearer's mind must be conditioned beforehand to the proper likes and dislikes by the nature of his fixed habits. To put it another way, the ethos proper to moral excellence must be preexistent. Finally, a complete and correct training leading toward moral excellence would be difficult to acquire, unless one had been brought up under a system of laws which provided for this. The education and activities of children must therefore be regulated by law. Contrary to what the Sophists profess, the selection of suitable laws requires intelligence. Deciding correctly is, moreover, of the greatest importance: musical-literary training provides a parallel example. Those who can pass detailed judgment correctly on the perfection and harmoniousness of a work of art are the persons trained to know such details; someone without this firsthand knowledge must be happy if it does not escape him whether, for example, a painting is well or badly executed. Now, laws are, so to speak, works of political art: this means that if one is to choose them well legislative experience is all but indispensable. To be sure, a theoretical study of constitutional law will presumably have the advantage of making the student better acquainted with the subject.[20]

These remarks seem to define clearly the limits of amateur judgment. Where music is concerned the expert alone can analyze critically the technical details of composition; the amateur has a hard enough time telling whether any given work creates a good or a bad general impression. At the same time, we must note that the last two sections of Book 10 (*E.N.* 10.22-23, 1181b12-23) do not propose a study of constitutional law through that direct experience on which Aristotle has just been insisting. Instead an academic survey is planned, less thorough than the Sophists' anthologies but not essentially different. The change surprises by its suddenness; yet few men in any age receive the opportunity to acquire a legislative turn of mind by actual experience as lawgivers. Furthermore, Aristotle was faced with the practical necessity of justifying his *Politics* and many separate constitutional treatises, of which the *Respublica Atheniensium* presumably is one. If we are undertaking to form a broad impression of his attitude toward music, we should note two points which Aristotle makes: the second field of constitutional study here proposed is "what sort of things preserve or destroy the state"; also, the study as a whole aims at determining "what laws and customs a state must have in order to embody perfect excellence." With this observation the *Nicomachean Ethics* closes.

The statement bears importantly on paideutic ethos since it indicates that the *Politics* proposes to evaluate music not theoretically but practically, as Plato had done. Plato, however, gives evidence of a certain limited dependence on the musical expert in questions of ethos;[21] his pupil accurately estimates the importance of the expert within the limits of his own proper science and takes care to keep him there—outside the province of moral excellence. Two statements from the *Politics* suggest the actual tendency of Aristotle's thought. By a theory of what might be termed aggregate excellence he concludes that "the general public is a better judge of poems and musical compositions" than the individual: different persons can judge different parts of the performance, and all of them collectively will be able to criticize it as a totality. There follows a qualified restatement: "in many cases" a crowd judges better than any single person because of the permanence and emotional stability of its collective decision. At once Aristotle adds conditions: such a crowd must be composed of freeborn persons who act according to law.[22] Plato says much the same thing, but he never shows anything other than flat disbelief in the validity of the crowd's opinion. His disagreement with Aristotle on this point is very marked.[23]

Shortly before his intensive discussion of the place music should occupy in education and the state generally, Aristotle considers why "the ancients" made it a part of paideia. He finds that it develops no skills or physical advantages benefiting work or health or martial valor. "It remains therefore that music is useful for rational enjoyment in leisure, into which [the ancients] do in fact evidently introduce it; for they give it a place in what they think is the form of rational enjoyment appropriate to the free," i.e., feasting.[24] Three quotations from the *Odyssey* follow to bolster this point, which indeed seems fairly taken. The Homeric poems consistently associate music with leisure, and the same may be said of Pindar's odes. Admittedly, neither the present statement nor any other in Aristotle's extant writings takes properly into account the liturgical use of music: this is his great error of omission. Such an approach contrasts sharply with the religous devotion of Plato's two extensive dialogues on the state.

O. Immisch, Teubner editor of the *Politics*, notes at the beginning of the long section dealing with music (1339a11-

1342b34) that it has been thought an excerpt from Aristotle's lost treatise "On Music." This section of the *Politics* opens with the very words of the title, Περὶ δὲ μουσικῆς. Whatever its origins, it forms the most valuable single treatment of musical paideia and paideutic ethos that has been preserved to us. Since the text is too long to be translated or even summarized, only the important passages will be considered.

Aristotle begins with an admission: the particular power of music is not readily defined, nor can one easily say for what purpose we should learn it. He then examines various possibilities. First, amusement and relaxation may be the proper ends of music. On such an analysis it would be like sleeping or getting drunk, pursuits which are not serious in themselves, pleasant though they may be.[25] A second possibility is that music tends to promote moral excellence, endowing our character with a certain quality by habituating us to a capacity for the correct type of enjoyment. This amounts to paideutic ethos. Finally, it may be that music contributes to our leisure pastimes and to intellectual culture. The *Ethics* considers music under the heading of ethical virtues; this is not invariably true of the *Politics*, which accuses only the aulos of imparting no intellectual benefit whatsoever.[26]

Though each category has its measure of validity, they will not all serve equally well to justify the place of music in paideia, as Aristotle at once demonstrates. He feels it is obvious that amusement (or "play") cannot be the end of paideia, since we learn not through play but through painful effort. This attempts to refute Plato's theory that a child's character can be shaped by the songs it learns, even though it cannot yet grasp serious matters. The two thinkers agree that amusement ought not to be the goal of education; Aristotle's difficulties come rather when he attempts at the same time to support his conclusion and to correct his teacher. Children do form patterns of habit in their games and in the songs which accompany their play: the really surprising thing is that only within the last hundred years have educators recognized and capitalized on a truth which was obvious to Plato, if not always to his pupil.[27]

Again, intellectual recreation seems to Aristotle a final realization of the training process, and consequently unsuitable for the formative years. Digressing, he weighs the contention that we undertake serious studies when we are children for the sake of amusement as adults. Elsewhere he dismisses this view as "silly" and "too utterly childish"; here the refutation takes the gentler form of questions. Why would a boy work hard to acquire a personal mastery of musical technique if such were the goal? Why should he not enjoy music and learn it through the skilled perfomances of professionals?[28] We shall find these questions answered in due course.

Passing to the debated issue of ethical power in music, Aristotle finds the same difficulty. Why train as a performer when one can acquire correct taste and critical ability by listening to others perform, as the Spartans do? They do not learn music, yet they are able—so they maintain—[29] to decide correctly whether melodies are good or bad. The same point applies to the use of music for refined enjoyment and intellectual entertainment. Indeed (he concludes), we think professional musicians vulgar, and we feel it unmanly to perform music except when we are drunk, or for amusement.[30]

Leaving his long digression, Aristotle returns to the main questions: does music deserve a place in education, and is it effective for education, for amusement, or for entertainment? "For all three, presumably," is the answer to the question about effectiveness. We cannot quarrel with amusement as a means to relaxation, and everyone will agree that entertainment ought to give pleasure. We all say, moreover, that music is one of the greatest pleasures we have, and we rightly use it to liven dinner parties or entertainments. Unfortunately, men have been known to make amusements an end, mistakenly seeking happiness in the attendant pleasures. Sometimes the reason for this is that certain kinds of pleasures do not so much look ahead to a final goal as backward, e.g., to hardships and pain now past. This will partially explain the handling music receives at times; another factor is music's usefulness for relaxation.[31]

Admitting that abuses may have occurred, Aristotle goes on to consider whether the essential nature of music is not more honorable than this incidental aspect would indicate. On this possibility, a second factor will be added to the pleasure that music gives naturally and indiscriminately: we must see if it somehow reaches also to the character (ethos) and the soul. There can be no question that it does so influence us, for our natures are qualified by many different types of music and notably by the melodies of Olympus, which, as everyone agrees, qualify the soul's ethos through the affective experience of divine infilling.[32] But divine inspiration does not admit of qualification in terms of "good" or "bad." So Plato argues, at least: when speaking of poets he admits and even stresses the genuineness of their inspiration, but he observes that they simply do not know whether their work is good or bad.[33] The inspired poetic vision is thus amoral for Plato, a thesis with which Aristotle might properly have dealt here. All he really has accomplished, however, is to show that the experience of divine infilling affects the soul's ethos. He has not made it clear that this proves anything about the ethical power of music in paideia, which after all did not specialize in revelations. One wonders why Aristotle chose the melodies of Olympus as his example; perhaps the dramatic vividness of their effect seemed best able to illustrate his point.

At all events, a second point follows immediately: everyone who listens to examples of musical mimesis experiences a corresponding state of feeling "even in the absence of a text, owing to the rhythms and melodies themselves." The quoted words render Susemihl's emendation of the standard text. Newman's attempts to defend the unemended text are criticized in an appendix: for the present we note that since Susemihl's reading makes Aristotle attribute ethical power to solo instrumental music it requires positive justification, especially in view of Plato's explicit opinions on this point. Actually there are three reasons why Aristotle should have spoken thus. First, he wished to reinforce his previous statement about the melodies of Olympus, which are aulos melodies. Accordingly, he explains this specific instance through the general theory of mimetic kindred feeling which it represents; it thus becomes possible, moveover, to proceed to an examination of secular music, really his sole interest. Second, he needed to correct the impression given by tragic and comic performances, where the single aulete almost invariably was heard as accompanist rather than soloist. Finally, Aristotle wished to refute Plato's contention that solo instrumental music has no discernible ethos.[34]

With this last reason firmly in mind he proceeds to repeat his point not once but twice, with additional detail. He maintains that rhythms and melodies contain representations, very like the realities they portray, of all the emotions and ethical states. Proof of their verisimilitude is the fact that we "change in our souls" when we hear them; and such emotional change has a close kinship with that which reality itself produces within us. Broadly speaking, only what the ear perceives has ethical power to any significant degree, but the melodies taken by themselves contain imitations (or "likenesses") of character. As proof of this Aristotle points out that the actual natures of the Harmoniai vary, so that the different ones affect us differently:

> Some of them make men noticeably mournful and restrained in mood, like the so-called Mixolydian; others, for

> example the relaxed modes, soften the temper of the active intelligence. Still another produces moderation and composure—Dorian seems to be the only one with such an effect—while Phrygian rouses religious ecstasy. These statements are made by persons who have devoted special study to this branch of education; and they are admirably stated, for these men take the proofs of their theories from actual experience. It is the same with rhythms: some have a markedly stable ethos, others an ethos which stirs the emotions; and of this latter class some are notably vulgar in their emotional effects while others better suit freeborn persons.

Aristotle at once proceeds to the conclusion that music can qualify the soul's ethos, and that the young must therefore be directed toward it and educated in it. Music he finds to be among the things that are pleasant by nature; "and we seem to have a certain affinity with modes and rhythms."[35]

Certain points in this unusually informative passage lend themselves to comment. One notes that throughout the entire section Aristotle's proofs relating to ethos remain determinedly empirical, with almost no admixture of musical psychology or any other kind of theory. The argument from common consent appears on more than one important occasion, and a surprising amount is taken for granted. Actually the core of Aristotle's argument is simply this: we must see whether music has the power to affect, i.e., to qualify, the soul's ethos; obviously it does—we all agree that the modes affect us variously, and experts have said which ethos results from any given mode or modal type; then our plan of education must include music. This hardly constitutes a great improvement upon Plato's views concerning ethos, and many questions suggest themselves.

One may well feel some curiosity about the facts of musical perception as they relate to ethos. According to a recurrent hypothesis of Aristotle's the soul, which exists only potentially until it actualizes its potential in thinking, never thinks without an image. The present passage calls mental images or forms *homoiômata*, "likenesses." Unfortunately Aristotle never explains the nature of these likenesses of emotional states and ethical attitudes. His general theory of perception, however, suggests two conclusions: the likenesses must be projections of forms within the soul of the agent; also, their influence upon the auditor (or patient as opposed to agent) takes the form of finally realizing the corresponding potential or predisposition within his nature.[36] All other factors being equal, what governs the success of this teleological process is the type and degree of the patient's habituation. Today the great majority of musicologists would reject out of hand the very existence of such likenesses—so far are we from understanding Hellenic views on ethos.

Aristotle states twice—three times, if we adopt Susemihl's insertion—that melodic ethos is a separate reality, and he is most explicit on this point. By all rights his proof should have dealt with the varying effects produced by different nomes, or melodic archetypes. Instead, it shifts at once to an argument a fortiori based on the modes. We can explain the shift, to be sure. For one thing, modal ethos apparently held the attention of aestheticians; the nomes never underwent comparable analysis, perhaps because they did not seem interrelated. Aristotle's specific examples of modal ethos generally follow Plato's account in the *Republic*. They are less full, but aside from the typically Aristotelian conception of Dorian as an ethical mean they differ only with regard to Phrygian. The really striking difference lies elsewhere, in Aristotle's all but direct admission that he has taken his summary from the empirical findings of expert musicologists. One assumes, moreover, that the brief mention of rhythmic ethos in the very next sentence derives from these same sources, especially since just the same sort of view is advanced. Plato, as we recall, took a precisely opposite course: he frankly left all details of rhythmic ethos to the special knowledge of Damon but acknowledged no indebtedness for the ethical valuation of the modes.

Who are the authorities mentioned in the text? The plural does not rule out Damon, since Aristotle would have known something about the Damonian school of harmonicists; and, as Susemihl noted (*ad loc.*) in his fourth edition of the *Politics,* they certainly do answer the description of persons who have "devoted special study to this branch of education." The main difficulty is, of course, Aristotle's absolute disagreement with Plato over the ethos and general respectability of Phrygian. One can find a solution, seemingly the only one possible, by supposing that the prevailing attitude toward the ethos of Phrygian shifted radically during the hundred years which separate the Periclean *floruit* of Damon from Aristotle's time.[37] If this did happen, there would have been nothing so very surprising about the Damonian theorists of the later fourth century reversing their master's position. We must admit that Damon himself cannot be made to stand back of both the *Republic* and the *Politics* without the exercise of considerable ingenuity. Still, his followers are the single most likely group of candidates, if any one group may be so called.

Aristotle's phrases offer no clues. The verb which describes his authorities is regularly translated "philosophize," but it need not refer to philosophers: decades before the *Politics* was written, Thucydides makes Pericles use this same word in the Funeral Oration, speaking for the whole Athenian citizen body. Plato can hardly be thought of, since apparently he did not command a specialist's knowledge of rhythmic ethos; the dialogues, moreover, nowhere suggest any attempt to amass empirical data on modal ethos by planned inductive experiments. Almost the only references in Plato and Aristotle which suggest that an empirical approach personally interested them have to do with Bacchic and Corybantic musical katharsis.

The details added by Aristotle should make identification

easier, but they offer no clear lead. Pythagorean musicology, for example, was harmonics—one could almost call it mystical mathematics; apparently it never had anything to do with character observation and induction. These two qualities, however, may lie behind what Athenaeus has preserved of the modal theories held by that disciple of Plato known as Heraclides Ponticus. The ethical associations which Heraclides so copiously sets forth are certainly based on observation (not necessarily his own); but he interprets the modes in terms of national character, employing a primitive method of argument which Plato and Aristotle alike tend to avoid. However the facts may stand, mention of those who "argue from observed facts" does accomplish one thing: it explains why Aristotle has felt free to omit theoretical explanation from the greater part of this entire section of the *Politics.* There is the added point that modal ethos represents the ethical aspect of sensation; and for Aristotle individual perception as such does not err.[38] His empirical handling of ethos strongly suggests that he could find no valid theoretical basis for analysis.

The remark that rhythms and modes seem to have a kind of affinity with the soul is not expanded. It is necessary that they should realize a potential within the soul, but Aristotle nowhere accounts for or discusses the origin and nature of such a rhythmic-harmonic predisposition. Even those passages of the *De Anima* which methodically disprove the theory that the soul is a Harmonia ignore the point. On this score Plato has worked out his scheme of rhythmic ethos more fully. To be sure, Aristotle may have intended an explanation for the portion of the *Politics* he did not live to finish, or may have given one in the lost work on music. The *Poetics* (1448b20-21) does say that our rhythmic and harmonic sense is a natural one, but goes no further.[39]

The next main section (ch. 6, 1340b20-1341b8) deals with the propriety of music lessons and the right choice of an instrument. Aristotle thinks it impossible, or at any rate difficult, to judge performances well unless one has at some time personally taken part in them. For this reason children should learn to perform music. Determining what material suits their age groups will be no great task. Their participation will be limited to student performances, and they ought not to be required to take part when they have reached mature years: by then they should be able "to judge of excellence and to experience enjoyment in a proper manner" on the basis of youthful studies. Some say that music makes men vulgar; and Aristotle concedes that some kinds may well be vulgarizing. One can only meet the objection by examining such points as the permissible extent of performance when civic excellence is the goal, or the proper melodies, rhythms, and instruments to use.[40]

It may be well to mention explicitly what Aristotle at first leaves implicit, namely, that much of the foregoing relates to the propriety of instrumental performances. It amounts to an attack on the display pieces of virtuoso kitharists and auletes, assuredly one of the types of music which he held to be vulgarizing. We shall consider later his direct references to these works and to the études which serve as a propaideutic for their mysteries. There can be no question of curbing vocal performance: the dramatic and other choruses, through whose ranks so many thousands of citizens passed, made up the second great bulwark of paideia,[41] while the use of skolia convivially had its own paideutic value.

The mature critical faculty, twice mentioned in the above passage, is on both occasions understood to be that which deals with ethical, not technical, excellence. One might have thought this obvious, but the Loeb translator renders the second instance wrongly. As for the charge of vulgarity, Aristotle himself has already joined in placing it.[42] Professionalism is the key word, and again instrumental music is meant. Under normal circumstances the voice cannot even attempt those technical feats which represent the natural end of instrumental technique, whereas an instrumentalist of very moderate attainments can realize them to some extent.[43] It was the solo arts of kithara playing and aulos playing that brought upon a man the name of vulgarian, and freeborn men supposedly did not practice them. A man might study with a music teacher in later life—Socrates himself did. His purpose, however, was simply to obtain the more advanced stages of paideia, unavailable to him during boyhood; he had no thought of becoming a solo kitharist.[44]

Aristotle continues with practical suggestions. These, he hopes, will prevent music from being overemphasized to the detriment of civic responsibilities and the other important duties of life. To begin with, the student must not labor to master études designed to groom him for professional appearances; neither should he pursue the "marvelous and extraordinary" feats of technique that first established themselves in the public competitions and have now filtered back into the educational system. It is the opposite sort of material which must be studied. Even this is to be used only until the student has learned to enjoy ethically good, i.e., profitable, melodies and rhythms. The aulos, moreover, can no more be considered for use than the kithara or the other professional instruments. It distracts the pupil from his studies, and it "is not a moralizing (literally, "ethical"), but an exciting, influence." It belongs therefore to occasions at which attendance brings purgation rather than instruction. Another point against it is the fact that an aulete cannot use a sung text. This, according to Aristotle, made a former generation bar its use by the young and by freeborn men. At first, in that surge of undiscriminating cultural interest which followed the Persian Wars, they had made use of the aulos. Once they had become better able to judge what conduced or did not conduce to moral excellence, and had learned through experience that the aulos did not, they came to disapprove of it. Many of the old instruments received the same treatment: any which required manual dexterity were judged unsuitable. Underlying the old story about Athena angrily throwing away a double aulos is probably the belief that education in aulos playing has no effect upon the intelligence.[45]

Earlier writers often mention the supposed bad effects of an excessive concern with music. Aristophanes satirizes the dilettante's infatuation both generally and specifically, portraying the young man who is too fatigued from musical exertions to think of manual labor and again bringing Agathon onto the stage as a lyre-twanging, saffron-robed effeminate. Plato, as we have seen, believed that preoccupation with the study of music and letters softens the character: he assigns a cowardly spirit as the natural attribute of a professional singer to the kithara.[46] We cannot, however, identify the "astounding" technical feats to which Aristotle refers with such sarcastic wonder. They must have been built up out of the stock devices, such as the tremolo and the abrupt melodic skip; extensive lists of these have survived. More important is the fact that they arose not out of the natural expression of a freeborn amateur but out of the professional's desire to catch popular fancy. Just as when a Meles or a Cinesias pandered to mass taste in dramatic poetry, so also in this purely musical instance the crowd educated itself. The unnatural and deplorable result was that the standards of its self-education were transferred to traditional paideia. Thus there came into existence a completely upside-down standard of values.

The sentences immediately preceding have been phrased from Plato's point of view, in order to suggest the relevance of Aristotle's brief remark to certain passages of the dialogues, for example *Laws* 659b5-c5 or 700d2-701a3. Both writers believe musical and literary training to be justified because it implants ethical criteria which will direct our musical enthusiasms in accordance with virtue when we are adults. "To take pleasure rightly" and "to discern what is excellent" are the twin goals, or rather the two aspects of the single goal.[47] It must have seemed a shocking miscarriage of the educational process when the crowd fashioned standards exactly opposite to these—for the ruin of the theater, as Plato frankly says—and later introduced them into paideia.

The musical material used ought, then, to be uncomplicated, and its use should continue no longer than necessary. It will not be needed, once the student has risen above the level of mere animal enjoyment and has come to recognize moral excellence in melody and rhythm. Aristotle joins with Plato in emphasizing the practical nature of the training; he differs from his master in the clarity with which he here distinguishes between the two levels of appreciation. The lower level is to be associated "even with animals, as well as with the great mass of slaves and children."[48] To use Platonic terms once more, they recognize and enjoy only what gives most pleasure. Of course the apparent distinction will not survive analysis. Both Plato and Aristotle conclude that pleasure is whatever habituation has made it: thus the good man alone knows the meaning of true pleasure. Neither thinker, however, adequately treats the point that habituation forms an essential part of education. Aristotle does say that we "learn some things by habituation and other things by conscious attention" (1332b10-11), but later he appears almost to have forgotten his claim.

As so often happens when one is dealing with Greek music, contemporary standards of judgment make it difficult to examine sympathetically this portion of Aristotle's analysis. Our cultured man esteems the music of his Western heritage not for the effect it may have on his character but because it affords him a refined pleasure, many aspects of which might fairly be called intellectual. He looks for four elements essential to extended composition: these are melodic line, rhythmic sequence, harmonic texture, and contrapuntal pattern. Hardly anyone who has carefully examined the written evidence at first hand believes that either harmony or counterpoint characterized Greek music. Leaving aside heterophony as relatively unimportant, we may say with broad truth that melody and rhythm were the two constituents of this art during its most celebrated age. Depth (harmonic or contrapuntal, or both) as well as length (melodic) characterizes our Western composition, and its vertical dimension is as important as its horizontal one; the music of the Hellenes knew but one dimension. When one deals with such an extraordinarily speculative and rational people, the resulting critical standards may well prove to have a basis quite different from anything that underlies our evaluation of our own music.[49]

We have seen that this did prove to be the case. Present-day music criticism and appreciation, no matter how profoundly based, has little or no relevance to either of Aristotle's levels. Very probably he would have felt compelled to assign it a special place on the lower, if a choice had to be made. The higher, that of ethical valuation, is peculiarly Greek and based on a peculiarly Greek complex of hypotheses, traditions, and associations.[50] Use of a one-dimensional form brought unusually keen awareness of melodic and rhythmic structure. In a highly developed culture this result becomes inevitable; comparative musicology can show many examples. The schematized or abstract form of melodic structure is the mode, the Harmonia; and this too was felt as a determinant of melodic character.

Bound up with the concepts of Melos and Harmonia were certain conclusions. These may or may not have had real validity, but they certainly seemed valid to the most acute minds of that remarkable age. Much of the belief in a theory of ethos was based on observation; disagreement occurred more often over the theoretical aspects of ethos than over the observed facts. To be sure, the whole problem was of lasting concern only to a comparatively small group of musicians and philosophers, most of them Athenians or resident in Athens. If we may judge from Aristophanes' warm and vivid portraits, the average man gave little thought to modal or rhythmic ethos, even if he had once gone to school (for which the phrase was *eis kitharistou,* it may be noted) and learned at least the elements of music. As it happened, however, the scholarly minority rather than the apathetic majority influenced the future course of musical aesthetics.

One should not suppose that Aristotle's way of analyzing the enjoyment of music disregards the markedly intellectual reaction familiar today. In fact, the *Politics* does have something to say about the intellectual contribution made by a knowledge of music. It first appears as a possibility: intellectual well-being is bracketed with refined diversion as one of the three presumed ends of music. Aristotle has stated earlier that reason and intelligence constitute the end of our being; that we must initiate and maintain our habits with reference to this end. Again, when he says that education in aulos playing has nothing to do with the intellect, the implied corollary may be that other forms of musical activity can make some intellectual contribution. But he has already reintroduced the earlier question of whether music serves for paideia, for play, or for recreation. "It may with good reason," he concludes, "be set under all three heads; it appears to participate [in them all]." Here intellectual well-being does not make an appearance: Aristotle speaks only of ways of social behavior.[51] The vital question thus remains unanswered: does instrumental music other than that of the aulos affect the active intelligence and contribute to intellectual well-being, even without a text? Since Aristotle divides the virtues into intellectual and ethical in the *Nicomachean Ethics,* and since he regularly deals with music under the second of these categories, we may presume he would answer no. It has been clear, moreover, that he holds a strong belief in the ethical power of purely instrumental music, a bolder stand than Plato is willing to take.

The fact that the aulos is rejected can surprise no one, particularly since a variety of reasons accompany the rejection.[52] One of these reasons, however, needs close scrutiny. It is the claim that aulos music has an exciting rather than a moralizing influence, and therefore suits occasions at which attendance brings not instruction but purgation—katharsis. These occasions apparently are the state religious observances, especially the Dionysiac festivals with their performances of tragedy.[53] Such, according to Aristotelian doctrine, is the proper setting for the "exciting" music of the aulos. When Aristotle denies that the aulos is moralizing or ethically effective, he really denies these qualities to tragedy as well;[54] and the fact that the element of habituation cannot be directly present supports this corollary.[55] Plato does appear to assign an ethical potential to tragedy, though not in any favorable sense. He calls it primarily hedonistic despite its awesome majesty, and he makes it almost impossible for tragic poets to obtain a chorus in his ideal Cretan city.[56] If a poet did convince the city authorities that he deserved to be heard, a kitharist rather than an aulete would provide the accompaniment for the public performance.

There appears to be considerable divergence between the two points of view. Plato clearly thinks of paideia as a lifelong process. Thus he can protest against vulgar dramatic performances on the ground that the audience ought constantly to be exposed to an ethic higher than their own. Taken in itself, this conviction must rank among the most exalted aspects of his paideutic doctrine; one regrets only that so few musical forms win approval for public performance. Aristotle, on the other hand, considers paideia in terms of elementary schooling, a childhood process with results which show their value during maturity. His distinctive theory of entelechy leads him to advance a suggestion which Plato would have found deeply shocking. It is that music for public performance should be no better than the type of audience which enjoys it.[57] There can be no doubt that Aristotle believed attendance at tragic performances to be an important experience in adult life, but he saw the goal of such attendance as purgation rather than education.

Ostensibly the kithara is banished as a professional's instrument; but if this reason had sufficed, Plato too would have banned it. The decisive reason must be the professionalism of "music" during the late fourth century, a development noted and deplored by Aristotle. This professionalizing trend may not have been so pronounced fifty years earlier. Moreover, the true lyre lacked sufficient carrying power to accompany the choric song that Plato so prominently discusses in the *Laws;* thus the absence of auloi made the kithara an absolute necessity. We shall not examine here Aristotle's historical exposition of the decline and fall of the aulos from popular favor. One claim nevertheless needs comment: when he maintains that the Greeks came to reject the aulos on ethical grounds, he probably exaggerates the importance of one factor among several. The real facts are not known.[58]

The final section (ch. 7, 1341b19-1342b34) of this treatise on music proposes to deal with modes and rhythms. Its extant portion goes only far enough to deal, perhaps incompletely, with the former. Lines 1341b19-26 give the three questions which will be considered, but textual corruption makes their precise meaning uncertain. A possible interpretation gives the headings as follows:[59] first, whether all the modes and rhythms should be used, or whether a division must be made; second, whether the same distinction or some other should apply to those persons who are working through a course of music and literature as part of their education; third, whether we should prefer melodic or rhythmic excellence. Some contemporary specialists and some of the philosophers who are versed in musical paideia have had much to say on this subject that is excellent, Aristotle believes. He leaves detailed analysis to them, proposing to treat the topic in broad outline only.[60]

As a preliminary he accepts the division of melodies, made by "some of those working in philosophy," into three categories. These are the "ethical" or moralizing, the "practical," productive of action, and finally the "enthusiastic" or "passionate," productive of divine infilling. He adopts also their disposition of the various modes under these headings and adds a triple division of his own. We learn that music serves no single and solitary proper end but a number of ends: these are paideia, katharsis, and diversion.[61]

From these hypotheses it is clear to him that the modes should all be used, but with discrimination. The most "ethical" types ought to see service in education, while the other classes of "active" and "passionate" will come into use when audiences are listening to professional performers.[62] These last two modal types, together with the corresponding melodies, must be assigned to those who enter public competitions; and, since there is a freeborn, educated element and also a vulgar element, the latter must be granted separate competitions and public spectacles. The souls of such persons are warped from the normal state; accordingly, those who compete before an audience of this kind must be allowed to use the sort of music which suits their listeners, seeing that everyone enjoys what is naturally suited to him. The corresponding deviations in mode and melody are those forms of (?)either which are highly strung ("syntonous") and irregularly colored.[63]

Education must employ the ethical modes and melodies, and Dorian is such a mode; yet we must accept any other mode which is approved by those who have a knowledge both of philosophy and of musical paideia. "Socrates, as he is represented in the *Republic*," does not do well to admit only Phrygian besides Dorian, especially after he has banished the aulos; for this mode has the same effect as the aulos—both are violently exciting and emotional (literally, "orgiastic and pathetic"). Poetry shows this to be so: every kind of Bacchic movement or similar activity is most naturally rendered on the aulos, while melodies in the Phrygian Harmonia realize the fitting modal expression of such activity. Everyone agrees that the modality of the dithyramb is Phrygian; the experts substantiate this with many examples. Notable among them is the story about Philoxenus, who tried to write a dithyramb in Dorian. He could not do so; the sheer force of nature took him back again into Phrygian, the mode which was suitable. It is also granted that Dorian possesses outstanding sedateness and a particularly manly ethos, while its relation to the other modes is that of a mean between extremes. Now since we extol such a mean and say that we should pursue it, it is clear that during our earlier training we should be schooled particularly in Dorian melodies.[64]

The last eighteen lines of the *Politics* (1342b17-34) were bracketed by Susemihl; Newman too came to regard them as an interpolation. If Aristotle did write them, he had experienced a radical change of convictions. They point out that we must undertake what is possible as well as suitable for the kind of person concerned, (?)rather than looking merely to suitability alone.[65] There are, moreover, divisions of age as well. Old men find the (?)high-pitched ("syntonous") modes no longer within their powers; nature suggests the relaxed varieties for persons of such years. This is why some musical authorities are right when they criticize Socrates' unwillingness to admit relaxed modes into education because he thought these modes made men drunk, as it were—not maddening them, after the fashion of ordinary drunkenness, but enfeebling them. It will not suffice, therefore, if we have a view merely to the later period of life and use modes and rhythms appropriate to it. We must also use any mode which suits the period of boyhood through its capacity for embodying orderliness together with education. Among all the modes this seems to be the case preeminently with Lydian. Thus moderation, possibility, and suitability clearly ought to be limiting principles in education.[66]

Of the three topics proposed at the beginning of this section, Aristotle's extant text deals with only two. We cannot predict his answer to the question whether melodic or rhythmic excellence has the greater importance. Plato appears to assign each its sphere of supremacy, and like Aristotle he constantly mentions the two together. Choric song, which for Plato (not necessarily for Aristotle) represented the supreme cultural expression of civic paideia, perfectly combines the two; it might accordingly seem artificial to make a distinction here. In the missing portion Aristotle may have attacked extreme partisan feeling on either side of the question. Certainly he does not share his teacher's fondness for using Harmonia of the soul, or of the sum total which a man's deeds and words represent; it would appear that mode was more consistently present to Plato's thought.

The triple division of melodies, with corresponding modes, shows much greater latitude than Plato anywhere permits. These categories presumably are meant to allow for the varied moods of aulos music used to accompany tragic performances: in the *Poetics* (1455b32-1456a3) the four types of tragedy include the "ethical" and the "emotional."[67] Yet the contemporary scholarly analysis which Aristotle reproduces speaks of "enthusiastic" melodies. The fact that he did not change this to "emotional" indicates perhaps that he wished to take into account liturgical music (the "sacred melodies" of 1342a9), for example that used in the Dionysiac rituals which so evidently interested both Plato and himself.[68]

The modes are not explicitly assigned to categories. We may, nevertheless, make certain choices with the presuppositions of the time as guides. Thus Dorian is eminently an ethical mode, Phrygian a passionate one. Lydian too is an ethical mode, according to the highly unexpected statement at the close of the text. The *Problems* (19.48, p. 108.10 Jan) specifically classes Hypophrygian among those modes which possess an "active" ethos; but this is later theory, not binding on the fourth century without connecting evidence. The "relaxed" modes will not readily come under any of the three headings. Aristotle treats their use as exceptional, a concession to the limited powers of the voice in old age. When he speaks in 1342a2 of a plurality of ethical modes, he is allowing room for Lydian as well as Dorian; whether Hypophrygian and other modes would also be included must remain conjectural. The whole subject of modal ethos avowedly is treated here at second hand; for his categories Aristotle depends on the theories of specialists. If he personally worked out a detailed theory of ethos as he did a theory of perception, his writings give little evidence of it.

The view that the goal of music may be education, purgation, or recreation may originate with Aristotle. It marks another flat disagreement with Platonic paideia: facts which Plato noted without considering them important are viewed in a new light, with new respect. Yet Plato did not entirely ignore the purgative and recreational functions of music. For example, he notes as observed fact the musical therapy of the Corybants which replaces "states of frenzy" with "sane attitudes" (*Laws* 791a8-b1). This distinction between a state or disposition (*diathesis*) and an attitude (*hexis*) is precisely the one Aristotle later used. What shows the difference in Plato's approach is his failure to make any use of the purgative capacity of music. Perhaps he thought it to be without civic relevance and thus classified it with Bacchic dancing; Aristotle thought otherwise.

As for the propriety of social amusement, Plato tends to show a stern and heavily critical attitude toward the activities associated with this term. Typical are his references to the use of music at symposia. He directly criticizes those who make their dinner parties occasions for vulgar musical displays,[69] and in the *Symposium* (176e6-8) he shows what should be done: the girl aulos player (who in actual fact was often a prostitute) is sent away into the inner part of the house to play "to herself, or to the other women." It must have been with such entertainment that the "slack" Lydian and Iastian were associated: this would explain their mention when Socrates asks which modes are "soft and convivial" (*Rep.* 398e9). That skolia were associated with such modes is highly doubtful. Their texts were hoary with tradition, to judge from the numerous examples cited by Aristophanes, and suggest perhaps a choice of Dorian. Through their use symposia might well be educative.

The nearest thing to social amusement that the Platonic state offers is the public musical competition; the *Laws* recognizes this as a permanent part of civic life. Choric song, also, supposedly will provide the participants with a harmless and beneficial pleasure. Essentially, however, the goal is instruction, not amusement. This is the difference between Platonic and Aristotelian musical theory which overshadows all others: for Aristotle paideia constitutes one goal, for Plato the only one. Aristotle's view makes its least exalted appearance in the double standard of musical performance. Although it is undeniably realistic by present-day standards, the distinction between concert hall and music hall ignores the broad implications of paideia in a way that Plato would have found inexpressibly cynical and shocking.[70] Subjective judgment has no proper place here; considered objectively, Aristotle's view represents one more symptom of that breakdown which the Greek city-state underwent from the late fifth century onward. The same may be said of the cultural idealism codified in Plato's dialogues, but this was symptomatic as a reaction, an unwillingness to tolerate ill-bred behavior.

When we examine the choice of modes and melodies for music which solicits popular favor, we find Aristotle's thought inconsistent. Elsewhere, in a passage previously discussed (1290a19-29), he speaks of the theory which some hold. According to this, there are properly speaking only two modes, Dorian and Phrygian; all the others are composite rearrangements. Men tend to classify constitutions in the same way; it would be more correct (Aristotle believes) to say that there are two well-constructed types of constitution or perhaps only one type, and that all the rest deviate either from the well-blended one or from the best one. Two examples follow: the more highly strung and despotic types are oligarchic; the relaxed and soft types are those dominated by the power of the masses.[71]

Returning to the present passage, we can now perceive that it twice strikes a puzzling note. First, consistency demands that it be the relaxed modes which win favor with the common crowd; this seems a fair inference from what was said earlier about constitutions. Yet Aristotle here claims just the opposite; moreover, we cannot easily suppose that the vulgar favorites could be those same modes later recommended for use in old age, and apparently approved for the earlier stages of life as well.[72] The terms "highly strung" and "irregularly colored," used to explain what kinds of mode and melody constitute deviations, involve still another difficulty. "Highly strung" was used both in a modal and a melodic context. Earlier, however, its modal association with constitutions was oligarchical. Here, as we have seen, the association must be with forms in which the commons held control, though previously this "demotic" element had characterized the relaxed modes. As for the mention of irregular coloring, this term properly applies neither to modes nor to melodies, but to genera. Plutarch (*Quaest. Conv.* 3.1.1) says the poet Agathon "reputedly was the first to introduce . . . the chromatic genus into tragedy." Aristotle may of course be attacking Agathon, and also whatever innovations the famous lines of Pherecrates lampoon.

Approval of the relaxed modes, apparently even for paideia, comes unexpectedly. Plato's *Laws* had already introduced the canon of feasibility, together with the provision for suitable music to sing in old age. The *Republic*, however, singles out two relaxed modes for rejection.[73] The writer of the present passage has not only a new criterion but a new way of following it out; for this portion of the *Politics* makes the central point that music should be a school subject so that during later life one can properly and intelligently enjoy performances by others.

The third wave, however, proves to be the commentator's undoing. This is the selection of Lydian as most orderly and educative of all the modes. Aristotle can hardly be credited with such a statement, in view of his remarks elsewhere about Dorian. Very probably the present sentence at least, or at any rate the part of it that deals with Dorian, was interpolated at a considerably later date. It does not belong within the pattern of musical thought during the late fourth century, so far as we can tell; but at some later period Lydian did gain the ascendancy, becoming the center of the modal system.[74] To an interpolator familiar with a modal complex dominated by Lydian, the present remarks may have seemed a justifiable addition.

One looks back over Aristotle's extensive comments on music with mixed feelings. His theories of sensation and alteration provide an impressive basis for procedure; scores of remarks on such vital points as ethos, modality, and educational policy are helpful when the student is struggling against odds to gain a reasonably clear picture of musical thought during the late Hellenic period. He recognized the importance of music for the purgation of emotion and for social amusement: without this recognition we would perhaps be misled by the forceful arguments of Plato, for whom Mistress Musica is ever the handmaid of theology, laboring at her lifelong task of paideia. Aristotle's whole approach to music, however, is a less thoroughly considered one than Plato's. Too much is accepted on the word of others, and inconsistencies are not wanting. If the pupil is more careful than the master about applying ethical and nonethical terms to questions of music, his works actually answer those questions less well than do the dialogues. It is as a supplement to Plato that Aristotle proves an invaluable aid for the study of musical ethos and paideia.

CHAPTER V

THE HIBEH MUSICAL PAPYRUS; PHILODEMUS

A specialized reading of the pre-Socratics and of Plato and Aristotle might leave a twofold impression: belief in modal ethos was general among intellectuals, and any disagreement which might have arisen came from differing views on the true ethical nature of a given mode. About sixty years ago, however, there came to light a papyrus containing what is often taken as a diatribe against the whole Damonian school. Since the original date of composition is believed on good grounds to be not much later than 390 B.C., it would appear that Plato's *Republic* was maintaining a position which already had been under sharp attack.[1]

Except for the version by Grenfell and Hunt, which contains questionable interpretations and is not easily accessible, no English translation of this significant document has been made. A line for line version is given here:

1 The thought has often occurred to me, men of (?)Hellas, how surprising it is
2 that certain persons pretend to knowledge outside their proper fields
3 without your realizing it. They say
4 that they are harmonicists, and they will select a number of pieces of vocal music
5 and compare them critically. Some they haphazardly
6 attack; others, equally at random, they praise highly.
7 They further say that one ought not to consider them instrumentalists

8 or singers; that this is something they let others
9 see to, while their own special province is the
10 theoretical aspect. As it actually turns out, however,
11 they show an immoderate enthusiasm for the things they "let others see to";
12 and as for the fields in which they claim to be strong, here their approach is improvised on the spur of the moment.
13 According to them, different kinds of melodies may
14 make men self-possessed, or wise in practical matters, or just,
15 or brave, or cowardly. They fail to realize that
16 the chromatic will not produce cowardice, any more than the enharmonic will produce bravery,
17 in those who employ it. Now, everyone knows
18 that the Aetolians and Dolopes and all those (?who meet) at
19 Thermopylae,[2] who employ the diatonic style of music,
20 are a more manly lot than the tragic actors, who
21 regularly sing in the enharmonic throughout. Thus
22 it is not true that the chromatic makes men cowardly or that the enharmonic makes them brave.
23 (These harmonicists) have gone so far as to fritter away a great deal of time
24 in string tuning. Their playing is much worse than that of the
25 professionals and so is their singing, while in their critical comparisons
26 there is nothing that any trained speaker could not improve upon in every respect.
27 As for what is called harmonics, the science towards which they
28 profess to have some sort of feeling, they cannot give any articulate account (of what they feel),
29 but are carried away by the performance and beat time —the wrong time—on
30 their plank seats to the actual sounds of the
31 psaltery. Moreover, their shamelessness has already led them to avow

32 that some melodies will have a characteristic associated especially with laurel, while others will resemble ivy.
33 And they go still further, asking if it is not obvious in such instances that a special type of cultivation exists, namely that of
34 mimetic excellence. Satyrs dancing to aulos accompaniment . . .

(Here the text breaks off.)

The papyrus itself dates from the period 280-240 B.C. How much earlier its contents may be is not easy to ascertain, but three separate points of evidence provide some basis for an estimate. First, the reference to enharmonic as regularly used in tragedy (20-21) proves a pre-Aristoxenian date, since enharmonic had been almost entirely superseded by chromatic in Aristoxenus' time.[3] Second, Wilhelm Crönert's thorough examination of the style of this diatribe reveals Isocratean form, construction, and terminology.[4] The author cannot have been Isocrates himself; for one thing, the neglect of hiatus argues against the possibility. Crönert attributes the work to a follower of Isocrates who lived at almost the same time as his master, before any strict Isocratean school had grown up. This would be early in the restoration of democratic government at Athens; the speech would thus date around the year 390. Though neither the speaker nor his opponents can be identified, the date indicates as the author a pupil of Damon's, perhaps that Draco whom Olympiodorus mentions.[5]

The third point of evidence derives from a proper understanding of line 30. The writer must be referring to the planks of the theater, drummed on by the aficionado who is carried away by the music.[6] This suggests that the contents of the papyrus do not merely antedate Aristoxenus but go back to some point not later than the middle of the fourth century, when the stone theater of Dionysus was built at Athens. Until this time the benches themselves had always been of wood, though solid earth foundations replaced the wooden supports after the seats collapsed in 499. This evidence suggests only a *terminus post quem,* not a precise date. Nevertheless, the Hibeh discourse is placed with considerable probability earlier than the widely mentioned reference to enharmonic in tragedy can place it. The fact that it omits any reference to a specific theater means, of course, that any conclusion drawn from line 30 must remain tentative.

Scholars have usually supposed that this speech attacks Damon or perhaps one of his pupils. If Crönert has argued correctly, Damon's dates are wrong for this; yet the question remains whether Draco or any other individual adherent of the Damonian school can have been the target. There seems no reason to suppose so. One gathers from the text itself only that a general attack has been made on a broad position and against a whole class of musical devotee—one might almost say sectary. The position must be that of the Damonian school, to be sure. All available evidence indicates that during the late fifth and early fourth centuries only two main groups existed: the harmonicists and their opponents the musical empiricists, later championed by Aristoxenus. Harmonicist views are regularly associated with Damon; from Plato and Aristides Quintilianus one may conjecture a good deal of Pythagorean and Sophistic (or at any rate Protagorean) influence, but direct proofs are lacking.

The Hibeh discourse proves especially valuable because it sets forth various aspects of harmonicist method and theory. The first is that of comparative criticism, referred to in line 5.[7] Though the judgments are here dismissed as arbitrary, the dismissal probably reveals mere ignorance of the criteria employed. These may well have seemed esoteric, if the Damonian system of evaluating melodies according to the presence or absence of "male" and "female" notes is an example. As for the insistence on amateur status and the fondness for theorizing (7-10), Damon's activities give a like impression; nor can there be any doubt about the association summoned up at the mention of melodies that are supposed to instill the major virtues or their opposites (13-15). Here a particular proof is the fact, hitherto unnoticed, that the writer specifically mentions the power of music to make men just. As Philodemus' remarks repeatedly show, this is Damonian though not Platonic.[8]

The sudden shift to a discussion of generic ethos (15-22) typifies the erratic quality of the whole diatribe. Here our main authorities cease to be helpful. Plato does not discuss the subject; his theorizing seems to assume a modal system too simple to admit the genera, though late evidence of quite uncertain value associates his name with one or another of them. Aristotle leaves unfinished the chapters on music in the *Politics*, without even his promised treatment of the rhythms. During Hadrian's reign Theon of Smyrna described the ethos of diatonic as majestic, powerful, and vigorous, and again as simple and noble and natural; chromatic he termed mournful and impassioned by comparison. He criticizes enharmonic as contrived, highly unmelodious, and lacking in naturalness compared with diatonic.[9] It would seem that he had no strictly ethical conception of enharmonic; his views on the other two genera are consonant with tradition. The author of the Hibeh diatribe makes no distinction between the ethos of chromatic and that of diatonic.

There follows the charge that harmonicists actually believe in musical associations with laurel or ivy (31-32). This is not, as previously supposed, an exaggerated reference to "program music." Laurel and ivy were universally acknowledged symbols, the one Apolline, the other Dionysiac. This musical symbolization of the contrast between the two great forces which characterized Greek religion is wholly relevant, despite the language of the diatribe, and its significance can hardly be overestimated. The rejection of mimetic excellence as a special end in music (33-34) at first appears to refer to the associations with laurel and ivy. But such is not the case; the topic is a new one, and we have maintained that the previous reference has nothing to do with direct mimesis. The Hibeh writer here attacks a genuinely Platonic doctrine, explicitly stated. He denies that the "rightness" of music lies in its mimetic excellence, as Plato claimed possibly a generation later.[10]

To sum up, the general criticisms of the Hibeh discourse attack harmonicist theory, not always Platonic but usually Damonian. When on the other hand its author singles out for ridicule a type of harmonicist, we cannot suppose that he means to describe serious representatives of any theory.[11] As a type these "enthusiasts" are familiar, for in musical-ethical belief as elsewhere extremism recurs eternally. Aristophanes and Euripides both mention it, and we shall see that Philodemus takes exception to similar extravagances. The prototype is as old as Western literature itself: the indolent, music-loving Paris whom Homer displays through Hector's criticisms.

Grenfell and Hunt accurately decribed the quality of argument throughout this discourse as unconvincing. The individual natures of the modes themselves receive no attention whatsoever; only genera are discussed in connection with ethos. Perhaps one ought not to have expected more of a period when the old Harmoniai had almost disappeared from the normal practice of music. The arguments themselves must be termed narrowly empirical, far inferior to those of Sextus Empiricus and Philodemus. When ridicule and exaggeration are stripped away, the Hibeh discourse lacks substance. Its violence may have impressed an audience of laymen, but it merits serious consideration only as a vivid document of the musical scene in Plato's day.[12]

During the Greco-Roman period the most important critic of the theory of musical ethos was Philodemus of Gadara, an Epicurean who lived during Cicero's time. From his treatise *On Music* in four volumes the papyri found at Herculaneum preserve fragments of Books 1 and 2, large sections of Book 3, and almost all of Book 4.[13] Although we should particularly like to have the missing portions of the early books, what is actually available contains much that has relevance to the present study; and some of Philodemus' comments, for example those concerning Damon or the question of verbal ambiguities, possess uncommon value for students of Hellenic music. Unfortunately, his polemic often abandons rational rebuttal for mere tirade, so that its considerable bulk proves to be less solid than might have been expected.

One finds a modicum of real or supposed musical-historical fact and theory, such as the claim that music was first and most intensively cultivated by the peoples of Sparta, Mantinea, and Pellana.[14] Here can be seen the underlying general belief that the stream of musical development flowed from Asia—notably from Phrygia and Lydia—into the Peloponnese. Philodemus does not mean to deny the undoubted Ionian influence, since his statement evidently includes only Greece proper.[15] When he says that music was first approved and then rejected, he may be referring to a sequence of events recorded nowhere else; it seems far more likely that he merely repeated what Aristotle had said about aulos playing and (quite without warrant) broadened the reference to deal with music generally.[16]

"Possibly others," Philodemus continues, "had found music a profitless pursuit even before this instance." The proof that originally followed, arguing from the attribution of music to the Muses, is available only in its beginning and so cannot be criticized. The evident fact that the ancients honored music is dismissed as having no significance: did not the Stoics esteem even divination, along with "a host of other things which confer no good, some of them leading to pronounced evil and held in dishonor by philosophy"?[17] This level of argument is not unusual in the treatise. Philodemus rarely offers points of detail concerning theory, such as the conclusion that music constitutes "a result of the quality of sound and cannot be a cause." He mentions enharmonic and chromatic genera, but only to point out their irrational nature—just the sort of attack that Epicurus himself launched.[18] Technical details such as crowd the pages of Cleonides and Gaudentius are wholly absent from the *De Musica.*

Philodemus sometimes argues by presenting only a part of the evidence: "Democritus, a peerless natural scientist among the ancients and no less accomplished as a historian, says music is a comparatively recent discovery; and the reason he gives for this is that it arose not out of necessity but out of . . . (a preexisting superfluity)." As it happens, Democritus also held that musical paideia is an important means of forming reverence in the young. Philodemus maintained exactly the opposite view, as we shall see. It would have been possible to cite Plato as well for the theory of an origin in superfluity; his version may embody some recollection of Democritean thought.[19] A final point is the denial that music imitates speech. Philodemus' terminology suggests that he meant to refer not to the general tenor of a discourse but to Plato's "tones and accents" of a brave and moderate man, imitated by Dorian and Phrygian.[20] A less likely possibility is that another, similar claim was involved. Once again, unfortunately, we lack the arguments brought forward in disproof; they were a part of the extensive lost portions of the earlier books.

Here as everywhere else, error—or what Epicurean criticism took to be error—comes under vigorous attack. At one point Philodemus makes plain what he feels is the basic fault: "As for the theoretical aspect, this is not understood by most persons. Moreover, its full development calls for careful treatment, which is lacking in those who stretch theory to absurd extremes." Since the absurdities of musical-ethical extremism were deplored as early as the first half of the fourth century, it would seem that a lunatic fringe constantly embarrassed the serious proponents of a restrained theory of ethos.[21]

Philodemus rightly notes a further complication: philosophers as such are not experts on music. Three centuries earlier Plato had freely recognized this, despite considerable play with the term *mousikos.* His excursions into Pythagorean number theory are known to all, though perhaps understood by none; but it is against the ancient theoreticians, not against the philosophers, that Philodemus directs his measured rejection of arguments from celestial mechanics:

> Even granting that the movement of the sun and moon and the distance between them have analogies with the movement (and spacing) of musical sounds, and that the zodiac (is comparable) to the system of division on the monochord, the fact of relationship is not established, since many factors which bear upon determining the nature of the analogy show the greatest conceivable difference.

None of the ancient theorists, he continues, has done anything more than

> give an inventory of what they learned from certain Pythagoreans. But if it has been shown, conversely, that they are in ignorance of celestial phenomena, then it is at once clear that they are truly insensible as regards musical theory.[22]

The sort of speculation discussed here is very like what Aristotle condemned; Aristides Quintilianus offers a wearying amount of it.

Word usage interested Philodemus. He mentions "intensification" or "moderation" of a condition. These terms may have been a standard part of the relevant technical vocabulary, though neither Plato nor Aristotle used them thus. Far more significant is a single partial sentence early in Book 3: ". . . and (?in) the verbal ambiguities which they themselves for the most part confounded alike in the modes and in the melodies and rhythms, as I showed in the preceding book." With this must be taken another excerpt from Book 3:

> For we think of bodily softness as not being the same thing as pliability, and of hardness as by no means identical with surface resistance. The one is true of wax candles, the other of an oar handle or a mattock—things which are irrational . . . Now, softness is imputed metaphorically to the soul's capacity for fear and lack of spirit and cowardice; hardness, again, (is used of the soul when it has come into a state of fearlessness or of courageous endurance).[23]

There can be little doubt that the verbal ambiguities of the former excerpt are the confused usages of "soft," "slack," "tense," and so on, of which the second passage cites two specific instances. Since we possess mere fragments of Book 2, we cannot reconstruct the exact course of Philodemus' argument. The precise physical sense in which such terms might be used obviously held a particular interest for him, however; and it would appear logical to suppose that he took the verbal confusion, applied to musical forms, as the result of a failure to distinguish between valid physical applications of certain terms and their (basically irrelevant) metaphorical uses.

At the same time, there is no question of his having given consideration to a view such as that of Schlesinger: according to her, terms of tautness or slackness referred originally to the muscular contractions or relaxations needed for producing equipartite modes on an aulos. Philodemus could not have done so, since the semitone scales of his own day did not involve these factors of performance. What he did achieve was important enough. He realized that when such thinkers as Damon, Plato, and Aristotle spoke of modes (for example) as "tense" or "relaxed" or the like, an unwitting linguistic confusion made any valid predication impossible. No other observation throughout the entire *De Musica* has comparable weight, for Philodemus' words also clearly show that such terms were applied not merely to the modes but to rhythms and to actual melodies. On the last point at any rate Plato and Aristotle are silent, as are all other sources prior to Aristides Quintilianus.

The surviving portions of the treatise do not treat modes and rhythms extensively. Plato's attack on the mischievous practices of the poet-composers reappears, with much of his actual language reproduced. If Kemke's restoration of the adjectives is correct, a fragment immediately following speaks of "the well-ordered Muse and the disordered";[24] the great Hellenic sources do not give this precise antithesis. Repeated occurrences of these adjectives and of the corresponding nouns in Aristophanes, Plato, and Aristotle suggest that here Philodemus may be preserving musical theory of the late fifth century. So also the opening of a discussion dealing with the ascription of ethos to purely instrumental music:

> I have heard some declare us foolish for supposing that (?)any philosophers or musical experts in their right minds hold that melody and rhythm without verbal significance turn us toward virtue, when (actually) they hold it is the text, set to melody and rhythm, which conduces in this manner: so Plato—explicitly, they say—in an attack upon uneducated philosophers.[25]

We may recall that Plato's condemnation of such music was essentially oblique, despite the vigor of his language. Broadly speaking, however, Philodemus has justly represented Plato's case. It might have been expected that he would go on to name Aristotle as chief among the proponents of this kind of ethos; instead, the argument takes quite a different turn.

Two other passages mention doctrines of modal ethos,

though they do not necessarily reflect Plato's dialogues.[26] The first runs as follows:

> . . . (and) moderateness and intensity of application, and that they have divided up the modes to fit each of these qualities (?and have proposed the theory) that every mode has a Tonos which relates to the emotions assumed to be present. Melodic composition, rhythms, and the rest are dealt with similarly. Therefore, as they maintain, our inner attitudes become familiarized with the modes in a kind of rapture (literally, "in the manner of one who is *entheos*," who has the god within him), and one mode is mediate and settled while another is of a (?torpid) kind.

Here we encounter for the first time the view that rapture, "enthusiasm" in its powerful original sense, regularly attends upon ethical habituation by means of the various types of character attributed to the modes. Plato has no mention of it, though isolated statements from the *Republic* and *Laws* might be wrongly generalized into such a conclusion. Neither is it Aristotelian: the *Politics* (1341b32-34) expressly adopts "the classification of melodies into ethical, active, and passionate which is made by some philosophers." Unless Philodemus has seriously misinterpreted such well-known evidence, his words indicate that a separate school of belief existed, having come into being perhaps after the fifth century. Here we have yet another warning against supposing that our modern phrase "theory of ethos" refers to the historical reality of a single doctrine.

The second of these two passages dealing with modal ethos matches the ethical theorists and their opponents against each other:

> Some, for example those of (?)Diogenes' belief, allege that one (?)kind of music is solemn, noble, single-natured, and pure, and that another is unmanly, vulgar, and illiberal; others term one severe and imperious, another gentle and

> persuasive. In either case they . . . attribute to music what is not there. Still others approach the matter more with an eye to the physical factors involved. They bid us isolate the auditory element from each of these types, on the ground that nothing of what is attributed to them belongs to either class through its own essential nature; and the same, they say, applies to the rhythms and to melodic composition. And certainly it is evident that music, though it may show the greatest variety of form . . . has never in itself made ethos manifest.

The opening lines echo both Plato and Aristotle, particularly the latter, without adding to our previous knowledge; the immediately following reference to those who concentrate attention on physical factors seems to point at Epicurus himself and his followers. Philodemus' final criticism is typically dogmatic, and no documentation or reasoning substantiates it.

Protagoras' dictum that the whole of life should be rhythmic and harmonious may be taken to be the source of a fragmentary and unidentified extract which mentions the view of music as "obviously serviceable for every part of life." Since Philodemus presents in a general form material from two specific statements of the Platonic Protagoras, his source probably does not antedate the dialogues. Still another passage, which on Gomperz' reconstruction should be attributed to Diogenes of Babylon, traces back to the first of Protagoras' sayings. Apparently Diogenes has claimed that music, rightly used, "will create a disposition which is harmonious and rhythmic in the highest degree." Philodemus' review of opposition evidence witnesses to the importance of Sophistic thought in forming theories of ethos. Seemingly original contributions by Diogenes complete this review, with counterarguments introduced into the same passage:

> Diogenes further claims that the poem of Crexus, which is not (originally) accompanied, turns out to be much more impressive when a musical setting is added; also that the

> Ephesian hymns and those sung by the choruses at Sparta will not have at all the same effect without . . . music. This, as he thought, amply sufficed to demonstrate music's power to move us. He did not stop to think how readily objections would be raised: first, that as far as impressiveness and the reasoning faculty are concerned music does not change a single thing but merely adds listening pleasure; second, that the change of feeling becomes manifest not on account of the melody but because of the honor paid to gods or men, which we presume to be an added factor; and third, that while this may perhaps occur, the reason . . .[27]

The reference to Crexus' poem must be to a single work, since the pseudo-Plutarchian *De Musica* speaks of him as a lyric poet, one of the rhythmic innovators. Philodemus' contention that music merely adds listening pleasure shows the adoption of a flatly Epicurean approach.

Only one other rebuttal deals principally with either rhythm or mode: this is the argument that if one examines dithyrambic Tropoi (modes?) one will find a great difference between the ethos of the Pindaric dithyramb and that of the Philoxenian, though the Tropos remains the same.[28] Since tradition associates the name of Philoxenus with modulation, the present statement may need explaining. Fortunately, Aristotle (*Pol.* 1342b9-12) has preserved the story of how Philoxenus tried to compose a dithyramb in Dorian but found himself compelled to revert to Phrygian, "the appropriate mode for this and all similar types of composition." It is possible, then, that Philoxenus, like Timotheus, passed through a conservative phase before launching the innovations which made his name a byword among traditionalists; thus Antiphanes hailed him as knowledgeable about what is truly *mousikê* (Athen. 643e). This praise is bestowed chiefly because he was a poet in the old sense and not merely a librettist who used other men's tunes (*allotria melê*, mistranslated by Gulick); one may conjecture that what Antiphanes admired was not meant to break drastically with tradition. Of course this is far from being proof positive: Antiphanes (*ca.* 407-333 B.C) died a half century after Philoxenus, and even as a *laudator temporis acti* he may have employed criteria rather different from those which applied in the older poet's day. He does mention (*ap.* Athen. 643d) Philoxenus' skilled use of *metabolai* and *chrômata.* The former must be "modulation," and it is doubtful that the latter can mean only "modification" of a simple melody, as *LSJ* proposes for this passage. The possibility that Antiphanes' praise is ironic complicates the whole matter further. All these difficulties seem nearest a solution if we keep to the initial conjecture that Philoxenus began as a conservative but became what Aristophanes (*Nub.* 333) called a "song-twister."

As for the attempt to substitute Dorian for Phrygian, apparently Pratinas did use Dorian for the celebrated hyporcheme to Dionysus, which directly attacks the aulos and indirectly the use of Phrygian. Experimenting with Dorian for types of composition associated with Dionysus was one method of handling the problem of his worship, but not the method which prevailed. We have maintained that Plato's approval of Phrygian is a wholly reasonable counterpart of the state control (meaning Apolline control, issuing from Delphi) of Dionysiac cult practices.

The *De Musica* contains scarcely more than a half dozen references to Damon, but their addition to the ancient evidence about him would be important almost from the standpoint of bulk alone. Damonian theory is presented more amply than in other sources, making it possible to see with special clearness how Damon and Plato differed on musical ethos.

For example, Damon "says that music will bring with it both (virtues and pleasures)."[29] Possibly the reference is only to the undifferentiated, universal pleasure gained from listening to music; Plato and Aristotle alike recognized that this existed. The text, however, has propounded a question about virtues and pleasures; Damon's remark replies to this. It is possible, then, that he viewed pleasure with that tolerance which we find in Aristotle, so unlike Plato's austere approach.

"If anyone thinks," says Philodemus at one point, "that even syllables are imitative . . ." Though the apodosis is not clear, the reference probably is to Damonian thought. The later portions of Aristides Quintilianus' treatise are filled with references to such forms of mimesis.[30] Once again, there is no indication that Plato himself ever subscribed to such doctrines.

Twice Damon is quoted as saying that "in singing and playing the lyre (a boy) ought properly to show not only courage and temperance but justice as well." To connect justice with music is absurd, Philodemus counters elsewhere.[31] If Plato had claimed that music conduces to justness, we would (he goes on) ask for proof; but he speaks differently, holding that the just has analogies with the musical. He claims neither that the musical man is just nor that the just man is musical, nor yet that either aspect assists the other where the two special fields of knowledge are concerned. (On Damon see also below, Appendix D.)

The relation between music and legislation apparently held less interest for Philodemus than for Plato. One finds nothing but an echo of various passages from the *Laws* when Philodemus refers to ". . . laying down a law that everyone should use it and introduce no innovation, (?and holding that) the current condition (*sc.* of music) differs widely from it." Connected with this, and deriving from two of the same passages (*Laws* 670, 803), is another excerpt: "He says that the lawful and serious (or "good") music was ordained primarily for the sake of honor shown to the divine, and in the second place for the paideia of the freeborn."[32] The main subject here probably is not Plato but Diogenes, Philodemus' immediate opponent. Admittedly it is the conclusion of the *Laws* that man, being the plaything of heaven, can live no better life than one of sacrificing, singing, and dancing in the gods' honor. Deliberately to rank paideia second is not Plato's way, however, and it may be argued that the lessened emphasis on musical paideia represents a later development taken up by Diogenes.

Philodemus' rebuttal comes as an attack upon the essential nature of music:

> And indeed music is not naturally either law-abiding or the opposite, like judgments or (?)things that one can see. Furthermore, if we violate the rules which some have ordained for it we are not thereby put at a disadvantage but rather at an advantage; observing these rules, on the other hand, brings not benefit but harm.

He presses the point home still more strongly when he contends that music naturally "equates with disorderliness and lack of restraint." Thus threnodies do not assuage grief or bring seemly and orderly behavior—they may intensify the sorrow.[33] Here Philodemus contradicts himself. If music is by nature neither law-abiding nor the reverse, it ought not to be connected with disorderliness and lack of restraint, since order is the embodiment of law. Philodemus is here attacking Plato's final work, and it is possible that he takes the notion of law narrowly.

Musical paideia itself and theories of ethos frequently engage his attention. He notes the view that music (*melos*) has some innate power to move us and rouse us to action. Elsewhere he refers to the argument from analogy that music influences us toward virtue and vice just as diet influences the body in matters of health or sickness. It is absolutely incredible, he retorts, that irrational things such as melodies should have the power to move us. Doubtless the same answer would meet Diogenes' claim that music can move our reasoning faculty.[34] A long passage of rebuttal sums up Philodemus' entire attitude on this question and elaborates his basic argument:

> And therefore the musical specialist who seeks the kind of understanding that will enable him to discern the nature of the various kinds of sense perception is looking for precise knowledge in things which do not have it, and his teaching on this matter is empty of meaning. The fact is that no melody, as melody (that is, with an irrational nature), rouses the soul from immobility and repose and brings it toward its natural ethical disposition, any more than it soothes or sets at rest the soul that is carried away by frenzy . . . Nor does melody have the power to divert the soul from one impulse to another or to cause intensification or lessening of the state in which the soul may find itself. For music is not an imitative thing, as some foolishly claim; nor does it, as Diogenes supposes, contain ethical likenesses that are non-imitative while showing in full all such ethical qualities . . . (as) magnificence (and) humbleness of spirit, or manliness and its opposite, or orderliness and boldness. This is no more true of music than it would be of cookery. And so (the various types of music) do not contain differentiated (ethical) attitudes, either by themselves or in combination or opposition, so far as auditory perception is concerned; the latter is the province of (?)artisans alone.[35]

From a Platonic point of view certain of these criticisms seem entirely apt. When Diogenes gives music power over the pure intellect he does what Plato never presumed to do. The attempt to grasp modal phenomena with precision ignores Plato's explicit statement that music will not yield exact knowledge (*Rep.* 522a3-b1). As he says in the *Laws* (889d1-2), it is a sort of "kindred image" of truth, not partaking of it to any great degree. But Diogenes also contends that the vehicles of musical ethos are likenesses which are not mimetic (26-28) and which at the same time make all ethical qualities manifest with the utmost clarity. Here we seem to find something of much greater importance. The point cannot be dismissed as a misunderstanding of Plato; actually it must be recognized as countering the Platonic view of mimesis. Diogenes' statement points to the existence of a separate school of thought, one whose key terms for "likeness" occur in the fragments of Damon's teaching and again in Aristotle. They are not used by Plato, who speaks directly of mimesis. It is difficult, however, to interpret the distinction involved in lines 26-28. We shall owe much to that scholar who can convincingly explain how these likenesses can manifest ethical qualities without employing mimesis.[36] At all events the present passage, besides its intrinsic importance, offers yet another instance of theory that is Damonian but not Platonic.

Philodemus' rebuttal here contains little except repeated denial of opposing views. When he concludes that musical ethos has no real existence relative to auditory perception, which is solely the artisan's province, it is scarcely easy to make out the positive implications.[37] Perhaps he means to say that theorizing about ethos is real enough, and that none but the common man judges honestly of what he hears in music. If so, he is rejecting that distrust and contempt with which Plato viewed "the many." But the matter remains conjectural.

One brief moment of sheer reason applied to the problem makes a solid contribution: "Inducing to action means impulse and choice; but melody does not, like reason, impel us rationally or implant a choice." It is absurd to say, Philodemus continues, that music "somehow affects the disposition not only of the body but of the mind as well." How can it even be claimed that the body is affected? A singer's altered facial expression does not prove this.[38]

Once again Philodemus has answered in a measure of agreement with the doctrines of the *Republic* and *Laws,* though he has adopted an Aristotelian approach.[39] Plato surely would agree that the power of music does not rationally impel or guide our choices. What Philodemus ignores is the whole positive side of the Platonic theory of ethos, the conviction that rhythmic and modal elements do implant a decided predisposition toward excellence. Impulse and choice differ only as aspects; together they manifest this predisposition through an immediate and instinctive recognition of the good, according to a celebrated passage of the *Republic* (401b1-402a4). Philodemus does not mention the theory; he regarded as nonsense the presuppositions which underlie it, for example that of the soul's motion. Less pardonable is his claim that music has no effect on the body: Philodemus ignored what unbiased students of musical phenomena, from the Hellenic period onward, have always recognized. It seems strange that as a resident of the Near East he had never observed the effects of native music.

We have met the opposition view that music "obviously" serves every aspect of life. Philodemus' counterarguments are these:

> Thus the conclusion that music is profitable (?for various kinds and classes of persons) does not obtain. If it actually does profit any group, that group is the common people. And the common people are not profited by every kind of music; nor is this true of the quantity of very elaborate music that is heard . . . and not by all but some Greeks, and under certain circumstances, and . . . now through hired performers.

This answers too shows a certain indebtedness to Aristotle, who had advocated one type of music for refined audiences and quite another type for vulgar hearers. It would be helpful to know the respects in which Philodemus felt the common people benefited from music. Taken together with his preceding description of auditory perception as the province solely of artisans, the present passage suggests he may have agreed with Aristotle that on the whole a crowd judges music better than any individual can. If pleasurableness is the criterion, it may relate to Philodemus' claim that the Greeks came to neglect music simply because it seemed to provide insufficient pleasure and relaxation.[40]

Background music, an all too familiar feature of contemporary life, supposedly aids many kinds of work. The *De Musica* might seem to be seconding this belief when it tells the story of an artist who succeeded in catching a likeness of his subject while he listened to the singing and playing of a kitharode. But Philodemus claims it is not permissible to attribute the success to the music, as Diogenes wishes to do. "Presumably Diogenes did not suppose that music endows men with added technical proficiency. If he did, he was simpleminded."[41] Diogenes may have claimed nothing more than that the kitharode's music had had a relaxing effect; the particular circumstances, however, suggest a conclusion based on mimetic ethos. In that event he would have gone well beyond any known claim advanced by Hellenic theorists.

For Philodemus, music is not to be accounted among things of serious worth: "On the contrary, most of it ends up at dinner parties." Later he cites Pindar's description of music as a delightful tidbit; he might have added Homer's observation that singing, playing and dancing are dainties of the feast. He does claim that Homeric evidence shows music to be a thing "fit for dinner parties."[42] Such a view, though it is obviously extreme and distorted, may contain more truth than the conjecture of modern scholars that Achilles and Phemius and Demodocus sang with conscious paideutic intent. One must remember that Philodemus had to combat the popular tendency to see Homer as a guide to every department of knowledge and conduct.

Music's relation to the major virtues concerns Philodemus no little: for all his skepticism, his outlook remains determinedly moral. He will readily grant Diogenes the point that "the most important thing in the impulse towards the good is liking and enjoying the things which one should." The agreement goes no further, however, for he holds that actually it is the special function of temperateness, and not of music, to discern "what is proper or not proper among men." The contrast with Plato becomes apparent at once when he continues, "As for those who say that music makes us gentle, softening our spirit and taking away its savageness, one must consider them utter fools; for it is only the instruction of reason which accomplishes this."[43]

While Philodemus sees an intimate connection between temperateness and instructive reason, he implicitly denies that "right education" in music can instill discretion through correct habituation, even though Plato in the *Republic* especially associates a temperate ethos with Phrygian. It is at once the merit and the marked shortcoming of Philodemus' method that he grants no power to the irrational. He further denies that music has anything to do with forming a reverent attitude:

> (There is the point that music) also was used by the ancients in educating youth, to form a preliminary outline of the virtues. Now, this point has already been dealt with, save perhaps as regards the quality of reverence; here we should like to have heard his explanation of just what ethical suppositions the application of literary and musical training does form, at any rate in its musical aspect (i.e., leaving the text aside).

We have noted Philodemus' insistence that Plato does not declare music conducive to a sense of justice. Gomperz has contributed a final item of evidence: when Aristophanes calls the plays of Aeschylus "full of Ares" he refers, according to Philodemus, to courage as popularly understood and not to the kind which "the philosopher" sanctioned.[44] Here "the philosopher" can hardly be anyone but Plato.

These strictures on reverence, justice, and courage do little to break down the Platonic scheme of reasoning. It pays the first two virtues scant notice in any case: the fact that Diogenes can set forth the rendering of homage to the gods as music's primary purpose shows how far he departed from Plato's line of thought. Both men reach the same broad conclusions; it is the altered approach which is significant. As for Aeschylus' portrayal of courage, one may answer that Plato bars tragedy from the first of his ideal states and grants it an entrance into the second only under conditions not likely to be met.

When he answers the claim that music has the incidental power to make us form bad habits, Philodemus may be taking his text from Aristotle. Presumably these habits would not appear if they did not truly exist, he argues, since "we have the causes of our own proper habits not from without but from within."[45] His view that a natural connection exists between music and the qualities of disorderliness and lack of restraint seems inconsistent with this line of argument. When we compare them with his treatment of the virtues, Philodemus' thoughts on the vices give an impression of not having been worked out. It is doubtless a commendable shortcoming.

On the closely related topic of psychic analysis Philodemus shows his usual impatience with Diogenes and similar theorists:

> These people divide up the parts of the soul in the most absurd way in the world. For one thing, it is not (right) to look to the forms of . . . melodic composition, which are in the realm of music, but music conceived wholly with relation to its end. For another, the parts of the soul are not arranged . . . as they claim; it is obvious foolishness to say that one part is settled and ordered while another is unrestrained and . . . passionate.

Symmetry among the parts of the soul he takes to be an impossible supposition.[46] What Philodemus attacks here is not Platonic doctrine at all but, as we have previously sought to show, a possible approach which Plato deliberately avoided. On the other hand, it may be pre-Platonic—Damonian, or even earlier—or as late as the time of Aristoxenus. Whatever its precise pedigree, the fact that Diogenes championed it provides one more example of his departure from Platonic theory.

Philodemus rejects the entire idea of parts of the soul, but the rejection is only to be expected in view of his Epicurean commitment.

The necessary subordination of text to music has Philodemus' unqualified support. A long passage, cited earlier, states emphatically that music adds nothing but listening pleasure. In the particular instance of erotic poetry he will not grant Diogenes' claim that music has power to stimulate; he attributes everything to the text. Diogenes, he says elsewhere, has no proofs to back up his theories: he has not shown that Ibycus, Anacreon, and other erotic poets corrupted young men by their melodies; actually it was their ideas which had this effect. Another passage, however, suggests that neither actor nor audience is tainted with moral evil by the text which is being presented. Dancing is dismissed: it makes no positive contribution to moral excellence.[47]

These statements form no consistent pattern of thought. Plato and Aristotle never dispute the fact that music regularly affords enjoyment: they differ from Philodemus precisely in that they assume this basic, undifferentiated pleasure and then go on to discuss certain higher levels. Philodemus may have shown common sense when he chose to reject such speculation, but he goes against all common sense when he denies that music can be erotically stimulating. Here it is Plato, Aristotle, and the Hellenic writers generally who prove to be the realists. Furthermore, when he seeks to show the text as all-powerful ethically, he brings his own efforts to nothing by maintaining a contradictory position: a dramatic poet (he argues) does the morals of his audience no harm, though erotic poets could and did corrupt men.[48]

When he is commenting on particular aspects of the theory of ethos, Philodemus' remarks apply to Plato more than once. Nevertheless, he does not disagree completely. Regarding supposed musical analogies with the position and movement of sun, moon, and zodiac he says, "The fact that one may see such a differentiated arrangement existing in the heavens seems to contribute nothing which would help one to acquire virtues or to correct one's moral habits." Surely this was not written without knowledge of Aristotle's treatment of the same point in his *Metaphysics* and *De Caelo.* These works dismiss such theorizing with comparative gentleness; perhaps Aristotle felt no wish to indict Plato for adopting the esoteric number theories of Pythagoreanism. Philodemus, however, directly attacks their relevance. Such an attitude is the only one possible for a thinker to whom the cosmological treatment of number, as found notably in the *Timaeus*, seems nothing but nonsense. His direct quarrel may have been not with Plato but with the neo-Pythagorean school, whose theorists "reduced music and its acoustical facts to a series of theological and metaphysical symbols" and upheld the belief in a *Weltharmonie.*[49]

Speaking apparently of music as characterized in the discussions of Diogenes and the ethical theorists, Philodemus claims it is "filled full of 'divine' inspiration and varnishing over, in a way that has no reason or order." The epithet "divine" is used sarcastically; so Plato had often used it.[50] On the particular topic of divine inspiration a number of passages noted earlier from the *Ion*, *Republic*, and *Laws* make it plain that Plato reacts with distrust. Here then, as in many other instances, it is Diogenes rather than Plato whom Philodemus reaches with his attacks.

Two passages dealing with modal ethos remain to be noted. One merely mentions "masculine and effeminate types of character (ethos)"; it directly follows a reference to "proper and improper types of melody." The other denies that anyone will achieve through music "a shift (literally, a "change" or "modulation") of emotions in virtue of which . . . and through which a given type of character is imputed to us." In his restoration of this passage Gomperz notes that Philodemus' denial is directed against such views as that of Aristotle, *Politics* 1340a22-23. He adds that the last part of the statement seems to be concerned with moral habits rather than emotions. To resolve this difficulty he appositely cites *Politics* 1340a10-12 on the melodies of Olympus.[51] The important part is the definition, which is specific and not general, of the emotion produced by these melodies as "the infilling of the soul's ethos." Here the difference becomes essentially a matter of aspect.

Modulation in the technical musical sense does not come under examination here, but it is a closely allied subject. Every post-Hellenic musicologist of the first rank deals seriously with it; where Philodemus' treatise is concerned, we may feel reasonably certain that the extensive lost portions of Book 2 contained attacks on the supposed *vis ethica* of modulation. Whatever the nature of his remarks, they cannot have been aimed at Plato (who mentions only Dorian and Phrygian with express approval) nor yet at Aristotle, unless the latter's own *De Musica* included a discussion of this topic. The target is not even Timotheus, who seems to be treated with respect. One concludes that Philodemus' quarrel was probably with the popular miracle tales of modal shifts. These became embedded in such sources as Athenaeus and pseudo-Plutarch; they may have been raised by Diogenes and his like to the supposed level of serious evidence supporting a theory of modal ethos.[52]

"Not everyone will be moved in the same way by the same music," we are told; then later, "In the case of what we hear there is no difference, broadly speaking"—we receive like impressions from like melodies, and we derive a like pleasure from them. There never has been any doubt that the second of these passages expresses Philodemus' own belief. Unfortunately the same conclusion was generally held regarding the first as well: it seemed foolish to suppose that Diogenes could possibly have spoken thus. We have now been shown, however, that very probably Diogenes did hold and express just this view. Thus we glimpse for a moment a late stage of the theory of ethos when music's power is thought to be highly individualized. This development we may not follow further; the subject deserves a separate study.[53] It may be worth noting that extensive modern tests have revealed extreme subjective variation and little else.

Gomperz has pointed out a notable correspondence between Aristotle's notion that "we seem to have a sort of innate affinity with mode and rhythm" and the bolder claim of Philodemus that "we have an innate affinity with music (literally, "the Muses"), one which does not have to be learned." "This is clearly shown," he goes on, "by the way infants are lulled to sleep with wordless singing."[54] Plato notes merely that such lullabies are very like aulos music. So far as one can tell, the fact did not strike him as proving any congenital feeling for the elements of music. But it is like Philodemus to be impressed by an empirical proof.[55] Plato held fast to a firm theoretical conviction that rhythm and modality form a part of the soul's structure. His own empiricism, so often overlooked, was real and striking; but here, as in every other important aspect of his thought, Plato sought to use observed proofs as flying buttresses for the central edifice, that of his theories.

Philodemus' comments on the actual affective force of music show that he has admitted a good deal. It does not seem unlikely that a reasoned elaboration of his views would have led to a theory of ethos which, though it might often be at variance with Platonic thought, nevertheless would present a comparable pattern and an area of agreement. Further speculation on this point would be unprofitable; yet we cannot stress too much the point that he did not view Plato as the archenemy.

It should now be possible to give a proper perspective to the views of Philodemus on musical paideia. A part of his opponent's thought has been cited already—Diogenes' supposed claim that the "lawful and serious" kind of music was ordained primarily for rendering honor to the divine and secondarily for the education of the freeborn.[56] This does not so much contradict Plato as assume a distinction which is fallacious in terms of Platonic thought. It furnishes impressive evidence that the old views on paideutic ethos had deteriorated under the Stoics, or even been supplanted by distinctly less philosophical considerations.

Certain of Philodemus' own comments on musical paideia may go back at least as far as Aristotle. "Many say," he tells us, "that those who lack natural capacity are not made one whit better" by music.[57] While the *Politics* does not deal with the problem posed by this deficiency, natural excellence is a vital, if tacit, hypothesis involved at the beginning of Book 2 of the *Nicomachean Ethics*, notably 1103a15-19. There the natural excellence assumed is of a moral kind; Philodemus presumably (though this is not certain) refers to contemporary ideas concerning such a person as the tone-deaf man, whose shortcoming is physical. The point deserves consideration in any case, since Plato normally assumes that all men possess an adequate rhythmic and harmonic sense. The *Laws* perhaps becomes more precise for a moment when Plato argues, at 829d1-4, that a morally and civically praiseworthy man will make a good music critic for the state's purposes even if he is not musically gifted by nature. But the reference is more probably to relative quickness at learning, a thing which need not be related to physical factors.

As for the supposed effect of musical paideia on grown men, Diogenes apparently had pointed out that the comic poets

> praise musical culture but abusively attack its absence in a man, and bar such a person from voting. The praise and abuse (comments Philodemus) is a fact; but as for the last point, this cannot be said . . . thus . . . (?)when they were

> boys and young men; for the first outlines of virtue were formed in them with a view to the virtue they would have later as men. As for the philosopher supposing that the (?)assertions of a pack of rascals are more worthy of belief than what he personally says, the fact speaks for itself.[58]

It is difficult to find passages from comic poetry which will serve to illustrate Diogenes' statement. The rebuttal does call to mind Aristotle's insistence in the *Politics*, especially 1340b35-39, that one should pursue a technical musical course during youth so as to develop moral and aesthetic judgment which will prove adequate to the needs of maturity. This again is a thoroughly Platonic precept, though each of the three thinkers develops the basic premise in his own way.

One brief statement embodies Philodemus' whole stand on the question of musical paideia: "It is not the theoretical knowledge of good and bad or suitable and unsuitable music (literally, "melodies") that educates, but philosophy working through literary and musical training."[59] The longer one considers this statement, the more strongly one feels that Plato would have thought it nearer his own position than much Aristotelian doctrine, and sounder by far than the cosmological fantasies of Damon and of Philodemus' opponent Diogenes. The great merit of Philodemus' treatment is that it permits glimpses of the later development of views on ethos, a development along lines which often were not Platonic at all, and that it confirms the independence of Plato's mature thought. Precisely because of his individuality, his discerning and distinctive use of contemporary theory, Plato is the touchstone for all subsequent musical analysis within the classical period.

It is against the background of the dialogues that we have attempted to see Philodemus. There emerges the figure of one who was a merciless and sometimes narrow critic of the Platonic theory of ethos, but not Plato's enemy. We find him holding the belief that music as such is irrational; that the text must never be subordinated to its setting; that musical theory has suffered absurd distortion; that music does not make us better at technical skills; that divine inspiration is a suspicious factor; that for the impulse toward the good it is of paramount importance to have the proper likes and dislikes.

These do not originate with Philodemus: they are fundamentals of Platonic theory. Clashes with Plato occur often enough and should not be minimized; yet an area of agreement remains. The evidence, if we have rightly interpreted it, witnesses to the fact that both men sought to fix a true and useful view of the nature of musical ethos. The sharpness of Philodemus' criticism points up what is irresponsible or incompletely developed in Plato's thought, even as the broader Platonic approach serves to reveal any narrowness on the part of Philodemus. Without the one we could not so well understand the other; the two views combine to grant an uncommonly valuable perspective. It does not seem unfitting, therefore, that a critical review of the *De Musica* should close with a word of appreciation for the contribution Philodemus has made to musical knowledge.[60]

CHAPTER VI
CONCLUSION

Among the various attitudes toward music considered in this study there exists no common denominator which can be termed the Hellenic theory of ethos. To use the term as a working concept may be thought allowable, but it is not allowable to retain that concept as Abert did in his pioneering study *Die Lehre vom Ethos.* One must admittedly grant that Damon and his school held systematic views on the power of music, views which plainly influenced the thinking of his own and later times. What the present writer cannot grant—what he has sought to refute—is the belief that Damonian theory dominated Plato's thought on this subject. While there may have been various approaches systematic enough to deserve the name of theories of ethos, these represent individual attempts. No basic theory existed, only a basic phenomenon: the real or supposed effects of music, which Greek writers sought to explain or utilize in their several ways. A major writer such as Plato borrows from several types of theory, yet the resulting body of doctrine is undeniably his own. If any unifying factor may be said to exist, it is a general belief in the real existence of musical ethos, broadly conceived, and often of modal ethos.

This body of general belief, so varied as regards details, proves to have a number of constituent parts. The basic Greek modes show ethnic origins; these were never forgotten, and on occasion—as in the conjectures of Heraclides Ponticus—a theory of ethos might be built up by interpretation in terms of ethnic character. For the most part, however, Greek writers seem to have ignored such an explanation of modal ethos as primitive and inadequate. The preference for Dorian reveals a certain amount of natural chauvinism; yet when the *Laches* claims that Dorian is "the one truly Hellenic mode," this proves to be the notion of a bluff field commander and not Plato's belief at all. Both Plato and Aristotle analyze the modes and their effects with reference to their actual use, their literary or other context; origins are passed over.

A closely related point is that of ethos by association. Upon examination this proves to be not one topic but a variety of topics, for the associative possibilities are many. To begin with, the Greeks would often characterize a mode according to the form of literary composition regularly connected with it. Plato does this to a minor extent, and even Aristotle seeks to demonstrate the ethos of Phrygian by citing its constant use in dithyrambic composition. To reason along such lines is to build on sand. We have seen, for example, that to a fifth-century lyric poet Phrygian may be just the right mode for a gay spring song; and Plato gives every indication of having flatly ignored the generally accepted associations attending upon this mode.

Again, it might appear that religious considerations would prove important. Such associations do receive mention, but they are not prominent. Though a broad division in Greek religion separates the worship of Apollo from the worship of Dionysus, music did not consistently acknowledge the separation. Plato hails music as "the gift of Apollo, Dionysus, and the Muses"; Pratinas actually seeks to establish Dorian as the rightful mode for hyporchemes and dithyrambs addressed to Dionysus.

The final possibility is perhaps the most obvious: that of ethical characterization of a mode through its actual technical characteristics. Such a procedure cannot of itself be associative.

It becomes so when the data of physical proportion, compass, and tonal center of gravity are treated as being significantly related to ethical terms, for example the idea of slackness or of the mean. We have sought to show that such transference of meaning never was warranted, that it resulted possibly from an inadequate technical grasp of music on the part of philosophers, and that it was just this practice which Philodemus rightly censured when he referred to verbal ambiguities. The special case of Pratinas, who speaks figuratively of Aeolian as a mean, is understandable only if his words are given an ethical rather than a musical context.

A good deal of evidence has been cited here to support the belief that paideutic ethos was considered a valid and highly significant function of music during the Hellenic age. Dissenting voices made themselves heard, to be sure, but it is clear that they constituted a minority. At the same time, majority opinion never displayed any clear tendency toward critical analysis of the modes. The strict selectiveness of a Plato is unique, and even with him the restrictions seem to arise out of an inflexible determination to achieve simplicity, not from any deep feeling against the majority of modes as such. Aristotle, on the other hand, welcomes the use of any mode that has the experts' stamp of approval, and he sees a possible usefulness for all.

The subject of music's power to affect men is eminently the province of philosopher and theorist, and the one direct statement that we have comes from Plato. Music, he points out, has decisive importance for elementary education because rhythm and mode "sink deep into the soul" and remain fixed there. Modern scientific research largely confirms the accuracy of his theorizing. Aristotle presents a closely reasoned scheme of perception and habituation within the framework of entelechy, but on the basic issue he can only recognize the soul's affinity with music. The same admission comes later from Philodemus, who seems to have read and remembered Aristotle on this point; and there is a faint, scattered echo, particularly of the Platonic view, even as late as Boethius.

So much may be said on the subject, but no more. A possible, though not essential, concomitant of any theory of paideutic musical ethos is the attributing of ethical qualities to music itself. We cannot state too emphatically that Hellenic theorists took great care to avoid doing this. Even when Aristotle argues for the affective ethical power of nonvocal music, he means to maintain not that melody as such is good or bad but that music has the power to influence the deliberate actions of men without a sung text. Philodemus' insistence on the irrational nature of music may have been a necessary antidote to the peculiar views of his opponent Diogenes. Against Plato and Aristotle, on the other hand, it is not needed once we have recognized the just indictment of ambiguous terminology.

Modern critics of Hellenic musicology have little patience with its attempts to handle the problem of ethos. They point out that no single approach will explain ethos, that one must take into account a wide variety of factors. This is true; nevertheless, classical theory should not be rated too low. Much of what it passed over may well represent deliberate omission. The listener's mood, for example, which is now regularly taken into account, may have seemed purely incidental and not at all a legitimate part of valid theory. Hellenic musical doctrine presents much to command admiration. Seldom dogmatic, it shows a firm conviction that theory must work together with actual observation. If it depends too much at times upon empirical proofs, it also avoids becoming mere analysis of the status quo. Seeking always the difficult balance between matter and spirit, between appearance and reality, it constitutes a worthy expression of the mind of Hellas during a period unparalleled in the history of Western thought.

APPENDICES

BIBLIOGRAPHY

NOTES

APPENDICES

APPENDIX A (SEE P. 118): MODALITY IN ARISTOTLE

A single statement in the *Politics* (1276b8-9) appears to be the only one in all his works that might indicate whether Aristotle's references presuppose interchangeable modes. The text (a translation is given below) is as follows: ἁρμονίαν τῶν αὐτῶν φθόγγων ἑτέραν εἶναι λέγομεν, ἂν ὁτὲ μὲν ᾖ Δώριος ὁτὲ δὲ Φρύγιος. J. Handschin, *Der Toncharakter* (Zurich, 1948), p. 350, rightly sees that Aristotle cannot be referring to transposition scales, which would have different pitch. The context shows that "die verschiedene Zusammensetzung bei physisch gleichbleibenden Elementen" is meant here, or so the argument runs. It is evident from his article "Tonart und Ethos" (in *Festschrift für Johannes Wolf* [Berlin, 1929], pp. 73-78) that E. M. von Hornbostel never considered the implication of Aristotle's words here, if he knew about them at all. Of his two invalid proofs, designed to show that ethos was based on absolute pitch rather than interval sequence, the first is a claim that "the ancients" spoke of a Dorian or Phrygian tone (φθόγγος). His ancients are Pliny the Elder, *H.N.* 2.20, and Martianus Capella, *De Nupt.* 2.196. One sympathizes with H. Abert's distress in 1929 over the fact that the new generation of musicologists for the most part did not know Greek.

Jowett translates Aristotle's words as follows: "A scale containing the same sounds is said to be different, accordingly as the Dorian or the Phrygian mode is employed." H. Rackham, the Loeb translator, gives this version: "A musical tune consisting of the same notes we call a different tune if at one time it is played in the Dorian mode and at another in the Phrygian." The latter interpretation, if correct, presupposes the old modality.

Several considerations indicate that it is not correct. First, *harmonia* does not mean "tune" according to any normal usage. Aristotle's exact discussion of its two proper senses and its metaphorical application has already been quoted. Second, the preceding text (*Pol.* 1276b1-8) contains the statement that if the state is an association of citizens under a constitution, a change in the form of constitution must mean that the state too has become different. Two analogies illustrate this point. One is that of a dramatic chorus: it is spoken of as different in its two differing uses (for tragedy or again for comedy), even though it may often be composed of the same persons. Similarly, we say of any other association or composite that it is different if the form of its composition (*sunthesis*) differs. The example of musical mode follows at this point.

K. Schlesinger's rendering in *The Greek Aulos* (London, 1939), p. 180, is ". . . we say a Harmonia of the same notes is different when it is Dorian and when it is Phrygian." Her explanation follows:

> The Harmonia of the same notes means, of course, the notes from Hypate Meson to Nete Diezeugmenon *kata thesin* or the strings of those names on the Kithara, but tuned *kata dunamin*—in one instance to the Dorian Harmonia, in the other to the Phrygian, and differentiated by their intervals. Evidence may be seen in this of the crying need of the theorist for the double nomenclature while the Modal System was in general use, quite independently of whether the actual names made known by Ptolemy were in use or not; they were the affair of the Theorist, while for the Musician, there was the tuning. Then we have a statement by Cicero: "But we can recognize the Harmonia from the intervals of sounds, the different grouping of which makes more Harmoniai."

Rackham's mistranslation is not vitally important; it must be clear that we can grasp Aristotle's meaning only through a correct understanding of φθόγγων and of the preceding reference to the "form of composition." The various renderings give the first of these terms variously, as either "sounds" or "notes." These are not, however, synonyms. The reference may be to the traditional names of the notes, as Schlesinger argues. If, on the other hand, actual sounds are referred to, Aristotle must be talking about octave-species. The alternatives are clear, and it is necessary only to choose between them.

Unfortunately this cannot be done. Both meanings are legitimate and common in the fourth century, and either might fit the present passage. The same is perhaps true of *sunthesis*, the term Cicero almost certainly had in mind when he attempted his own description of mode (*Tusc.* 1.18): *harmoniam autem ex intervallis sonorum nosse possumus, quorum varia compositio etiam harmonias efficit plures.* Both *varia compositio* and altered *sunthesis*, however, most naturally suggest a varied arrangement of components which are not of necessity altered individually. It is unlikely that Cicero would have been familiar with any but a highly tempered modal system.

Two other passages from Aristotle are relevant to the larger problem; both have already been mentioned briefly. First, Dorian is spoken of as a mean between modal extremes (*Pol.* 1342b14 τὸ μέσον μὲν τῶν ὑπερβολῶν). Here Aristotle can only be referring to the Greater Complete System, where the other modes were derived by extension, as species, from the Dorian Harmonia. This Dorian scale pattern, no longer a true mode but instead a sequence of intervals, was centrally located within the complex; some scholars have thought that its Mese was also the Mese of the other six species. The second passage (*Fg.* 47 Rose, 25 Ross; *ap.* ps.-Plut. *Mus.* 23, p. 121.28-29 Lasserre, p. 18.25-27 Ziegler) says of mode that its "parts, magnitudes, and excesses are manifest according to number and (?)equal measure." The final word, *isometrian*, occurs nowhere else, and its meaning has occasioned some dispute.

The translation given here is that of Schlesinger, p. 171, who regards this statement as the single most important piece of evidence supporting her theory of equipartition. (It is not entirely fair, however, to say that she "based her conception of the Greek modal system on this passage," as I. Düring does in his review of Lasserre.) The difficulty is that it does not fit well with what follows, namely, "for melodies are arranged (literally, "rhythmized") in two tetrachords." Düring takes *isometria* to mean instead "a well-balanced structure of the whole." His rendering makes a perfect join between the two parts of the statement, but it would seem really to be a translation of *summetria*, not of *isometria*. On this point, then, a final decision is difficult indeed.

The three passages just examined fail to make clear that Aristotle spoke of distinct modes without common denominators of sequence and interval. They do suggest that he had in mind the later, interchangeable scales which his pupil Aristoxenus was to call *eidê*, octave-species, rather than Harmoniai. This is not necessarily to say that the Harmoniai were unknown to Aristotle; it does propose that his actual references are probably to the species, tempered sequences admitting of free modulation within a more or less standardized scale pattern. One further point of evidence may be added: the *Metaphysics* (1093b3-4) speaks of the aulos as having a compass of twenty-four notes, which seems to imply a three-octave range. This cannot be taken for granted, since Aristotle may be thinking of an instrument with intercalated finger holes or auxiliary mechanisms; but a range of twenty-four notes is hardly comprehensible in terms of the old modality under any circumstances.

APPENDIX B (SEE P. 126): ARIST. *Pol.* 1340a13-14

The text reads καὶ χωρὶς τῶν ῥυθμῶν καὶ τῶν μελῶν αὐτῶν. Several MSS indicate a lacuna between χωρίς and the immediately following τῶν. Susemihl proposed the insertion of τῶν λόγων διά; Rackham, *ad loc.*, approves of this as a probable correction, although his translation does not use it. The choice of reading is important here, since accepting the text as it stands would radically modify a basic proposition of Aristotle's theory of ethos. With Susemihl's conjecture the emended text would read: ". . . even without a text, owing to the rhythms and melodies themselves." In *The Politics of Aristotle* (Oxford, 1902), III, 537, W. L. Newman vigorously defends the unemended text; his arguments must now be considered.

The first of these is the claim that "mere imitative sounds" arouse within us the feeling which they imitate, even without rhythmic or melodic factors. The point is questionable taken as a whole, and—to deal with specifics—mere imitative sounds are not music. Newman consequently has no warrant for equating the two. To illustrate his point he cites an anecdote from Plutarch (*De Cohib. Ira* 6): "a single tone" from a slave's pitch pipe would restore composure to Gaius Gracchus when he had become harsh and angry while speaking in public. This proves nothing about music. One note from a pitch pipe cannot produce any ethically meaningful state of feeling. Its purpose here could have been to warn Gracchus that his voice had gone shrill and abandoned the effective central portion of the spoken register; but the story is hardly credible.

Aristotle has just spoken of the effect which Olympus' melodies have on the soul's ethos. According to Newman, he adds the present (unemended) remark to keep the reader from supposing that the ethical capacity of music is not connected with its power to imitate ethical states but with "its accompaniments of melody and rhythm." "Accompaniments" is a strange word: if we take away what Newman calls "melody" and "rhythm," the remainder is noise, not music. Plato (who normally uses the terms ῥυθμός and ἁρμονία) repeatedly makes it clear that they are the two basic constituents of music. As for Plato's explanation of the vital importance of music for paideia (*Rep.* 401d5-e8, a passage which Newman notes), the reason he mentions these two factors is that they are the ones which serve as media for the mimesis of ethical states. Finally, Newman's line of reasoning requires him to give μελοποιΐα a special and narrowed meaning in 1341b23, when there is no need to do so. K. Svoboda, *L'Esthétique d'Aristote* (Brno [Brünn], 1927), p. 179, n. 3, finds Newman to be in error on this point and notes that the MS used by Moerbeke had a lacuna after χωρίς. Svoboda's suggestion that the gap might equally well be filled by τῶν κινημάτων διά does not commend itself.

APPENDIX C (SEE P. 276): HIBEH MUSICAL PAPYRUS 30 τὸ ὑποκείμενον σανίδιον

This phrase has regularly been misinterpreted or left unclear. C. von Jan (*Griechische Saiteninstrumente,* p. 19; cited in H. Abert, "Ein neuer musikalischer Papyrusfund," *Zeitschrift der internationalen Musikgesellschaft,* 8 [1906]: 82) thought it referred to a bridge on the psaltery itself; but a psaltery has no bridge. M. Untersteiner (*Sofisti: testimonianze e frammenti,* fasc. 3 [Florence, 1954], p. 211) translates 31 *psaltêrion* simply by *cetra,* but this is incorrect. Considering the Apolline-Dionysiac antithesis to which the writer refers obliquely at the close of the fragment, it appears possible that the mention of an emphatically un-Hellenic instrument rather than a lyre or kithara conveys deliberate mockery. Even if we could suppose that the reference is to the lower part of the wooden body of a psaltery, rapping against this surface would necessarily be intermittent, like the thumb technique used by flamenco guitarists today. The text, however, says (30) that it occurs "simultaneously with the very sounds."

The more generally accepted view is that of Abert, who supposed that an individual performer used a board lying on the ground to mark the rhythm with his foot, even as auletes beat time with their wooden shoe clappers in the theater. Like von Jan, Abert supposed the reference to be to performers; it is actually to members of the audience. The aulete's clapper constitutes only a specious analogy, for the notorious weakness of the aulos was its inability to achieve a clear rhythmic outline, the one real virtue of instruments such as the kithara. Since the human voice has a similar weakness, the chorus leader's clapper sandal served as an intermittent metronome.

A fourth-century inscription from Delphi (*SIG* 244B61) uses *sanis* in just the sense needed. The diminutive form *sani-*

dion is less normal, but there is no reason to suppose that it could not have been employed with the same meaning. Dramatic festivals took up the theaters for only a few days each year; at other times they were constantly used for various kinds of civic events, not least for musical competitions. As for the relevance of the interpretation proposed here, one need only turn to the *Characters* of Theophrastus and note how the buffoon reacts to music (*Char.* 11.11; for his misbehavior at the theater, see 11.3): "When aulos music is being performed he will be the only person present who claps time." The Hibeh diatribe attacks not only witless pretensions to expert musical knowledge but boorishness as well.

APPENDIX D (SEE P. 162): PHLD. *Mus.* 4.34.1-5, 1.11.17-19, PP. 104, 7K.

The reference Philodemus makes to Damon's speech before the Areopagites is well known: "Now if Damon said this kind of thing before the real Areopagites and not made-up ones, then he was befooling them grievously." T. Gomperz, *Zu Philodem's Büchern von der Musik: Ein kritischer Beitrag* (Vienna, 1885), p. 9, supplements our meager information on this point. Noting that 1.11.17 ends with οἱ παίζον-, he suggests that the passage can be filled out with certainty as follows:

οἱ παίζον-
τες ταύτην τ)ὴν ἄκ(ρ)οτον
κατὰ Δά)μωνα (π)αι(γ)νίαν . . .

(Lasserre, p. 76, follows Wilamowitz in reading ἄσωτον, on the basis of interpreting the MS as α.οτον. Gomperz' reading, which van Krevelen adopts, is considerably more likely.) Gomperz goes on to claim that if this reading is correct we have at last a proof of Damon's literary activity. The rarity of *akrotos* and *paignia* indicates a quotation, he believes. We cannot, however, say from what source it has been taken if such is the case. The terms appear to be post-Hellenic: *akrotos* is otherwise known only from Hesychius, who defines it quite differently, while the closest parallel to *paignia* referring to a literary trifle is Plato's use of *paignion* in the plural (*Legg.* 816e10-817a1) to describe the collective impression made by comedy. D. A. van Krevelen, *Philodemus—De Muziek* (diss. Amsterdam, 1939), p. 13, sees here a possible suggestion of a politely silent audience, *een ideeal publiek.* We may well question whether any Greek would have thought a silent audience ideal.

There are two possible meanings for *akrotos,* one "not applauded" and the other "incapable of being applauded" or "not to be applauded." The first of these gets no support from Philodemus' later reference (4.34.1-5, p. 104 K.; translated in the first sentence, above). The second, however, tallies with Philodemus' suspicion that the audience of Areopagites may have been only a pretended one. Thus the choice seems to lie between a speech actually delivered to the members of the Areopagus and a speech supposedly addressed to them but made public only as a written work—an academic display, almost in the category of *suasoriae.* Philodemus gives the impression of favoring the latter view. If so, his adjective shows that the speech was not meant to be heard publicly; that is, it was "not (meant) to be applauded."

It might be asked why Damon should have addressed any speech to the Areopagus, even as a pretense. Possibly the decree of 458 permitted this body to retain supervisory power over education, a subject of obvious concern to the famous theorist. One would have a difficult time either proving or disproving the competence of the Areopagus to summon Damon, especially since Solon had given it such broad areas of new authority. In "Οἱ περὶ Δάμωνα," (*RhM,* 40 [1885]:311-12) Buecheler supports Philodemus, calling the speech an epideictic literary contrivance; so later Wilamowitz, *Griechische Verskunst* (Berlin, 1921), p. 59. Buecheler attributes it not to Damon but to members of the Damonian school writing shortly before the year 423. He argues that there cannot seriously be any question of the Areopagus supervising education during the period of Damon and Ephialtes. It is true that the *Respublica Atheniensium* (25.2) says that "all the acquired powers in virtue of which it was the guardian of the state" were taken away from the Areopagus at Ephialtes' instigation; but control over education may have been among its hereditary powers (as van Krevelen believes, p. 217). Had the Areopagites possessed no such power in Damon's time, a speech before them on the rightful nature of *mousikê* would have been absurd, even as a literary device. Buecheler's position has gained acceptance also from W. Nestle (*Vom Mythos zum Logos* [Stuttgart, 1940], p. 436 and n. 41), who nevertheless stresses the historical reality that he sees underlying the writing of this epideictic fiction. Citing pseudo-Xenophon, *Respublica Atheniensium* 1.13, he makes the point that the *dêmos* very probably regarded the musical practices of the aristocracy with suspicion—an aspect that has usually been overlooked.

Except for Buecheler and Nestle, the scholars thus far mentioned all assume the Damonian authorship of this work. H. Koller (*Die Mimesis in der Antike* [Bern, 1954], pp. 155-56) has stated their belief anew; but in a criticism of Koller's study A. Neubecker (*Die Bewertung der Musik bei Stoikern und Epikureern* [diss. Berlin, 1956], pp. 91-93, cf. p. 66) points out that the assumption, taken for granted ever since the time of Wilamowitz, is not warranted: we may well be dealing here with the work of another writer, who has Damon appear. For the theory that the Areopagus speech is one of the dialogues of "Heraclides Ponticus" see Buecheler, p. 311, and more recently R. Philippson, *RE,* XIX, 2457-60, art. "Philodemus."

APPENDIX E (SEE P. 217): COMMENTS ON P. BONAVENTURA MEYER, ʽAPMONIA: *Bedeutungsgeschichte des Wortes von Homer bis Aristoteles* (DISS. FREIBURG; ZÜRICH, 1932)

The printed form of this study is a reduced version of the original. It lacks the first half of the text, which deals with writers through the fifth century (these are, however, included in the summary, pp. 53-56) except for the Pythagoreans; an appendix has also been omitted. The sections which remain include a brief treatment of Pythagorean doctrine (9-13) but are devoted principally to Plato and Aristotle (14-46).

As the basic meaning of *harmonia* Meyer, going on the generally accepted version of its etymology, gives "[die] Zusammenfügung verschiedener Töne, bzw. Saiten zu einem Wohlklang, bzw. zu einer Einheit, Tonart." The "so-called Pythagoreans"—Meyer follows Frank closely—used this etymological concept to explain the metaphysical concept of *harmonia* which they had created, so that it now broadly designated the combining of different and contrary elements into a unity. Cosmology, psychology, even geometry, saw applications of this new use. The term itself was also taken as synonymous with various virtues. Here one sees the influence of popular belief; yet the references of Heraclitus and Democritus already contain suggestions of an ethical coloring.

At the conclusion of his summary Meyer proposes three main stages as characteristic of the process by which *harmonia* took on an altered significance. The earliest references show its etymological meaning predominant. It was taken over into music during the sixth century first as "mode" and then as "music," while the etymological use faded into the background. At the close of the fifth century and the beginning of the fourth, it developed into a technical term with various meanings for scholarly and artistic activity. Bearing the last of these points especially in mind, we may note what the summary has to say about Plato and Aristotle (55-56):

> With Plato . . . the concept of ἁρμονία underwent its most extensive differentiation of meaning. He made use of almost all its traditional conceptual values . . . and fitted it into his doctrine as *a technical term of scholarly and artistic activity* [here and elsewhere, italics are the author's]. While the question of priority among . . . these concepts really admits of no final settlement, I believe on the basis of Frank's inquiries that Plato may have given priority . . . to the *mathematical* idea of harmony (*number*) and to the musical idea

derived from it of *octave, consonance,* absolute *scale,* and *world-soul.* We are indebted to Plato for important explanations of the relation of harmony to rhythm, μέλος, music, melody, and συμφωνία . . .

Aristotle did not appreciably widen the conceptual range of *harmonia:* in fact, he reduced its traditional meanings to a select few. The commonest of these is the *musical* meaning —the harmonic factor in music (especially as regards the combination ἁρμονία καὶ ῥυθμός), mode, scale. In individual cases he extends the basic *etymological* conception when he offers his critique of the various theories concerning the soul. Here he fixes the meaning of harmony as the fitting together (*Zusammenpassen*) of diverse factors into a well-ordered whole, particularly as this finds expression in physical *health* and then as the *relationship* or *principle* of this unifying and blending process.

Individual points taken from the detailed treatment of Plato and Aristotle will be noted; my own comments are occasionally added in parentheses. First, for Plato *harmonia,* like *sumphônia,* is a favorite metaphor for aesthetic, ethical, or logical agreement. Its fundamental distinguishing characteristic as he uses it—the sense out of which all the others develop—is that of a fitting together. This may be intensified to a union achieved by fusion, or it may gain preciseness through the presence of mathematical proportion. Aristotle basically agrees with this concept; he also stresses the idea of mixture (*sunthesis, krasis, mixis*), distinguishing between harmony as the *product* and again as the *formal principle* of the process.

Where mathematics are concerned, Plato thought in terms of objective numerical proportions existing a priori. The consonant intervals within the octave were therefore pure mathematical constructs; the "*Timaeus* scale" represents the ultimate embodiment of this a priori scale. (Meyer, perhaps following Frank too closely, is much inclined to describe Plato's contributions with such terms as *phantastisch.* It is a case not so much of misstatement as of failure to redress the balance: one would not realize from Meyer's study that Plato could be a realist in musical matters. Had his theories of rhythm been fully covered, a different final impression might have resulted. Meyer is nevertheless quite right to stress the point that Plato's *musica speculativa* had little or no connection with music as actually performed.) The Platonic conception is thus a double one: *harmonia* represents both number concept and scale, as mathematics joins with music.

Under the heading of aesthetics Meyer notes that while Plato does not use *harmonia* as an aesthetic term, he does use it in such a way that the laws of aesthetics necessarily lead to it. Like his teacher, Aristotle nowhere gives it an explicitly aesthetic meaning. (This last point may deserve even more emphasis than it receives. As for Plato, the reference to *ästhetische Gesetze* might lead one to suppose that aesthetics was one of the formal provinces of Plato's conscious thought.) When he deals with Platonic poetics, Meyer suggests a variety of meanings. He bases that of *Ton* on *Rep.* 397c4, where *harmoniôn* is taken as denoting *Tonarten* in the "wider sense" of *Tönen.* (This seems inadmissible, as does the following argument for such a usage in Aristotle. Meyer may not have been aware that Plato was referring to musically accompanied declamation, including actual theatrical performance "in all seriousness, and before an audience" [397a3-4].)

As we know, both philosophers use *harmonia* with the greatest frequency to mean "mode." In *Rep.* 400a6 Plato mentions four types of musical sounds "whence all the Harmoniai [are derived]"; Meyer takes these *eidê* to be actual modes. (This is an altered version of the explanation given by Westphal, whose priority is not acknowledged. It fails to convince: presumably one does not derive the Harmoniai from themselves. See Adam's note *ad loc.* The passage remains a crux.) Neither Plato nor Aristotle uses *tonos* in the technical sense of transposition scale, nor can we tell from their uses of *harmonia* whether they are referring to Tonoi or to modes. There is no differentiation: *harmonia* may have either meaning. Generally, however, the second obtains. We reach this conclusion from the fact that the two writers are so often concerned with the paideutic role of ethos, which must have required varied sequences of intervals. (It is clear, especially from n. 96, that by "mode [*Tonart*]" Meyer means octave-species: he does not seem to be aware of any earlier stage. This is the kind of thinking that prompted J. Chailley to write of "the myth of the Greek modes.") Meyer deals confidently with *harmonia* as a reference to genus in Plato, and claims that chromatic is twice scorned as "the sweet (or "sweetened") Muse." (*Laws* 802c5-6 and *Rep.* 607a5. Neither has any necessary application to chromatic, and the context strongly suggests that they are general references. Adam, *ad loc.,* takes the second broadly.) The equation of *harmonia* with *sumphônia* is treated at some length. (With the exception of portions of Scheltema's article on antiphony, this brief discussion is the only solid treatment of the subject that I have found. Meyer does not refer to heterophony [*Heterophonie*], a coinage of the comparative musicologists that was just coming into use.)

So brief a sampling no doubt fails to do even the rudest justice to a work of such great scope and complexity. Meyer's study represents a major achievement: it is not likely to be replaced. Nevertheless, one should not accept its claims uncritically. It shows no awareness of any field but classical philology—this at a time when much had already been achieved in the new field of comparative musicology. As a result it seems more dated than need have been the case. Probably its most notable deficiency is the author's complete failure to realize that *harmonia* as mode (*Tonart*) must have represented an entire complex of factors, not merely a scale pattern.

BIBLIOGRAPHY

Articles in Bursian's *Jahresbericht* provide extensive periodic bibliographies of Greek music, together with commentary. See C. Jan, 104: 1-75 (covers 1884-1899); E. Graf, 118:212-35 (1899-1902); H. Abert, 144:1-74 (1903-1908) and 193:1-59 (1909-1921); K. Fellerer, 246:1-42 (1921-1931, with a few later entries). R. P. Winnington-Ingram has compiled the most recent survey, "Ancient Greek Music 1932-1957," *Lustrum,* 3 (1958): 6-57, 259-60. A number of modern references not listed elsewhere will be found in the extensive bibliographical section of J. Kunst, *Ethnomusicology* (The Hague, 1959). Abbreviations of classical periodicals regularly follow Marouzeau, *L'Année Philologique.*

Abert, Hermann, "Der Gegenstand der Forschung über die antike Musik," *Gesammelte Schriften und Vorträge,* ed. Friedrich Blume (Halle, 1929), pp. 35-58.

——— *Die Lehre vom Ethos in der griechischen Musik* (Leipzig, 1899).

——— "Die Musik der Griechen," *Ges. Schr. u. Vortr.,* pp. 22-34.

——— "Ein neuer musikalischer Papyrusfund," *Zeitschrift der Internationalen Musikgesellschaft,* 8 (1906): 79-83.

——— "Die Stellung der Musik in der antiken Kultur," *Ges. Schr. u. Vortr.,* pp. 1-21. (*Die Antike,* 2 [1926]: 136-54.)

Adam, James, ed., *The Republic of Plato,* 2 vols. (Cambridge, 1929).

Ahlvers, Adolf, *Zahl und Klang bei Platon* (Bern, 1952).

Amsel, Gustav, *De vi atque indole rhythmorum* (Breslau, 1887). (Breslauer philologische Abhandlungen, Band 1, Heft 3.)

Anderson, W. D., "The Importance of Damonian Theory in Plato's Thought," *TAPA,* 86 (1955): 88-102.

Arbatsky, Yuri, Jaap Kunst, and J. H. Hanford, "Hellenic Influence in Folk Music of the Modern Balkans," *Athene,* 16 (1955): 3-6, 17.

BIBLIOGRAPHY

Arnim, Heinrich von, ed., *Stoicorum Veterum Fragmenta*, 3 vols. (Leipzig, 1905).

Auda, Antoine, *Les modes et les tons de la musique et spécialement de la musique médiévale* (Brussels, 1931). (Académie Royale de Belgique, Classe des Beaux Arts, Mémoires, Coll. in-8, tome III, fasc. 1.)

Barbour, J. Murray, "The Principles of Greek Notation," *Journal of the American Musicological Society*, 13 (1960): 1-17.

Barclay, William, *Educational Ideals in the Ancient World* (London, 1959).

Bartók, Bela, *Hungarian Folk Music*, tr. M. D. Calvocoressi (London, 1931).

Batra, Rai Bahadur R. L., *The Science and Art of Indian Music* (Lahore, n.d.).

Beazley, J. D., "Hydria-Fragments in Corinth," *Hesperia*, 24 (1955): 305-19.

Beck, F. A. G., *Greek Education 450-350 B.C.* (London, 1964).

Becker, Oskar, "Frühgriechische Mathematik und Musiklehre," *Archiv für Musikwissenschaft*, 14 (1957): 156-64.

Behn, Friedrich, "Die Laute im Altertum und frühen Mittelalter," *Zeitschrift für Musikwissenschaft*, 1 (1918): 89-109.

——— *Musikleben im Altertum und frühen Mittelalter* (Stuttgart, 1954).

Belvianes, Marcel, *Sociologie de la musique* (Paris, 1951).

Bénard, Charles, *L'Esthétique d'Aristote* (Paris, 1887).

Biehle, Herbert, "Les éléments esthétiques de l'art vocal de l'antiquité," *Revue de Musicologie*, 14 (1930): 22-35.

Bodley, N. B., "The Auloi of Meroë," *AJA*, 50 (1946): 217-40.

Boeckh, August, *De metris Pindari* (Leipzig, 1821).

Borthwick, E. K., "ΚΑΤΑΛΗΨΙΣ—A Neglected Term in Greek Music," *CQ*, 11 (1959): 23-29.

Boyancé, Pierre, *Le culte des Muses chez les philosophes grecs* (Paris, 1937).

——— "La religion astrale de Platon à Cicéron," *REG*, 65 (1952): 312-49.

Bowra, C. M. (Sir Maurice), *Primitive Song* (New York, 1963).

——— *Problems in Greek Poetry* (Oxford, 1953).

Broneer, Oscar, "Isthmia Excavations, 1952," *Hesperia*, 22 (1953): 182-95.

Buecheler, Franz, "Οἱ περὶ Δάμωνα," *RhM*, 40 (1885): 309-12.

Burnet, John, *Early Greek Philosophy* (London, 1945; first edn. 1892).

——— *The Ethics of Aristotle* (London, 1900).

——— ed., *Plato's Phaedo* (Oxford, 1911).

Bury, R. G., "The Theory of Education in Plato's *Laws*," *REG*, 50 (1937): 304-20.

Busse, Adolf, "Zur Musikästhetik des Aristoteles," *RhM*, 77 (1928): 34-50.

Butcher, S. H., *Aristotle's Theory of Poetry and Fine Art* (London, 1898).

Bywater, Ingram, *Aristotle on the Art of Poetry* (Oxford, 1909).

Campbell, D. A., "Flutes and Elegiac Couplets," *JHS*, 84 (1964): 63-68.

Caskey, L. D., "Archaeological Notes: Recent Acquisitions of the Museum of Fine Arts, Boston," *AJA*, 41 (1937): 525-27.

Cazden, Norman, "Pythagoras and Aristoxenus Reconciled," *Journal of the American Musicological Society*, 11 (1958): 95-105.

Chailley, Jacques, "A propos de Thémison," *Revue de Musicologie*, 40 (1958): 15-26. [Part 2. See on Machabey.]

——— *L'Imbroglio des modes* (Paris, 1960).

——— "La musique de la tragédie grecque devant une découverture épigraphique," *Revue de Musicologie*, 39 (1957): 6-9.

——— "Le mythe des modes grecs," *Acta Musicologica*, 28 (1956): 137-63.

Chrimes, Katharine M. T., *Ancient Sparta* (New York, 1952).

Clements, E., "The Interpretation of Greek Music," *JHS*, 42 (1922): 133-66.

Coleman-Norton, P. R., "Music and Musicians Among the Greeks," *Musica*, 2 (1935): 175-89.

Combarieu, Jules, *Histoire de la musique*, 3 vols. (Paris, 1938).

——— *La musique et la magie* (Paris, 1909).

Cornford, F. M., *Principium Sapientiae* (Cambridge, 1952).

Crocker, Richard L., "Pythagorean Mathematics and Music," *Journal of Aesthetics and Art Criticism*, 22 (1963-64): 189-98, 325-35.

——— review of E. A. Lippman, *Musical Thought in Ancient Greece*, in *Musical Quarterly*, 51 (1965): 432-36.

Crönert, Wilhelm, "Die Hibehrede über die Musik," *Hermes*, 44 (1909): 503-21.

Croissant, Jeanne, *Aristote et les mystères* (Liège and Paris, 1932).

Curtis, John, "The Double Flutes," *JHS*, 34 (1914): 89-105.

——— "Reconstruction of the *Greater Perfect System*," *JHS*, 44 (1924): 10-23.

Dale, Amy M., *The Lyric Metres of Greek Drama* (Cambridge, 1948).

Darack, Arthur, "Aesthetics of Music: Early Greek Views," unpub. diss. University of Indiana, 1951.

De Lacy, P. H. and E. A., *Philodemus: On Methods of Inference* (Lancaster, 1941).

Denniston, J. D., "Some Recent Theories of the Greek Modes," *CQ*, 7 (1913): 83-99.

Deubner, Ludwig, "Terpander und die siebensaitige Leier," *PhW*, 50 (1930): 1566-67.

Diehl, E., ". . . fuerunt ante Homerum poetae," *RhM*, 89 (1940): 81-114.

Diels, Hermann and Walther Kranz, eds., *Die Fragmente der Vorsokratiker*, 3 vols. (8th edition, Berlin, 1956).

Dirlmeier, F., "Κάθαρσις παθημάτων," *Hermes*, 75 (1940): 81-92.

Dodds, E. R., ed., *Euripides: The Bacchae* (Oxford, 1944).

——— *The Greeks and the Irrational* (Boston, 1957).

Doutzaris, P., "La rythmique dans la poésie et la musique des grecs anciens," *REG*, 47 (1934): 297-345.

Duchemin, Jacqueline, *La houlette et la lyre: Recherche sur les origines pastorales de la poésie*, vol. I: *Hermès et Apollon* (Paris, 1960).

——— *Pindare, poète et prophète* (Paris, 1956). (Collection d'études anciennes.)

Düring, Ingemar, "Greek Music: Its Fundamental Features and Its Significance," *Journal of World History*, 3 (1956): 302-29.

——— "Studies in Musical Terminology in 5th Century Literature," *Eranos*, 43 (1945): 176-97.

——— review of François Lasserre, ed., *Plutarque: De la musique*, in *Gnomon*, 27 (1955): 431-36.

Edmonds, J. M., ed., *Elegy and Iambus*, 2 vols. (London and Cambridge, Mass., 1944). (Loeb Classical Library.)

——— ed., *Lyra Graeca*, 3 vols. (London and New York, 1928). (Loeb Classical Library.)

Ehrenberg, V. L., *Sophocles and Pericles* (Oxford, 1954).

Eitrem, S., L. Amundsen, and R. P. Winnington-Ingram, eds., *Fragments of Unknown Greek Tragic Texts with Musical Notation* (*P. Osl. inv. no. 1413*) (Oslo, 1955).

Ellis, Catherine J., *Aboriginal Music Making* (Adelaide, 1964).

——— "Pre-Instrumental Scales," *Ethnomusicology*, 9 (1965): 126-37.

Else, G. F., *Aristotle's Poetics: The Argument* (Cambridge, Mass., 1963).

——— " 'Imitation' in the Fifth Century," *CP*, 53 (1958): 73-90.

England, E. B., *The Laws of Plato*, 2 vols. (Manchester, 1921).

Farmer, H. G., *Sa'adyah Gaon on the Influence of Music* (London, 1948).

Feaver, D. D., "The Musical Setting of Euripides' *Orestes*," *AJP*, 81 (1960): 1-15.

Festugière, A. J., "L'Ame et la musique d'après Aristide Quintilien," *TAPA*, 85 (1954): 55-78.

Fränkel, Hermann, *Dichtung und Philosophie des frühen Griechentums* (New York, 1951).

Freeman, Kathleen, *Ancilla to the Pre-Socratic Philosophers* (Oxford, 1948).

——— *Companion to the Pre-Socratic Philosophers* (Oxford, 1946).

Freeman, Kenneth, *Schools of Hellas* (London, 1908).

Friedländer, Paul, *Die Melodie zu Pindars erstem pythischen Gedicht* (Leipzig, 1934). (Berichte über die Verhandlungen der sächsischen Akademie der Wissenschaften, Philologisch-Historische Klasse 86, Heft 4.)

Fyfe, W. Hamilton, ed., *Aristotle: The Poetics* (London and Cambridge, Mass., 1939). (Loeb Classical Library.)

Gamberini, Leopoldo, *La parola e la musica nell' antichità* (Florence, 1962). (Historiae Musicae Cultores, Bibliotheca No. 15.)

Geiringer, Karl, *Musical Instruments* (New York, 1945).

Georgiades, Thrasybulos, *Greek Music, Verse and Dance*, tr. Erwin Benedikt and M. L. Martinez (New York, n.d.).

——— *Der griechische Rhythmus* (Hamburg, 1949).

——— *Musik und Rhythmus bei den Griechen: Zum Ursprung der abendländischen Musik* (Hamburg, 1958). (Rowohlts deutsche Enzyklopädie No. 61.)

Giani, Romualdo, and Carlo del Grande, "Relazione melodica di strofe e antistrofe nel coro greco," *Riv. di Fil.*, 59, N.S. 9 (31): 185-206.

Girard, Paul, *L'Education athénienne* (Paris, 1891).

Gombosi, Otto, "Key, Mode, Species," *Journal of the American Musicological Society*, 4 (1951): 20-26.

——— "The Melody of Pindar's 'Golden Lyre,'" *Musical Quarterly*, 26 (1940): 381-92.

——— "New Light on Ancient Greek Music," *Papers Read at the International Congress of Musicology . . .* 1939, ed. Arthur Mendel, Gustave Reese, and Gilbert Chase (New York, 1944), pp. 168-83.

——— *Tonarten und Stimmungen der antiken Musik* (Copenhagen, 1939).

Gomperz, Theodor, *Zu Philodem's Büchern von der Musik: Ein kritischer Beitrag* (Vienna, 1885).

Graf, Ernst, *De Graecorum veterum re musica quaestionum capita duo* (Marburg, 1889).

Grande, Carlo del, "Damone metrico," *Filologia Minore* (Milan and Naples, 1956), pp. 197-214. (*Giornale italiano di filologia,* 1 [1948]: 3-16.)

——— *Espressione musicale dei poeti greci* (Naples, 1932).

Greif, Francisque, "Etudes sur la musique antique," *REG,* 22 (1909): 89-139.

——— "Etudes sur la musique antique (cont.)," *REG,* 23 (1910): 1-48.

Grenfell, B. P., and A. S. Hunt, *The Hibeh Papyri* (London, 1906).

Grieser, Heinz, *Nomos: Ein Beitrag zur griechischen Musikgeschichte* (diss. Heidelberg, 1937).

Groningen, B. A. van, "A propos de Terpandre," *Mnemosyne,* 8 (1955): 177-91.

Guillemin, M., and J. Duchesne, "Sur l'origine asiatique de la cithare grecque," *AC,* 4 (1935): 117-24.

Gundert, Hermann, *Pindar und sein Dichterberuf* (Frankfurt, 1935).

Guthrie, W. K. C., *The Greek Philosophers from Thales to Aristotle* (New York, 1960).

——— *A History of Greek Philosophy,* vol. I (Cambridge, 1962).

Hackforth, Richard, tr., *Plato's Phaedo* (Cambridge, 1955).

Hadow, Sir W. H., ed., *Oxford History of Music,* Introductory Volume (Oxford, 1929).

Haigh, A. E., *The Attic Theatre* (Oxford, 1907).

Hamlyn, D. W., "Aristotle's Account of Aesthesis in the *De Anima,*" *CQ,* 9 (1959): 6-16.

Handschin, Jacques, "Musikalische Miszellen," *Philologus,* N.S. 40 (1931): 52-67.

——— *Der Toncharakter* (Zürich, 1948).

Harap, Louis, "Some Hellenic Ideas on Music and Character," *Musical Quarterly,* 24 (1938): 153-68.

Hartlaub, G. F., "Musik und Plastik bei den Griechen," *Zeitschrift für Ästhetik,* 30 (1936): 135-78.

Henderson, M. Isobel, "Ancient Greek Music," chapter in *The New Oxford History of Music,* I, 336-403. (See on Westrup.)

——— "The Growth of Ancient Greek Music," *Music Review,* 4 (1943): 4-13.

——— "The Growth of the Greek 'APMONIAI," *CQ,* 36 (1942): 94-101.

Higgins, R. A. and R. P. Winnington-Ingram, "Lute-Players in Greek Art," *JHS,* 85 (1965): 62-71.

Hornbostel, E. M. von, "Phonographierte tunesische Melodien," *Zeitschrift der Internationalen Musikgesellschaft,* 8 (1907): 41-43.

——— "Tonart und Ethos," in *Festschrift für Johannes Wolf* (Berlin, 1929), pp. 73-78.

Howard, A. A., "The Αὐλός or Tibia," *HSPh*, 4 (1893): 1-60.

Huber-Abrahamowicz, Elfriede, *Das Problem der Kunst bei Platon* (diss. Basel, 1954).

Huchzermeyer, Helmut, *Aulos und Kithara in der griechischen Musik bis zum Ausgang der klassischen Zeit* (diss. Münster-Westph., 1931).

Husmann, Heinrich, "Antike und Orient in ihrer Bedeutung für die europäische Musik," in *Kongressbericht der Gesellschaft für Musikforschung* (Hamburg, 1956), pp. 24-33.

——— *Grundlagen der antiken und orientalischen Musikkultur* (Berlin, 1961).

Idelsohn, A. Z., *Jewish Music* (New York, 1929).

Jaeger, W. W., *Paideia*, tr. Gilbert Highet, 3 vols. (New York, 1943).

Jan, Karl von, ed., *Musici Scriptores Graeci* (Hildesheim, 1962; original printing Leipzig, 1895).

Janssens, A. J., "Aristoteles en de oudere muziekaesthetiek," *Philologische Studien*, 6-7 (1934-1935): 108-32.

——— "Die muziekaesthetische papyrus van Hibeh," *Philologische Studien*, 11-12 (1939-1940): 90-111.

——— "De Muziekpsycholoog Damoon van Oa," *Tijdschrift voor Philosophie*, 3 (1941): 499-566, 649-712.

Jeanmaire, Henri, *Dionysos: Histoire du culte de Bacchus* (Paris, 1951).

Joachim, H. H., *Aristotle: The Nicomachean Ethics*, ed. D. A. Rees (Oxford, 1951).

Kahl, Alexis, *Die Philosophie der Musik nach Aristoteles* (diss. Leipzig, 1902).

Kleingünther, Adolf, "ΠΡΩΤΟΣ 'ΕΥΡΕΤΗΣ, Untersuchungen zur Geschichte einer Fragestellung," *Philologus*, Supplementband XXVI, Heft 1 (Leipzig, 1933).

Koller, Ernst, "Musse und musische Paideia," *MH*, 13 (1956): 1-37, 94-124.

Koller, Hermann, *Die Mimesis in der Antike: Nachahmung, Darstellung* (Bern, 1954).

——— *Musik und Dichtung im alten Griechenland* (Bern and Munich, 1963).

Koster, W. J. W., *Rhythme en metrum bij de Grieken van Damon tot Aristoxenus* (Groningen, 1940).

Kraus, Walther, "Die Auffassung des Dichterberufs im frühen Griechentum," *WS*, 68 (1955): 65-87.

Krevelen, D. A. van, *Philodemus—De Muziek: Met Vertaling en Commentaar* (diss. Amsterdam; Hilversum, 1939).

Lachmann, Robert, *Musik des Orients* (Breslau, 1929).

Laloy, Louis, *Aristoxène de Tarente, disciple d'Aristote, et la musique de l'antiquité* (diss. Paris, 1904).

——— *La musique chinoise* (Paris, 1909).

Laroche, Emmanuel, *Histoire de la racine* NEM- *en grec ancien* (νέμω, νέμεσις, νόμος, νομίζω) (Paris, 1949). (Etudes et commentaires, 6.)

Lasserre, François, ed., *Plutarque: De la musique* (Olten and Lausanne, 1954).

Lechner, Matthias, *Erziehung und Bildung in der griechisch-römischen Antike* (Munich, 1933).

Levin, Flora R., "The Hendecachord of Ion of Chios," *TAPA*, 92 (1961): 295-307.

Levis, J. H., *Foundations of Chinese Musical Art* (repr. New York, 1963; first publ. Peking, 1936).

Lippman, E. A., *Musical Thought in Ancient Greece* (New York and London, 1964).

——— "Symbolism in Music," *Musical Quarterly*, 29 (1953): 554-75.

List, George, "The Boundaries of Speech and Song," *Ethnomusicology*, 7 (1963): 1-16.

Livingstone, R. W. (Sir Richard), *Plato and Modern Education* (Cambridge, 1944).

Lohmann, Johannes, "Die griechische Musik als mathematische Form," *Archiv für Musikwissenschaft*, 14 (1957): 147-55.

Longman, G. A., "The Musical Papyrus: Euripides, *Orestes* 332-40," *CQ*, N.S. 12 (1962): 61-66.

Luschnat, Otto, *Zum Text von Philodems Schrift De Musica* (Berlin, 1953).

Machabey, Armand, "A propos de Thémison," *Revue de Musicologie*, 40 (1958): 3-14. (Part 1. See on Chailley.)

Marrou, H. I., *A History of Education in Antiquity*, tr. George Lamb (London and New York, 1956).

——— *Saint Augustin et la fin du monde antique* (Paris, 1937).

——— review of Kathleen Schlesinger, *The Greek Aulos*, in *REG*, 52 (1940): 87-92.

Martin, Emile, *Essai sur les rythmes de la chanson grecque antique* (Paris, 1953).

Marx, Friedrich, "Critica et Hermeneutica," *RhM*, 83 (1934): 376-79.

——— "Musik aus der griechischen Tragödie," *RhM*, 82 (1933): 230-46.

Meyer, P. Bonaventura, 'APMONIA, *Bedeutungsgeschichte des Wortes von Homer bis Aristoteles* (diss. Freiburg; Zürich, 1932).

Monro, D. B., *The Modes of Ancient Greek Music* (Oxford, 1894).

Montargis, Frédéric, *De Platone musico* (diss. Paris, 1886).

Moraux, Paul, "La 'mimesis' dans les théories anciennes de la danse, de la musique, et de la poésie," *Etudes Classiques*, 23 (1955): 3-13.

Morrow, Glenn R., *Plato's Cretan City* (Princeton, 1960).

Mountford, J. F., "Greek Music and Its Relation to Modern Times," *JHS*, 40 (1920): 13-42.

——— "The Musical Scales of Plato's *Republic*," *CQ*, 17 (1923): 125-36.

——— "A New Fragment of Greek Music in Cairo," *JHS*, 51 (1931): 91-100.

Moutsopoulos, Evanghélos, *La musique dans l'oeuvre de Platon* (Paris, 1959).

Müller, Gerhard, *Studien zu den platonischen Nomoi* (Munich, 1951).

Nestle, Wilhelm, *Vom Mythos zum Logos* (Stuttgart, 1940).

Neubecker, Annemarie, *Die Bewertung der Musik bei Stoikern und Epikureern: Eine Analyse von Philodems Schrift De Musica* (diss. Berlin, 1956).

Newman, W. L., ed., *The Politics of Aristotle*, 4 vols. (Oxford, 1887-1902).

Nilsson, M. P., *A History of Greek Religion* (Oxford, 1925).

Norwood, Gilbert, *Pindar* (Berkeley and Los Angeles, 1945).

Page, D. L., ed., *Poetae Melici Graeci* (Oxford, 1962).

Parry, C. H. H., *The Evolution of the Art of Music* (New York, 1930).

Pearl, O. M., and R. P. Winnington-Ingram, "A Michigan Papyrus with Musical Notation," *Journal of Egyptian Archaeology*, 51 (1965): 179-95.

Perls, Hugo, "Μοῦσα: Etude sur l'esthétique de Platon," *Revue Philosophique*, 117 (1934): 259-84, 441-71.

Philippson, R., art. "Philodemus," *RE*, XIX, 2457-2460.

Pianko, G., "La musica nelle commedie di Aristofane," *Eos*, 47 (1954): 23-34.

Pickard-Cambridge, A. W. (Sir Arthur), *Dithyramb, Tragedy and Comedy* (Oxford, 1927).

——— *The Dramatic Festivals of Athens* (Oxford, 1955).

Pike, K. L., *Tone Languages* (Ann Arbor, 1948).

Pöhlmann, Egert, *Griechische Musikfragmente: Ein Weg zur alt-*

griechischen Musik (Nuremberg, 1960). (Erlanger Beiträge zur Sprach- und Kunstwissenschaft, Band VIII.)

Pohlenz, Max, "Τὸ πρέπον: Ein Beitrag zur Geschichte des griechischen Geistes," *Göttingen Gelehrten Nachrichten* (Berlin, 1933), pp. 53-92.

——— "Das Satyrspiel und Pratinas von Phleious," *Göttingen Gelehrten Nachrichten* (Berlin, 1927), pp. 298-321.

Popley, H. A., *The Music of India* (Calcutta, 1921).

Potiron, Henri, review of Antoine Auda, *Les gammes musicales,* in *Revue Internationale de Musique,* 12 (1952): 90-97.

Powell, J. U., and E. A. Barber, eds., *New Chapters in the History of Greek Literature* (Oxford, 1921; Second Series, Oxford, 1929; Third Series, Oxford, 1933).

Powers, H. S., "Mode and Raga," *Musical Quarterly,* 44 (1958): 448-60.

Quasten, Johannes, *Musik und Gesang in den Kulten der heidnischen Antike und christlichen Frühzeit* (Münster-Westph., 1930).

Radermacher, Ludwig, "Ein Bruchstück des Damon," *WS,* 56 (1938): 110-11.

——— "Metrisches—I. Damon und das ἡρῷον," *WS,* 59 (1941): 1-3.

Rankin, H. D., "Plato and Man the Puppet," *Eranos,* 60 (1962): 127-31.

Reese, Gustave, *Music in the Middle Ages* (New York, 1940).

Regner, Johannes, *Platons Musiktheorie: Eine Studie zur griechischen Musikgeschichte* (diss. Halle, 1924).

Reinach, Théodore, "Euripides und der Choreut," *Hermes,* 45 (1910): 151-55.

——— art. "Lyra," Daremberg-Saglio, III², 1437-51. (Charles Daremberg, Edmond Saglio, and Edmond Pottier, eds., *Dictionnaire des antiquités grecques et romaines,* 5 vols. in 9 [Paris, 1904].)

——— *La musique grecque* (Paris, 1926).

——— art. "Tibia," Daremberg-Saglio, V, 300-32.

Reisch, E., *De musicis graecorum certaminibus* (diss. Vienna, 1885).

Renehan, Robert, "The Derivation of ῥυθμός," *CP,* 58 (1963): 36-38.

Richter, Lukas, "Die Beziehung zwischen Theorie und Praxis der Musik im aristotelischen Protreptikos," *Hermes,* 88 (1960): 177-88.

——— "Platons Stellung zur praktischen und spekulativen Musiktheorie seiner Zeit," in *Bericht über den Internationalen*

Musikwissenschaftlichen Kongress: Hamburg 1956, ed. Walter Gerstenberg and others (Kassel and Basel, 1957), pp. 196-202.
——— *Zur Wissenschaftlehre von der Musik bei Platon und Aristoteles* (Berlin, 1961).
Rivaud, Albert, "Etudes platoniciennes, II: Platon et la musique," *Revue d'Histoire de la Philosophie*, 3 (1929): 1-30.
Robin, Léon, *Aristote* (Paris, 1944).
Romagnoli, Ettore, *Nel regno d'Orfeo: Studi sulla lirica e la musica greca* (Bologna, 1921).
Roos, Ervin, *Die tragische Orchestik im Zerrbild der altattischen Komödie* (diss. Lund, 1951).
Ross, W. D., *Aristotle* (London, 1945).
——— ed., *Aristotle: De Anima* (Oxford, 1961).
——— ed., *Aristotle's Metaphysics*, 2 vols. (Oxford, 1924).
Ruelle, C.-E., "Le papyrus musical de Hibeh," *Revue de Philologie*, 31 (1907): 235-40.
——— "Sextus Empiricus contre les musiciens," *REG*, 11 (1898): 138-58.
Ryffel, E., "Eukosmia," *MH*, 4 (1947): 23-38.
Sachs, Curt, *A History of Musical Instruments* (New York, 1940).
——— *Die Musik der Antike* (Wildpark-Potsdam, 1928).
——— *Die Musik des Altertums* (Breslau, 1924).
——— *Rhythm and Tempo* (New York, 1953).
——— *The Rise of Music in the Ancient World East and West* (New York, 1943).
——— *Vergleichende Musikwissenschaft in ihren Grundzügen* (Leipzig, 1930). (Musikpädagogische Bibliothek, ed. Leo Kestenberg, Heft 8.)
——— *Vergleichende Musikwissenschaft: Musik der Fremdkulturen* (Heidelberg, 1959).
——— *The Wellsprings of Music*, ed. Jaap Kunst (The Hague, 1962).
Sanden, Heinrich, *Antike Polyphonie* (Heidelberg, 1957).
Scheltema, H. J., "De antiphonia," *Mnemosyne*, 60 (1932): 239-53.
Schipper, Edith W., "*Mimesis* in the Arts in Plato's *Laws*," *Journal of Aesthetics and Art Criticism*, 32 (1963): 199-202.
Schlesinger, Kathleen, "Further Notes on Aristoxenus and Musical Intervals," *CQ*, 27 (1933): 88-96.
——— *The Greek Aulos* (London, 1939).
Schmiedel, Peter, "Ein unsymmetrisches Tonsystem," in *Bericht* . . . , pp. 202-3. (See on Richter.)
Schneider, Marius, "Entstehung der Tonsysteme," in *Bericht* . . . , pp. 203-11. (See on Richter.)
——— and J. W. Schöttländer, "Über die Anwendung der

Tonalitätskreistheorie auf die Musik der orientalischen Hochkulturen und der Antike," *Zeitschrift für Vergleichende Musikwissenschaft,* 3 (1935): 50-75.

Schoen, Max, *The Psychology of Music* (New York, 1940).

Schönewolf, Helmut, *Der jungattische Dithyrambos: Wesen, Wirkung, Gegenwirkung* (diss. Giessen, 1938).

Schuhl, P. M., "Platon et la musique de son temps," *Revue Internationale de Philosophie,* 9 (1955): 276-87.

Sedgwick, W. B., "A Note on the Performance of Greek Vocal Music," *Class. et Med.* 11 (1950): 222-26.

Shero, L. P., review of Otto Gombosi, *Tonarten und Stimmungen der antiken Musik,* in *CP,* 48 (1953): 178-83.

Shirlaw, Matthew, "The Music and Tone Systems of Ancient Greece," *Music Review,* 4 (1943): 14-27.

——— "The Music and Tone-Systems of Ancient Greece," *Music and Letters,* 32 (1951): 131-39.

Shorey, Paul, "Plato's *Laws* and the Unity of Plato's Thought," *CP,* 9 (1914): 345-69.

Snell, Bruno, "Die Sprache Heraklits," *Hermes,* 61 (1926): 353-81.

Spiegel, Walter, *Die Bedeutung der Musik für die griechische Erziehung im klassischen Altertum* (diss. Erlangen; Berlin, 1910).

Stenzel, Julius, *Platon der Erzieher* (Hamburg, 1961; first publ. 1928).

Stewart, J. A., *Notes on the Nicomachean Ethics of Aristotle,* 2 vols. (Oxford, 1892).

Svoboda, Karl, *L'Esthétique d'Aristote* (Brno [Brünn], 1927).

Tannery, Paul, "Sur les intervalles de la musique grecque," *REG,* 15 (1902): 336-52.

Taylor, A. E., *Plato* (London, 1926).

Thomson, George, *Greek Lyric Metre* (Cambridge, 1929).

Tiby, Ottavio, *La musica in Grecia e a Roma* (Florence, 1942).

Turner, R. L., "A Note on the Word Accent in Greek Music," *CR,* 29 (1915): 195-96.

Untersteiner, Mario, *Sofisti: testimonianze e frammenti,* fasc. 3 (Florence, 1954).

——— *The Sophists,* tr. Kathleen Freeman (New York, 1954).

Vetter, Walther, *Antike Musik* (Munich, 1935).

——— "Die antike Musik in der Beleuchtung durch Aristoteles," *Archiv für Musikforschung,* 1 (1936): 2-41.

——— "Antike Polyphonie?" in *Bericht über den Siebenten Internationalen Musikwissenschaftlichen Kongress Köln 1958,* ed. Gerald Abraham and others (Kassel, Basel, London and New York, 1959), pp. 290-93.

——— art. "Ethos," *Die Musik in Geschichte und Gegenwart*, vol. III (Kassel, 1954), cols. 1581-91.

——— arts. "Musik," "Musikunterricht," *RE*, XVI, 823-88.

——— "Die Musik im Erziehungsplane der griechischen Antike," *Deutsche Musikkultur*, 7 (1942): 33-42.

——— "Die Musik im platonischen Staate," *Neue Jahrbücher für Wissenschaft und Jugendbildung*, 11 (1935): 316-20.

Vogel, Martin, "Anregendes Griechentum," *Die Musikforschung*, 15 (1962): 1-11.

——— "Die Zahl Sieben in der spekulativen Musiktheorie" (unpubl. diss. University of Bonn, 1954).

Voss, Otto, *De Heraclidis Pontici vita et scriptis* (diss. Rostock, 1896).

Waerden, B. L. van der, "Die Harmonielehre der Pythagoreer," *Hermes*, 78 (1943): 163-99.

Wagner, Rudolf, review of Otto Gombosi, *Tonarten und Stimmungen*, in *Gnomon*, 27 (1955): 111-15.

Warry, J. G., *Greek Aesthetic Theory* (New York, 1962).

Wegner, Max, *Die Musikinstrumente des alten Orients* (Münster-Westph., 1950). (Orbis Antiquus, Heft 2.)

——— *Das Musikleben der Griechen* (Berlin, 1949).

Wehrli, Fritz, ed., *Die Schule des Aristoteles: Texte und Kommentar*, 10 vols. (Basel, 1944-1959).

Weil, Henri, and Théodore Reinach, eds., *Plutarque: De la musique* (Paris, 1900).

Wellesz, Egon, *A History of Byzantine Music and Hymnography* (Oxford, 1961).

Werner, Eric, *The Sacred Bridge* (London and New York, 1959).

Westrup, J. A., and others, eds., *The New Oxford History of Music*. Vol. I: *Ancient and Oriental Music*, ed. Egon Wellesz (London, 1957).

Whitman, C. H., *Aristophanes and the Comic Hero* (Cambridge, Mass., 1964).

Wilamowitz-Möllendorff, Ulrich von, *Griechische Verskunst* (Berlin, 1921).

——— "Lesefrüchte," *Hermes*, 63 (1928): 369-90.

——— *Pindaros* (Berlin, 1911).

——— *Platon*, 2 vols. (Berlin, 1919).

Wilkinson, L. P., "Philodemus on *Ethos* in Music," *CQ*, 32 (1938): 174-81.

Williams, C. F. Abdy, *The Aristoxenian Theory of Musical Rhythm* (Cambridge, 1911).

Winnington-Ingram, R. P., "Ancient Greek Music 1932-1957," *Lustrum*, 3 (1958): 6-57, 259-60.

——— "Aristoxenus and the Intervals of Greek Music," *CQ*, 26 (1932): 195-208.

——— "Die Enharmonik der Griechen," *Die Musikforschung*, 18 (1965): 60-64.

——— *Euripides and Dionysus* (Cambridge, 1936).

——— art. "Greek Music (Ancient)," *Grove's Dictionary of Music and Musicians*, ed. Eric Blom, 9 vols. (New York, 1955), III, 770-81.

——— *Mode in Ancient Greek Music* (Cambridge, 1936).

——— "The Pentatonic Tuning of the Greek Lyre: A Theory Examined," *CQ*, 6 (1956): 169-86.

——— "The Spondeion Scale," *CQ*, 22 (1928): 83-91.

——— review of Otto Gombosi, *Tonarten und Stimmungen*, in *CR*, 66, N.S. 2 (1952): 34-36.

——— review of M. Isobel Henderson, chapter on ancient Greek music in *The New Oxford History of Music*, vol. I; in *Gnomon*, 30 (1958): 243-47.

——— review of Hermann Koller, *Musik und Dichtung*, in *CR*, 79, N.S. 15 (1965): 193-95.

——— review of Kathleen Schlesinger, *The Greek Aulos*, in *CR*, 53 (1939): 185-86.

——— (See also under Higgins, R. A., and Pearl, O. M.)

Wolf, Ernst, "Zur Etymologie von ῥυθμός und seiner Bedeutung in der älteren griechischen Literatur," *WS*, 68 (1955): 99-119.

Wright, F. A., "The Technical Vocabulary of Dance and Song," *CR*, 30 (1916): 9-10.

Young, T. Campbell, *The Making of Musical Instruments* (London, 1939).

NOTES

I. INTRODUCTION

1. Herman Koller (*Musik und Dichtung im alten Griechenland* [Bern and Munich, 1963], p. 9) has shown the uniqueness of Greek music through a comparison involving the musical terminology of ancient India and the Arabic-speaking countries. There are words for such component elements as dance (*nrtya, raquasa*) and song (*gîta*) but no word for "music" in the unitary, inclusive sense familiar to us—let alone the much wider sense of the Hellenic term *mousikê*, for which we might almost give "culture" as an equivalent.

2. For the differing views on this fragment see n. 4.

3. The first reference to ethos in this musical sense may have been made by the fifth-century specialist Damon, who is discussed in ch. ii and at length in ch. iii; on the passage see p. 40. Egon Wellesz (*A History of Byzantine Music and Hymnography*, 2nd edn. [Oxford, 1961], p. 46, n. 1) gives the Greek text. He claims that this is also the first occurrence of *harmonia;* but here the speaker seems rather to be Aristides Quintilianus, the late commentator who quotes or paraphrases Damon. How much of the actual phrasing is Damonian cannot easily be determined.

4. The evidence on this much debated question has been assembled and discussed with notable economy by Egert Pöhlmann (*Griechische Musikfragmente: Ein Weg zur altgriechischen Musik* [Nürnberg, 1960]). On A. M. Dale's comments and the article by D. D. Feaver, both concerned with the *Orestes* fragment, see n. 61 to ch. ii. Leopoldo Gamberini's *La parola e la musica nell' antichità* (Florence, 1962) is a collection of fanciful conjectures of melodic patterns intuited from vowel coloring in the poets. The "speech melody" is first noted by Aristotle's pupil Aristoxenus in his *Harmonics* (p. 18 Meibom).

5. See Friedrich Behn, *Musikleben im Altertum und frühen Mittelalter* (Stuttgart, 1954), pp. 85-91. The most detailed de-

scription of the *kollopes* and their use is that given by Théodore Reinach in Daremberg-Saglio, art. "Lyra," III^2, 1443. (Charles Daremberg, Edmond Saglio, and Edmond Pottier, eds., *Dictionnaire des antiquités grecques et romaines*, 5 vols. in 9 [Paris, 1904]. "Lyra": vol. III, pt. 2, pp. 1437-51.)

6. Cic. *N.D.* 2.59.149. See R. P. Winnington-Ingram, "Ancient Greek Music 1932-1957," *Lustrum*, 3 (1958): 14-15, and M. Guillemin and J. Duchesne, "Sur l'origine asiatique de la cithare grecque," *AC*, 4 (1935): 117-24. The spelling "kithara" will be used throughout. With few exceptions, classical authors and works are abbreviated in accordance with Liddell-Scott-Jones, *Greek-English Lexicon*, 9th edn. (Oxford, 1948) and *Harpers' Latin Dictionary*. The former will be referred to as *LSJ*.

7. Eric Werner (*The Sacred Bridge* [London and New York, 1959]) has convincingly established this distinction: see pp. 375, 378, 405.

8. Neither Homer's poems nor the vase paintings of the late Geometric period indicate any early use of the plectrum (*plêktron*) or pick. Pindar, at the beginning of the fifth century, is the first writer to mention it, although it appears on a seventh-century amphora: see Max Wegner, *Das Musikleben der Griechen* (Berlin, 1949), pl. 1c, and n. 6 to ch. iii. Tradition ascribed its invention to Sappho (Suid., *s.v.* 1).

9. The parallel is not with the neck strap of the modern guitar but with a rifle sling. Reinach (Daremberg-Saglio, III^2, 1446-47) twice explains that the strap engaged the performer's left wrist. Probably the clearest and most detailed explanation of the use of the *telamôn* is that given by Otto Gombosi in "New Light on Ancient Greek Music," in *Papers Read at the International Congress of Musicology* . . . 1939 (New York, 1944), p. 180. See n. 65 to ch. ii on his claims (pp. 169-170) that the idea of a rotating yoke (above, p. 5) is nonsensical and that the true function of the terminal grips was to compress the two uprights. Certainly one cannot simply assume that the yoke was rotated, as François Lasserre does (ed., *Plutarque: De la musique* [Olten and Lausanne, 1954], p. 38) when he speaks confidently of ensemble tuning.

10. Professor Winnington-Ingram has reminded me of the variation in degree of curvature displayed by the barbiton. He cites Wegner, pls. 9 and 15a, for the straighter and more rounded forms. The contrast can be seen even more clearly in the two parts of pl. 15: 15a shows Dionysus holding a barbiton which has broadly bowed and unusually thick arms, while in 15b the instrument which the poet Alcaeus is playing has slender arms with a more restrained curve—it resembles generally the barbiton which I have described

above in the text. Certain contrasts between kithara and lyre may come to mind. The greater string length of the barbiton means that its basic pitch must have been lower than that of either of these other instruments. Pindar (*Fg.* 125 Schroeder, 110 Bowra) speaks of the sound of its plucked strings (*psalmon*) as "answering the high pektis (ἀντίφθογγον ὑψηλᾶς . . . πακτίδος)." Here the use of the epithet suggests that Pindar intended to convey a contrast in pitch. Reinach (Daremberg-Saglio, III[2], 1440, 1450) holds that this lyre was not a *barbiton* (or *barbitos*), which he classes among the polychordal instruments; he cautions against trying to give it any special name. His references, however, show nothing relevant that is earlier than Theocritus (16.45 βάρβιτον ἐς πολύχορδον). In a long and massively documented note, Ervin Roos (*Die tragische Orchestik im Zerrbild der altattischen Komödie* [diss. Lund, 1951], p. 216 and esp. n. 15) argues that when we find the barbiton instead of the double aulos in representations of a Dionysiac procession or theater scene, we are not to suppose that stringed instruments actually replaced the aulos. It is rather (he maintains) a case of the artist selecting what has special interest: the aulos was always present. See Exkurs II, "Phrynichos, die flötende Kröte und das 'Hyporchema' des Pratinas" (pp. 209-35); this includes an extended encomium of the green toad that cannot fail to charm the most churlish scholar.

11. Roos, p. 216 and nn. 3-14, furnishes extensive documentation to show that the aulos was indispensable for all Dionysiac activities. As for the clash between indigenous and Oriental cultures, probably neither Apollo nor his instruments originated in Greece, despite what the Greeks believed; but it is the belief, not the fact, that has been important. On the physiological basis of the antithesis see p. 152 and n. 10. In *Musik und Rhythmus bei den Griechen* (Hamburg, 1958), pp. 22-23, the Munich musicologist Thrasybulos Georgiades has memorably contrasted aulos and kithara in terms of subjectivity and objectivity, without mentioning Dionysus or Apollo. Aulos music is a representation of personality, "unseres Ich"; lyre playing expresses our wondering awareness of the world about us, and here music appears rather as a mirror of the cosmic harmony. In this antinomy, according to Georgiades, are contained all the possibilities of music. On the various ways the double aulos might have been played, including the *tibiae impares*, see Behn (*Musikleben*, p. 103). Heinrich Husmann (*Grundlagen der antiken und orientalischen Musikkultur* [Berlin, 1961], p. 69) wrongly maintains that from the outset auloi had a two-octave range permitting the seven octave-species to be played. In his lengthy study of the aulos (Daremberg-Saglio, V, 300-32, art. "Tibia") Reinach notes that the

Phrygian variety never became popular with the Greeks, being confined to Dionysiac cult and the exotic rites of Cybele (p. 301). While the ordinary pipe was always made of cane, from the fifth century onward aulos makers increasingly used metal to give greater strength and (so they believed) to reinforce the tone (pp. 302-3).

12. See Wegner, *Musikleben*, pp. 58-59. He suggests that this fact explains Io's mention (A. *Pr.* 574) of a *kêroplastos donax*, a "wax-formed reed pipe" such as shepherds used.

13. For a possible exception, the only one known to me, see L. D. Caskey, "Archaeological Notes: Recent Acquisitions of the Museum of Fine Arts, Boston," *AJA*, 41 (1937): 525-27.

14. This is not a lost secret of the ancients, like electrum or Greek fire; it requires nothing much more than agility of the soft palate.

15. See Thrasybulos Georgiades, *Der griechische Rhythmus* (Hamburg, 1949), and on rhythmic ethos Gustav Amsel, *De vi atque indole rhythmorum* (Breslau, 1887).

16. *New Oxford History of Music*, ed. J. A. Westrup and others, vol. I: *Ancient and Oriental Music*, ed. Egon Wellesz (London, 1957), p. 15. See also Schneider's "Entstehung der Tonsysteme," *Bericht über den Internationalen Musikwissenschaftlichen Kongress: Hamburg 1956* (Kassel and Basel, 1957), pp. 203-11. More recently Husmann, p. 197, has propounded the theory that ancient peoples in the classical and Oriental countries all show the same sequence of development: Indo-Germanic or Mongol invaders have substituted the harmonic system for the tempered system of the indigenous cultures. One could wish that Husmann had worked out this challenging idea, which comes at the end of his study and unexpectedly.

17. See Catherine J. Ellis, "Pre-Instrumental Scales" (*Ethnomusicology*, 9 [1965]: 126-37, esp. 127-28), on the choral music of aborigines in Central Australia. *Aboriginal Music Making* (Adelaide, 1964), by the same author, deals with similar points in a more general way.

18. The unit of subdivision of the whole tone was the *diesis*, which we conventionally translate by "quarter tone." Aristoxenus was not certain about its size: he regarded it as being very often a quarter tone but acknowledged important exceptions to his rule; see W. D. Ross, n. on Arist. *Met.* 1016b22. Aristoxenus was very careful to note that it did not exist in any absolute sense (*haplôs*). This may indicate that the question had not yet been resolved in the schools, as Louis Laloy contends (*Aristoxène de Tarente, disciple d'Aristote, et la musique de l'antiquité* [diss. Paris, 1904], p. 111). R. P. Winnington-Ingram ("Aristoxenus and the Intervals

of Greek Music," *CQ*, 26 [1932]: 195-208) and Kathleen Schlesinger ("Further Notes on Aristoxenus and Musical Intervals," *CQ*, 27 [1933]: 88-96) set forth two opposed views on Aristoxenus' method. For an account of the unsatisfactory qualities in his approach see J. F. Mountford's Introduction (pp. xv-xxvii) to Schlesinger, *The Greek Aulos* (London, 1939). Mrs. M. I. Henderson champions Aristoxenus—going far beyond Laloy's estimate of him—throughout much of her admirable chapter on Greek music in the *New Oxford History of Music*, vol. I (see n. 16). Laloy, p. 119, strongly maintains that musical practice knew nothing of the theorists' tempered scales with intervals precisely equal or commensurable: "the theoretical scales therefore could not measure the *actual* diatonic or chromatic." Aristoxenus (*Harm.* 2, p. 35 M.) tells us that the teachers of theory were content to use the time-honored method of trial and error, instructing their students in lyre tuning by direct example. "The space separating the consonant sounds of the scale," says Laloy later (pp. 134-35), "was a veritable *terra incognita* where various paths could be traced out at random." It was not realized that the degrees of a modal scale, characterized solely by position, might be mutually bound by any relationship.

19. A.Q. *Mus.* 1.9, p. 19.1-10 (with diagram of notation, pp. 19-20) Winnington-Ingram (W.). Letters in italic type indicate a note raised by a quarter tone. My schematization follows Winnington-Ingram's in *Mode in Ancient Greek Music* (Cambridge, 1936), p. 22. He takes the Lydian as having been noted in the Hypolydian key, a fourth lower than the diagram indicates. The other scales, taken to be in Lydian, actually begin on G (Dorian, Phrygian) or E (the rest); all are given in the natural key (*ibid.*, n. 2) for purposes of ready comparison. Otto Gombosi (*Tonarten und Stimmungen der antiken Musik* [Copenhagen, 1939], p. 112) also transposes all the scales for convenience, but has precisely opposite conclusions regarding the original keys.

20. F. Bellermann, *Die Tonleitern und Musiknoten der Griechen* (Berlin, 1847), pp. 65ff; cited in Rudolf Schäfke, ed., *Aristeides Quintilianus: Von der Musik* (Berlin, 1937), p. 191, n. 1, and in Lasserre, p. 40. See Husmann, p. 81 and n. 1; he rightly remarks that in such matters one can hardly treat poets as competent, let alone authoritative (p. 65, n. 2). Theories of errors in the tradition used by Aristides: Husmann, p. 81, cf. p. 65. Jacques Chailley ("Le mythe des modes grecs," *Acta Musicologica*, 28 [1956]: 154) sees that these scales must have differed from those of the Perfect System. Their melodic character and vocal timbre were, he believes, sufficiently distinctive to let them be identified at once and to produce their moral effect upon nonprofessional listeners. This con-

clusion would seem to follow necessarily from Plato's remarks. More debatable is the claim (*ibid.*) that both system and pitch characterized these scales. See more recently the same author's *L'Imbroglio des modes* (Paris, 1960), pp. 10, 42. For instances of Javanese scales exceeding the octave or falling short of it, see n. 14 to ch. ii. The ancient *spondeion* scale provides another example of this. Martin Vogel ("Anregendes Griechentum," *Die Musikforschung*, 15 [1962]: 1-11) argues that the pre-Aristoxenian enharmonic had intervals in pure tuning; R. P. Winnington-Ingram contends that this was the genus of the *spondeiazôn tropos* and discusses its gapped nature ("The Spondeion Scale," *CQ*, 22 [1928]: 83-91).

21. *Harm.* 2, pp. 39-40 M. The text is cited by Pöhlmann, pp. 12-13. For a heterodox theory of the antiquity and practicality of Greek musical notation see his ch. i *passim;* see also Laloy, pp. 108-9, and cf. Henderson, p. 358.

22. The suggestion that Aristides misinterpreted *petteia* is Mrs. Henderson's (p. 376 and n. 1). Curt Sachs has succinctly stated the case for thetic-dynamic tension as a meaningful melodic principle in *The Rise of Music in the Ancient World East and West* (New York, 1943), pp. 234, 250-51. On Ptolemy's use of the two nomenclatures and systems of classification see Winnington-Ingram, *Mode*, pp. 6-8, 64-65.

23. For a countering view see Gustave Reese, *Music in the Middle Ages* (New York, 1940), p. 25, n. 55. He explains ethos in terms of melodic cadences, on the assumption that Mese may be considered a tonic, and follows von Hornbostel in believing that symbolism accounted for certain associations. His survey of Greek music (see ch. ii, "Greece and Rome," pp. 11-53) is carefully reasoned and thoroughly documented; while there will be differences of opinion on many points such as Sachs' theory of lyre tuning, much of the discussion is still rewarding. It provides one of the most extensive treatments of species and Tonoi available outside specialized works, and students of Greek music must regret Professor Reese's decision to omit the chapter from the new edition of his book. Specialists will perhaps be more likely to know a number of the positions he has developed from having noted their separate occurrences in the published work of Gombosi. It is not generally realized that Reese had worked out many of these hypotheses before coming to know Gombosi's arguments.

24. See Laloy, p. 102, n. 1; H. I. Marrou, review of Kathleen Schlesinger, *The Greek Aulos*, in *REG*, 52 (1940): 91; Martin Vogel, "Die Zahl Sieben in der spekulativen Musiktheorie" (unpubl. diss. Bonn, 1954), pp. 10-14. On Wead and von Hornbostel see n. 25. Vogel, p. 13, has said the final word on equiparti-

tion: "Das Prinzip der gleichmässigen Teilung weder zur Deutung der griechischen Musik noch zum Aufbau eines hochentwickelten Tonsystems ausreicht." The difficulty of judging Schlesinger's work is stated by R. P. Winnington-Ingram in his review of *The Greek Aulos:* see *CR*, 53 (1939): 185-86.

25. See Peter Schmiedel, "Ein unsymmetrisches Tonsystem," *Bericht über den Internationalen Musikwissenschaftlichen Kongress: Hamburg 1956* (Kassel and Basel, 1957), pp. 202-3. Curt Sachs (*Vergleichende Musikwissenschaft: Musik der Fremdkulturen* [Heidelberg, 1959], p. 10) briefly indicates the conclusions regarding equipartition that were reached by C. K. Wead in 1900 and by E. M. von Hornbostel in 1928. Husmann's *Kammerton* (see n. 34) recalls von Hornbostel's well-known theory of a *Massnorm.*

26. The idea of a manner or style, as one sees it in *tropos,* should not be taken as a sufficient explanation of modal ethos. The comment of Mrs. Isobel Henderson that "the ethos of a composition is simply what we should call its style" ("The Growth of Ancient Greek Music," *Music Review,* 4 [1943]: 12) oversimplifies considerably. Her recent extended treatment of Greek music (see nn. 16 and 18) dismisses ethos in a few sentences.

27. His reference applies mainly to contemporary techniques of performance in use among non-Western peoples, but Curt Sachs' mention of "das Näseln, Jodeln, Vibrieren, Stossen, Gleiten, das fast noch mehr als der Bau der Stücke das wesentliche Merkmal der einzelnen Tonsprachen ist" has relevance for Greek music. (*Vergleichende Musikwissenschaft* [see n. 25], p. 9). Idelsohn's definition of mode (*Jewish Music* [New York, 1929], pp. 25-26) is cited by Reese, p. 10; see also H. S. Powers, "Mode and Raga," *Musical Quarterly,* 44 (1958): 449-50.

28. Husmann, p. 51: "das Skelett, das übrigbleibt, nachdem die ganze praktische Wirklichkeit abgestreift worden ist."

29. I was not able to obtain a copy of P. Bonaventura Meyer's 'APMONIA: *Bedeutungsgeschichte des Wortes von Homer bis Aristoteles* (diss. Freiburg; Zürich, 1932) until the final revision of text and notes had been completed. In Appendix E, I have attempted to take account of some of the conclusions reached in this important work.

30. Chailley, "Le mythe," p. 162. I have added numerals to my translation.

31. See Husmann, pp. 84-85, and esp. Martin Vogel, *Die Enharmonik der Griechen* (Düsseldorf, 1963), critically discussed by R. P. Winnington-Ingram in "Die Enharmonik der Griechen," *Die Musikforschung,* 18 (1965): 60-64. I have not had direct access to Vogel's book.

32. J. Curtis, "Reconstruction of the *Greater Perfect System*," *JHS*, 44 (1924): 16.

33. At Athens the auletes were regularly non-Athenians; they came from Boeotia in particular, a point to which we shall recur. See Roos, p. 221 and n. 1, and also below, n. 61 to ch. iii.

34. It should be remembered that the species or *eidê* were sequences of intervals within the System: they had nothing to do with pitch as we now understand the term. For the study of Greek music absolute pitch no longer constitutes a meaningful issue; it is difficult, accordingly, to find any theoretical provision for pitch unless the Tonoi are assigned this role. When Husmann (pp. 60 and 65, n. 4) speaks of the "absolute pitch" of the Tonoi and of the supposed *Kammerton*, one hears the overly faithful pupil of von Hornbostel.

35. Henderson, pp. 347-58. See R. P. Winnington-Ingram's review in *Gnomon*, 30 (1958): 243-47. On p. 246 he briefly raises a number of questions concerning her treatment of the Tonoi.

36. For a significant reference in Plato see n. 6 to ch. iii. Laloy, p. 6 and n. 2, points out that in musical training a sharp distinction was drawn between amateurs and professional artists, so that the freeborn Athenian generally received only a rather elementary musical training. He could not play an instrumental solo, nor did he know the formulas for free accompaniment or the rules of composition. A passage in the *Laws* (812d1-e6; see pp. 96-97) shows that various master musicians of Plato's day would teach their pupils these imposing secrets.

37. Writing with Oriental music chiefly in mind, Curt Sachs (*Vergleichende Musikwissenschaft in ihren Grundzügen* [Leipzig, 1930], p. 68) has eloquently and concisely stated the cosmological basis of ethos doctrines: "Die Welt ist eine Einheit; alles Menschliche hängt unlösbar im Kosmischen, und auch die Charaktere, Temperamente und Tugenden werden durch den Weltlauf und den Gang der Gestirne bestimmt. Die Weltordnung aber kann musikalisch nachgebildet werden, und der gelungenen Nachbildung eignet die gleiche Kraft wie dem grossen Ganzen." Sachs does not, however, differentiate between Greeks and Orientals. As a consequence, he explicitly includes the former in his statement (p. 69) that the astrological significance of a mode determines its ethos. This connection may conceivably apply to Damon; it has no relevance to the poets of the fifth century or the philosophers of the fourth. Like the equation of ethos with style (see n. 26), it is inadequate as an explanation. Sachs (*ibid.*) finds the earlier interpretation of ethos in terms of varying sequences of intervals to be unacceptable on several counts. He notes that the *slendro* scale

of Java (see n. 14 to ch. ii), with absolutely equal intervals, is divided into modes each of which supposedly has a specific ethos. We shall not attempt to deal with the possible origins of musical ethos in magical beliefs. On this point see Jules Combarieu, *Histoire de la musique* (Paris, 1938), I, 3-4, and in connection with Pythagorean teachings Karl Svoboda, *L'Esthétique d'Aristote* (Brno [Brünn], 1927), pp. 177-78. G. F. Hartlaub ("Musik und Plastik bei den Griechen," *Zeitschrift für Ästhetik*, 30 [1936]: 163-64) discusses modal ethos uncritically and attempts to explain it in terms of "die astrale Bedeutung der Grundtöne"; this is fantasy.

II. FROM PINDAR TO ARISTOPHANES

1. *Fg.* 198a Schroeder, 187 Bowra: "Famous Thebes taught (*epaideusan*) me to be no stranger indeed to the Muses nor unacquainted with them." In *Paideia* (tr. Gilbert Highet [New York, 1943], I, 287, n. 1) Werner Jaeger calls this fragment "an important proof of the fact that in the time of Pindar and Aeschylus even in Boeotia the word *paideuô* already implied the musical (and, of course, also the gymnastic) culture which constituted its principal content for the Periclean period." Pindar he describes (I, 124) as "the greatest master of the art of educating and encouraging men through praise of noble deeds." His views on Pindar as educator have called forth outspoken disagreement from Gilbert Norwood (*Pindar* [Berkeley and Los Angeles, 1945], pp. 46-47). Walther Kraus ("Die Auffassung des Dichterberufs im frühen Griechentum," *WS*, 68 [1955]: 65-87), who is less at variance with Jaeger, believes there is no cause for surprise if Pindar does not appear in an expressly paideutic role, since the poet of the victory odes is the spokesman of a grateful people. We may well question this: it was not *das Volk* who hired a Pindar or a Bacchylides to write epinician odes. According to Hermann Gundert (*Pindar und sein Dichterberuf* [Frankfurt, 1925], p. 57), Pindar's verse never has the quality of didactic poetry, but when he used the gnomic sayings of Homer or Hesiod he was conscious of acting as a teacher of his people. The phrase *mousikan orthan* (*Fg.* 32 S., 13 B.) is suggestive. See also Lasserre, pp. 47-49, who notes another fragment (132 Turyn = 124c S., 111 B.) which praises the barbiton as calming the violent speech and moods of drunkenness. He makes *P.* 12 the origin of mimetic theory; this account of an auletic nome can hardly be associated with Aristotelian doctrine.

2. *Mode in Ancient Greek Music* (Cambridge, 1936), pp. 81, 3. Mrs. Henderson ("The Growth of the Greek 'ΑΡΜΟΝΙΑΙ," *CQ*, 36 [1942]: 97) speculates on the Hellenization of foreign modes

and justly maintains that modes have their basic affinity not with scales but with melodization. Robert Lachmann (*Musik des Orients* [Breslau, 1929], p. 50) suggests that apparently the modal patterns did not always permit of natural and easy application to Greek melodic structure; but this may be putting the cart before the horse. Winnington-Ingram's explanation of mode in relation to melody (*melos*) is well supplemented by Mrs. Henderson's quotation and comment in "The Growth of Ancient Greek Music," p. 4 and n. 2: "The Harmonia is defined by Heraclides Ponticus (*ap.* Athen. 624d): 'The course (ἀγωγή) of the Melodia which the Dorians composed was called the Dorian Harmonia.' A Melodia was a corpus of songs; its 'course' was the series of notes used in those songs, taken and arranged in order of pitch." The unknown Academician from Heraclea Pontica was active during the later part of the fourth century; Mrs. Henderson (p. 10) rightly observes that he treats the Harmoniai of his own time as full octave-species. Μελῳδία should not be confused with μέλος, which denotes the individual "song" or "melody." "Le mode," says Antoine Auda, "forme l'essence, l'âme de la mélodie" (*Les modes et les tons de la musique* [Brussels, 1931], p. 19); see n. 69 to ch. iii on Laroche. On the problem of defining modality and on the Harmoniai from a comparative point of view, see Chailley, *L'Imbroglio des modes*, p. 5. On Heraclides see also n. 17 to ch. iii.

3. The difference between practical scales (*Gebrauchsleitern*) and the extended, "ideal" scales of instrumental tuning is brought out by Lachmann, p. 36. He further points out (p. 61) that even practical scales, central notes, and tonal compass "remain nothing but lifeless data if we do not know the melodies in which they attain to determinate form." The musicologist's criterion referred to in the text is illustrated by E. M. von Hornbostel's "Phonographierte tunesische Melodien," *Zeitschrift der Internationalen Musikgesellschaft*, 8 (1907): 41-43, on the actual practice of music among Arab peoples.

4. Better than any single term in English for Tropos is the German *Melodiewendung*. So Oriental music, which regularly uses elaborate figurations, nevertheless seeks to avoid falsifying any of the essential characteristics of the melodic and rhythmic type. The traditional music of India, for example, keeps its development within the bounds of the particular *raga* (rhythmic-melodic pattern) which has been chosen. See H. S. Powers, "Mode and Raga," *Musical Quarterly*, 44 (1958): 448-60. Aside from the present instance, Tropos appears to be used only twice as synonymous with Harmonia (ps.-Plut. *Mus.* 17, p. 13.27 Ziegler; Bacch. *Isag.* 46, p. 303.3 Jan), unless Dionysius of Halicarnassus (*De*

Comp. Verb. 19) offers another example. In keeping with the explanation of *O.* 14.17 offered in the text is Laloy's comment (p. 89, n. 1) that the modal dative phrase Λυδῷ . . . τρόπῳ must mean "à la mode de Lydie," not "dans le mode lydien." See also Laloy, p. 95, on the puzzling references to the "Dorian lyre" and also to "Aeolian melodies" in *O.* 1.17, 105. The combination witnesses to some undeniable degree of systematization.

5. See Arist. *Poet.* 1459b35-36. The excesses of the Hellenistic commentators are not in question here. Laloy, p. 88, proposes that "Lasus of Hermione, Pindar's teacher, already was familiar with the theory of the modes and had doubtless set it forth in his *Harmonika*, earliest of all Greek treatises on music." This is of course sheer conjecture. On Lasus see p. 46.

6. Sources are cited according to the chapter and item numerations in the B sections of Diels-Kranz. (Hermann Diels and Walther Kranz, eds., *Die Fragmente der Vorsokratiker*, 3 vols. [8th edn., Berlin, 1956].) The translations are those of Kathleen Freeman, *Ancilla to the Pre-Socratic Philosophers* (Oxford, 1948). For the titles of the two tetralogies on music confidently ascribed to Democritus, see 68B15c, 25a.

7. Wellesz, p. 46. He gives as the source of his definition Aristotle's *De Anima*, sections 407b-408a: the only relevant portion is 407b30-31. See the notes in Ross's edition (Sir David Ross, ed., *Aristotle: De Anima* [Oxford, 1961], pp. 195-96). The theory as we have it in the *Phaedo* goes counter to established Pythagorean belief. See Burnet, nn. on *Phaedo* 85d3, 86b5-6; also Laloy, pp. 22-23. Claudianus Mamertus represents Philolaus as having declared that the soul is joined to the body "through Number and likewise incorporeal Harmony" (44B22). On the relationship between body and soul see Ross, *Aristotle* (London, 1945), p. 132. See also n. 59.

8. See n. 20 to ch. iii. The central doctrines attributed to Philolaus are cited, with the Greek text of the key phrases added, by Georgiades, *Musik und Rhythmus*, pp. 91-92. Many scholars deny or dispute the authenticity of some of the fragments which purport to give Philolaus' doctrines; I believe that the validity of the general picture presented here is nevertheless not compromised to any serious extent.

9. The early *mousikoi* got their general doctrines from the Pythagoreans, who were the only thinkers to have offered even a tentative explanation of musical phenomena: "un musicien philosophe ne pouvait être que pythagoricien" (Laloy, p. 78).

10. Aristotle regards habituation and human nature (*ethos* [ἔθος] and *phusis*) as synonymous, or extremely alike at the very least (*E.N.* 1152a30-33).

11. Professor Winnington-Ingram has suggested to me that this presumably refers to melody which follows the scale order.

12. See Carlo del Grande, "Damone metrico," in *Filologia minore* (Milan and Naples, 1956), pp. 197-214; originally in *Giornale italiano di filologia*, 1 (1948): 3-16.

13. Hermann Koller, *Die Mimesis in der Antike* (Bern, 1954), has attempted to show that Damon's teachings are by far the most important single force in the development of the concept of mimesis. Several scholars have refuted his thesis. G. F. Else ("'Imitation' in the Fifth Century," *CP*, 53 [1958]: 73-90) presents a convincing case for the idea that mimesis is a Platonic rather than a Damonian concept, and comes from drama. On this interpretation (see esp. p. 85), Damon's contribution was the musically based concept of assimilation, probably expressed with the help of the terms which we find associated with his name in the *Republic:* ὁμοίωσις or ὁμοιότης (ὁμοιοῦσθαι) and πρέπον or τὸ πρέπον (πρεπόντως, πρέπουσαι). The continuing importance of these ideas of likeness, already so striking in the fragments, thus appears with a special clarity.

14. Aristides had an evident fondness for male-female dualism, imputing it to diverse aspects of the cosmos. In Oriental music, however, such differentiation does actually occur. The Javanese divide the notes of a central scale between two instruments according to the male-female cosmic antithesis: one instrument has the even tones resulting from a cycle of fifths, while the other has the odd tones. See Lachmann, p. 22. Jacques Handschin, *Der Toncharakter* (Zurich, 1948), gives further examples, taken from China and Bali as well as Java. This *Umschichtleiter* or "alternating scale," with its unvarying interval of 156 cents, is schematized and discussed by Curt Sachs (*Vergleichende Musikwissenschaft in ihren Grundzügen*, pp. 27-29; for examples of "male" and "female" divisions in primitive music see his *Vergleichende Musikwissenschaft: Musik der Fremdkulturen*, pp. 25-26). He shows how this scale, which exceeded the octave limit (see n. 20 to ch. i), was replaced by the earlier form of the *slendro*. This fell short of the octave, having five intervals of 234 cents. It gave way in turn to the later *slendro* with its five intervals of 240 cents, a full octave. The development with constantly uniform intervals here is not comparable, obviously, with what happened to the *harmoniai*. A parallel begins to appear only in the next stage, that of the *pelog* scale with its varied intervals. There is no evidence that the male-female antithesis dates from any early period of Greek music. On individualism as a late theory see p. 173.

15. As the supplied words show, Damon's statement contains a

very strange ellipsis. It does not seem likely, however, that the usual translation is wrong.

16. Max Wegner, *Die Musikinstrumente des alten Orients* (Münster-Westph., 1950), pp. 46-51, refutes Sachs' claim that Greek music was an Oriental importation.

17. Thucydides says that Spartans went into battle to the sound of the aulos (5.70) and with *polemikoi nomoi* (5.69.2). The scholiast explains this phrase as "battle songs," though it has been taken to mean "military usages." One may question the belief that the text of elegy had become divorced from music at so early a date as *ca.* 640. This point cannot easily be settled, since the separation seems to have been a gradual process. According to Chamaeleon (*ap.* Athen. 620c) the works of Homer, Hesiod, Archilochus, Mimnermus, and Phocylides were actually sung. This comes, however, from his treatise "On Stesichorus"; we cannot be sure that he was speaking of any period earlier than the time of Stesichorus, who apparently made musical settings for the performance of Homeric epic. In a recent article ("Flutes and Elegiac Couplets," *JHS*, 84 [1964]: 63-68) D. A. Campbell has argued strongly against the accepted view that early Greek elegiac poetry normally had an aulos accompaniment. He uses some points already made by other scholars, e.g., the confusion between the two senses of *elegos* and the possibility that Thucydides was not referring to elegiacs.

18. See Archil. *Fg.* 190 Edm. (on Pyrrhus) and n. 75 to ch. iii.

19. Musicological studies of primitive peoples the world over have shown that this basic division which Plato seeks to establish is not mere theory, but precisely recognizes a fact of human expression in movement. In *Rhythm and Tempo* (New York, 1953), pp. 50-51, Curt Sachs gives many well-documented examples. Lucian's description (*Salt.* 12, p. 275 Jacobitz), the earliest empirical evidence, is as follows: "First an ephebe dances the 'high-spirited' steps (*ta neanika*) and whatever figures he will later make use of in war. Then a maiden follows, demonstrating the women's dance performed with neatness and order. Thus the ring dance (*hormos*) is a blend of moderateness and courageous spirit." Possibly Plato, whose terminology reappears here, had in mind contemporary performances of this dance when he wrote.

20. 6 Diehl (3 Edmonds); *ap.* Cleonid. *Harm.* 12, p. 19 Menge (in Karl von Jan, ed., *Musici Scriptores Graeci* [Hildesheim, 1962; original printing Leipzig, 1895], p. 202.11-12). According to Suidas, Ion began to produce tragedies in Ol. 82 (452-449). Poets often made their dramatic debut as very young men, Aristophanes before he was twenty; hence the lines which are given here could well date from a later period, as they ought from a technical

musical point of view. Friedrich Marx ("Critica et Hermeneutica," *RhM*, 83 (1934): 376-79) does not believe these two distichs are the work of Ion and takes the "crossways" (*triodous*, literally "three-ways") to refer to tetrachords. His arguments seem neither constructive nor plausible. Timotheus explicitly claims for himself the addition of an eleventh string or note (6e D. [15 Page = 791: see n. 22], lines 229-31; 19 E., lines 240-3), while Ion does not; but Schlesinger, pp. 143-44, errs in claiming that Ion used a ten-stringed kithara. *Dekabamona taxin*, which refers to the intervals, can be misleading. J. M. Edmonds (ed., *Elegy and Iambus* [London and Cambridge, Mass., 1944], I, 432) capitalizes *harmonias*, conjecturing a metaphor from the crossways of Hecate; but it is unlikely that Ion means to refer merely to harmoniousness in general.

21. For a useful collection of the evidence see Flora R. Levin, "The Hendecachord of Ion of Chios," *TAPA*, 92 (1961): 295-307. Her discussion takes no account of the fundamental ambiguity involved in the noun *chordê* and the *-chordos* epithets, and Schlesinger's hypothesis of equipartition is treated as fact; but on a number of counts her article is a welcome addition to the studies of this problem.

22. 1 Bergk (5 E.); *ap.* Str., p. 618 Meineke. D. L. Page (ed., *Poetae Melici Graeci* [Oxford, 1962], p. 363) does not recognize as Terpander's either these lines or the two which praise Sparta as the home of the Muse and of Justice (see n. 23). As in n. 20, both systems of numeration in Page's collection are cited. The first is by individual author; the second represents the total sequence of items.

23. Terpander: 6 E. (3 B.); *ap.* Plut. *Lycurg.* 21. See n. 22. Alcman: 100 D. (35 B., 62 E., 41 P. = 41); *ap.* Plut. *Lycurg.* 21.

24. Alcman, on Apollo playing the aulos: 102 B. (51 P. = 51); *ap.* ps.-Plut. *Mus.* 14, p. 117.28-29 Lasserre, p. 12.8-9 Ziegler (Plut. *Mor.* vi.3); Pl. *Legg.* 672c8-d3. M. P. Nilsson (*A History of Greek Religion* [Oxford, 1925], pp. 108-9) writes vividly of the absorption and taming of Dionysiac ecstasy by the serene liturgy of Apollo. See also Henri Jeanmaire, *Dionysos* (Paris, 1951), pp. 187-97.

25. Only a century before Plato, the comic poet Epicharmus (*Fg.* 75 Kaibel; *ap.* Athen. 184f) portrayed Athena accompanying the Dioscuri on the aulos. Earlier still, the Boeotian lyric poetess Corinna (29 B. [17 E., 15 P. = 668]; *ap.* ps.-Plut. *Mus.* 14, p. 117.29-30 L., p. 12.9-11 Z.), traditionally Pindar's adviser, sang of how Athena taught Apollo to play the aulos. This seems to have been a legend local to Boeotia, as Wegner (*Musikleben*, p. 16) believes; Greek artists never showed Apollo with the pipes.

26. The Phrygian tune: 14 D. (37 B., 37 E., 35 P. = 212); *ap.*

Schol. Ar. *Pax* 797ff. The swallow's note: 13 D. (36 B., 38 E., 34 P. = 211); *ap*. Schol. Ar. *Pax* 800.

27. 1 D. (1 B., 1 E., 1 P. = 702); *ap*. Athen. 624e-f. On Lasus see n. 5.

28. 1 D. (1 B., 1 E., 1 P. = 708); *ap*. Athen. 617c-f. Max Pohlenz ("Das Satyrspiel und Pratinas von Phleius," *Göttingen Gelehrten Nachrichten* [Berlin, 1927], pp. 298-321) interprets this hyporcheme as a work performed by two choruses or semichoruses. A conventional group enters first, singing slow and solemn anapests to the usual aulos accompaniment. They are taken to task for this by a band of satyrs who suddenly invade the scene. The text of the work is explained by Pohlenz as a protest against the emergence, under Phrynichus, of a new and disturbing art form. According to this theory it was tragedy, accordingly, that called forth such criticisms as οὐδὲν πρὸς Διόνυσον (*nihil ad Dionysum*); and so the Dionysiac play subdivided into two forms, the serious and the comic, which were and would remain distinct. In his analysis of literary origins Pohlenz may be correct—there are separate grounds for believing that the phrase quoted above referred to tragedy—but his actual interpretation of the text of Pratinas is most questionable. In the first place, his explanation of the role of the aulos is weak. Moreover, his theory would mean that the opening of the poem must be derogatory of the speakers themselves, surely an unlikely possibility. As Pohlenz says (p. 315), the τάδε of line 1 is deictic; but the "outrage" and "tumult" of line 2 do not suit a solemn parodos. The opening of Pratinas' hyporcheme is all of a piece, and the impression it makes is not that of a reference to tragic choral lyric. The exhaustive study of Pratinas' lines by Roos gives reason to believe them part of a satyr play (see pp. 232-33 of his study), although his detailed reconstruction is unconvincing in a number of respects. Del Grande puts forward the same general explanation in "Damone metrico" (*Filologia minore*, p. 184). See, however, n. 30. Lasserre, pp. 45-47, takes no note of Roos in his study of the hyporcheme.

29. "The rhythm," says George Thomson, "cannot be determined without the aid of the music which accompanied it" (*Greek Lyric Metre* [Cambridge, 1929], p. 2). A century earlier, August Boeckh had actually called the whole metrical scheme of this hyporcheme *elegantissimum* (*De metris Pindari* [Leipzig, 1821], p. 271). In the same way, Emile Martin has defended the rhythms of Timotheus' *Persae* (*Essai sur les rythmes de la chanson grecque antique* [Paris, 1953], pp. 327-39).

30. Jeanmaire (p. 233) cites in translation the text of a votive epigram which celebrates the victory of a dithyrambic chorus in

the Great Dionysia of 485. The aulos modality is stated as Dorian; accordingly, Pratinas did not lack a precedent. Roos (p. 215) correctly maintains that the hyporcheme is a protest not against the aulos as such, but against the way it was being used. Both Roos (esp. pp. 233-35) and Hermann Koller (*Musik und Dichtung*, p. 144) maintain what R. P. Winnington-Ingram calls the "all too fashionable view" that the so-called hyporcheme actually comes from a satyr play (see n. 28) and uses two choruses, one of them kitharodic. See Winnington-Ingram's review of Koller, *CR*, N.S. 15 (1965): 195.

31. A. W. Pickard-Cambridge (*Dithyramb, Tragedy and Comedy* [Oxford, 1927], p. 48) conjectures that "as the dithyramb was further removed from the Bacchic revel to which it had at first belonged, and became part of an orderly civic festival, the wildness of the music may have abated."

32. Whether directly or indirectly, knowingly or unknowingly, it must have been from Pratinas that Claudio Monteverdi took his guiding principle, "L'orazione sia padrona dell' armonia e non serva" (cited by Hermann Koller, *Musik und Dichtung*, p. 11, without reference to any specific Greek author). Thus it appears that Pratinas was a real, if unacknowledged, force in the initial development of opera as a musical form.

33. 4 D. (5 B., 5 E., 5 P. = 712); *ap.* Athen. 624f-625a.

34. Much the same thing is true of Hypophrygian, where dynamic Mese came on the second degree. Curt Sachs (*The Rise of Music in the Ancient World East and West* [New York, 1943], p. 226) notes that of all the scales none had a lower center of gravity than Hypodorian. Hermann Abert (*Die Lehre vom Ethos in der griechischen Musik* [Leipzig, 1899], p. 73) suggests that the delicacy of the Greek feeling for pure melody appears in the sweeping ethical distinctions posited between modes using Mese as a proper tonic, yet ending on Hypate, and again those in which Mese functions equally as a *finalis*. This seems extremely speculative; it suggests the influence of the Gregorianists, whose current assumptions and terminology in dealing with Greek modality Jacques Chailley has recently criticized (cf. pp. 28-29 and n. 30 to ch. i). Matthew Shirlaw ("The Music and Tone Systems of Ancient Greece," *Music Review*, 4 [1943]: 14-27) argues that no firmly established tonic existed in Greek music and derives the existence of the modes from this fact. The hypothesis of dynamic Mese is still uncertain, regrettably (see p. 20). If we could accept it, we might more easily be able to explain the statement in the *Problems* of the Aristotelian school that singers to the kithara favored Hypodorian and Hypophrygian (19.48, p. 109.3 Jan; cf. 19.30).

The reader who may wonder why the present study has not made greater use of Abert's celebrated treatise will find a number of the reasons set forth in detail by A. J. Janssens, "Aristoteles en de oudere Muziekaesthetik," *Philologische Studien*, 6 (1934-35): 127-30. One representative objection (p. 129) may be cited, as particularly telling: "De ethosleer wordt aldus voorgesteld als een homogeen geheel, zonder ontwikkeling in den tijd en in de ruimte" —Abert's study is synthetic and analytical, lacking the historical dimension that such a treatment should have.

35. On this passage see Boeckh, pp. 224-25, and Abert, *Lehre*, p. 22, where the analysis is similar to that offered here. D. B. Monro failed to perceive the associative basis and so was led to conclude that Aeolian was a scale of medium pitch. J. F. Mountford ("Greek Music and Its Relation to Modern Times," *JHS*, 40 [1920]: 13-42) believes the real meaning of "tense," "relaxed," and "slack" in Greek musical usage is ethical, so that no need or proper reason exists to refer them to pitch at all. There is no evidence for this view, which runs counter to normal semantic development. Laloy, pp. 100-3, argues that *epaneimenê*, *suntonos*, and *chalara* refer to an alteration of intervals, while *oxus* and *barus* designate pitch differences. It is difficult to disprove this as a technical explanation; yet we must at all times be wary of treating poets as if they were musicologists. See n. 20 to ch. i, on Husmann.

36. Plato (*Rep.* 398e2) couples Syntonolydian with Mixolydian. Svoboda (p. 188, n. 5) follows Bergk in taking *suntonon* here as an actual reference to Syntonolydian; this is possible. He is certainly right in claiming that this adjective should not be taken with *iasti*, and also in his belief that *aneimenan* is a characterization of the Iastian Harmonia.

37. Socrates' attacks, *Nub.* 331, 333; the older dithyramb and paideia, *Nub.* 985-88. Helmut Schönewolf (*Der jungattische Dithyrambos* [diss. Giessen, 1938], pp. 21-22) declares the text to be incomprehensible at line 334 unless *kampê* is understood as a reference to strophic division. That is, the poem is "twisted" out of its proper direction and fails to achieve the responsion of an antistrophe.

38. The Lydian *nomos* and Dorian: 2 D. (2 B., 2-3 E., 2 P. = 806); *ap.* Athen. 617b. The pattern was contrived, says Telestes, "with shifting-shaped reeds (*aiolomorphois kalamois*)." This may be the sole reference in Greek poetry to the double-reed straw mouthpiece of the earlier and simpler aulos. Originally a single straw, it came to have two separate blades in this middle stage before the introduction of the beating-reed mouthpiece. High pitch in the "Lydian hymn": 4 D. (5 B., 5 E., 6 P. = 810); *ap.* Athen.

626a. With particular reference to *oxus* and its use by Telestes, Laloy (p. 99 and n. 1, cf. pp. 123-24) supposes that certain modes had a predilection for certain regions (*topoi*) of the voice which revealed their character. See also n. 35.

39. So far as the story (Plut. *Inst. Lac.* 17) of the ephor at the Carneia threatening to cut off Timotheus' excess kithara strings has any validity, it tells against the possibility. A poet must not be held accountable for technical expertise (see n. 35, and also n. 20 to ch. i), and Telestes may be referring only to melodies of the Lydian Harmonia which usually kept to the higher portion of their compass. On Timotheus and the ephor see also n. 44.

40. Timotheus as a conservative: 6e D. (15 P. = 791), *Pers.*, lines 216-17; 19 E., lines 229-30. Contradicted: 7 D. (12 B., 24 E., 20 P. = 796); *ap.* Athen. 122d.

41. The text: Pherecr. 145 Kock, 145 Edmonds (J. M. Edmonds, ed., *The Fragments of Attic Comedy*, 3 vols. [Leiden, 1957], I, 262-65), 2.326 Meineke; *ap.* ps.-Plut. *Mus.* 30, p. 125.1-28, 31-33 L., pp. 24.6-25.5, 25.9-11 Z. Edmonds rearranges the text on chronological grounds, but his reasoning is probably false: see Lasserre, p. 173, on such attempted corrections. An important discussion of the *Chiron* fragment is Ingemar Düring's "Studies in Musical Terminology in 5th Century Literature," *Eranos*, 43 (1945): 176-97. Schönewolf's notes to his translation of the fragment (see pp. 67-69) are stimulating on one or two points: he suggests that in line 16 "twelve" is mentioned simply as a round number. *Dutzend* and "dozen" both are comparable. With regard to the incessant modulations, Aristophanes (*Thesm.* 100) refers in much the same way to constant changes of melodic direction; if Pherecrates had his reference in mind, the year 411 would be a *terminus post quem*. Düring (p. 196) believes Pherecrates was speaking of chromatic melodies. The epithet *exarmonios* used in the *Chiron* excerpt is the antonym of *enarmonios* in the sense of "melodious"; see Pl. *Legg.* 654a2.

42. Here Edmonds translates ἐν with the dative as "between." This seems less correct than "in," since cola as well as strophes were subject to modulation. His rendering clearly is governed by his theory of instrumental interludes. The same notion of the *kampai* leads him to mistranslate the scholiast's definition of them as περιῳδαί; see *LSJ* for the correct meaning. In such matters as these his new edition of the comic fragments (see n. 41) represents no advance.

43. The *niglaros* is literally a boatswain's pipe, to judge from Ar. *Ach.* 554. Its plural use here suggests the strained sound of the high notes when sung; Schönewolf (*ad loc.*) translates by *Triller-*

pfeifen. Düring, p. 196, cites Eupolis, *Fg.* 110 K. (120 E.) *niglareuôn kroumata.* This, he says, refers to octave tones produced by shortening the strings with the left hand; apparently an induced first harmonic is meant. In the end we may agree with Reinach that *niglaros* was applied to an instrumental technique, the precise nature of which is not known. Whether it may also have been used of a vocal technique or malpractice is unclear; Düring interprets the passage in the *Acharnians* as a reference to the "call," not the pipe, of the boatswain. The scholiast there explains *niglaros* as *krouma kai melos;* Lasserre, p. 174, takes this seriously as evidence.

44. *Pers.* 229-31 (241-43 E.); see n. 20. The epithet *hendekakroumatos* is a Timothean coinage. Helmut Huchzermeyer (*Aulos und Kithara . . .* [diss. Münster-Westph. 1931], p. 6) holds that *krouma* used in reference to a stringed instrument is no earlier than Euripides, if that early; see *Etym. Magn.* p. 153, 31 on Ar. *Thesm.* 120, where the word occurs. *Krouma* and *krouein* he takes as deriving originally from the terminology applied to percussion instruments; Lachmann's view (p. 67) is related. Düring (pp. 181, 192) contends that the kithara retained a seven-stringed form throughout the classical period, and that the addition of strings beyond this number was an experiment which met strong resistance. The whole problem is greatly complicated by the fact that Greek musical terminology did not clearly distinguish between notes and strings. Timotheus' grouping of added strings all at one extreme of the Dorian sequence may be reflected in Plutarch's story (*Inst. Lac.* 17) that an ephor at the Carneia asked him from which end the offending excess strings should be cut off; see n. 39.

45. Tragic and comic choruses are another matter. The great festivals of Dionysus used the civic amphitheaters only a few days each year, while *CIA* II, 553 shows that there were dithyrambic choruses not only at the urban Dionysia (with ten choruses) but at the Thargelia, Prometheia, and Hephaesteia as well. To this list should be added the Panathenaea; and *CIA* II, 1367, a later inscription, shows that they came to be featured at the Lenaea as well. These contests were tribal and continued to be so until the second century of our era; but the *eleutheroi* were early superseded, in part at least, by professionals. See Pickard-Cambridge, *The Dramatic Festivals of Athens* (Oxford, 1953), pp. 74-75. Aristides Quintilianus (p. 30.3 W.) equates the dithyrambic style with the median range of the voice. Commenting on this, Abert (*Lehre,* p. 73) says, "Since the chorus was made up of nonprofessionals, the choice naturally could not have fallen on any other range of the voice than a middle one, which contained the normal compass of

the male voice." His words, though generally true, will not describe the dithyrambs and nomes of Timotheus.

46. *Probl.* 19.15, pp. 86.2-87.7 Jan. Edmonds' generally similar translation of this passage (*Lyra Graeca* [London and New York, 1928], III, 295) must be used with caution on one or two points, especially as regards the rendering of *enarmonia.* Schönewolf, p. 13, finds in the latter half of the first paragraph evidence for his belief that *mimeisthai* does not denote dramatic representation, which he believes is an acquired meaning added to the primary ethical one. So sweeping a conclusion would seem to be unwarranted, but Schönewolf rightly interprets the present reference as being to *Klangmalerei* and mentions Plato's attack upon this sort of excess (*Legg.* 669c-d).

47. The *Scylla:* 23 D. (3 B., 7 E., 23 P. = 799); *ap.* Arist. *Rhet.* 1415a12. Metrically meaningless lines: e.g., 10 D. (7 B., 27 E., 23 P. = 799). Hephaestion (*Poëm.* 3 Consbruch) says that the kitharodic nomes of Timotheus are written "at random" and "without any definite meter." This is of course extreme, but it does represent something of the impression conveyed by the *Persae.* On Martin's minority view see above, n. 29. The pseudo-Plutarchian *De Musica* (4, p. 113.5-6 L., p. 4.12-14 Z.) explains that Timotheus mixed hexameters with dithyrambic rhythms in his first kitharodic nomes, "so as not to seem to be breaking the laws of the ancient *mousikê* at the outset." A valuable discussion of the *Persae*, especially from this point of view, is contributed by C. J. Ellingham to *New Chapters in the History of Greek Literature* (Oxford, 1921).

48. This fact, together with the unsuitability for dancing, would have guaranteed Timotheus the hostile reception he is supposed to have been accorded by the Spartans (above, n. 39), who introduced choral singing into Greece from Crete. Concerning the general effect of his "new music" Pickard-Cambridge (*Festivals*, p. 266) conjectures that "the obscurity imparted to the words of the tragic chorus (i.e., through music of the Timothean sort) was one, among others, of the causes of its rapid decline in the fourth century. Poets might not care to compose what their hearers could not follow." Jeanmaire, p. 233, reasonably suggests that the noisy accompaniment of the later dithyramb prevented its text from being heard properly.

49. Their achievement was not wholly a negative one. Walther Vetter (*RE* XVI, 870) has stressed its positive side, perhaps with more charity than most scholars would show.

50. Timotheus' handling of the kitharodic nome may have been one of the reasons for Aristotle's wish to ban the kithara from education, a radical step indeed. Wilamowitz (*Griechische Vers-*

kunst [Berlin, 1921], p. 111) has commented on the great difference between the roles of aulos and kithara in this respect: "Actually the music which the aulete played, music in which . . . repetition of the melody was customary, could hardly give any impetus to innovations. The kitharode, on the other hand, who was himself just as much of a practicing artist, had not strophic poetry but epic verse . . . It was natural as a next step to make use of the abundance of highly varied verse types which meantime came into being. Thus Phrynis began the work, and Timotheus completed it." Polybius (4.20.9) states that among the Arcadians the nomes composed by Timotheus and Philoxenus are taught as a second stage of "musical" education. This seems startling at first, but (as Professor Winnington-Ingram has suggested to me) Timotheus had quite possibly become "classical" for the Arcadians of Polybius' day.

51. Proclus (*ap.* Phot. *Bibl.* 320a33) writes of a later period, not datable, in which the nome has become "orderly and systematic in its construction," being pervaded by Apollo. "Each type uses its special modes, the dithyramb Phrygian and Hypophrygian, the nome the Lydian system of the kitharodes." The latter reference presumably is not to Lydian alone but to the whole Lydian group of modes, or at any rate all that remained in use. Proclus' authority was sufficiently late so that Lydian had come to occupy the central place of honor held in the fifth century by Dorian. Proclus states further that Timotheus brought the nome to "its present condition"; actually a considerable number of changes must have been effected during the intervening period.

52. A. E. Haigh (*The Attic Theatre* [Oxford, 1907], p. 321) takes this passage as proof that Aeschylus used Iastian. His whole survey of the modes in drama (pp. 310-11) is uncritical.

53. *Chordê* probably is used here *in malam partem*, paralleling the references to Odysseus' "bending the bow" by Hellenistic comic poets. This sense is not attested in *LSJ;* but see *s.v.*, II.2, and for *arcus* so used with reference to Penelope see Ov. *Am.* 1.8.47-48. The use of *nervus* as *membrum virile* is well known. It regularly means "bowstring" rather than "bow," but the latter use occurs in Valerius Flaccus, 3.182. Edmonds (I, 265) is aware of sexual *double entendre* or direct statement in the verbs at least. For these Lasserre (pp. 172, 174) makes a better case, using the reading ἀπέλυσε κἀνέλυσε; this has greater musical significance. He describes the two verbs as "operations successives encore que presque identiques d'un déshabillage," and rightly notes also that in line 4 ἀνῆκε alludes to loosing the virgin zone as well as to slackening

lyre strings. Where the technical musical status of *chalaros* is concerned, Pl. *Rep.* 398e10 constitutes the crux.

54. The same question inevitably arises with regard to Phrygian, the next mode after Dorian in the opposite direction. Düring (pp. 180-81) holds that the literal reference is to the low pitch of Melanippides' compositions; he interprets Ar. *Nub.* 968 on the same principle. See n. 64.

55. The Boeotian nome, *Ach.* 14; the nome of Olympus, *Eq.* 9; the nome to Pan, *Av.* 745. For an exhaustive list of specific nomes see Emmanuel Laroche, *Histoire de la racine* NEM- *en grec ancien* (νέμω, νέμεσις, νόμος, νομίζω) (Paris, 1949), pp. 167-68.

56. Ps.-Plut. *Mus.* 5, p. 113.15-16 L., p. 4.26-27 Z. B. A. van Groningen ("A propos de Terpandre," *Mnemosyne*, 8 [1955]: 188) represents the nomes of Terpander as having been extremely simple and regular verbally, metrically, and melodically.

57. He states his position bluntly several times, although the evidence seems to be limited to a single play, the *Frogs*—lines 366, 1286 (the first occurrence of the *tophlattothrat* refrain), and perhaps 1302. In lines 1281-82 of this play, Euripides receives severe criticism for taking his choral lyrics partly from kitharodic nomes.

58. This historical fact must be balanced against Sachs' warning (*Rise of Music*, p. 47) that "melody is not an abstract conception to be indiscriminately realized either on instruments or with human voices." There are, and presumably have always been, areas of composition in which a melody may be ambiguous from this point of view. Folk song, for example, has constantly been treated instrumentally by the most renowned composers; and one will hardly understand Bach's arias without Schweitzer's comment that they represent a concept of melodization which is neither vocal nor instrumental, but the common denominator of both.

59. In his commentary on *Phaedo* 85-86 Richard Hackforth (*Plato's Phaedo* [Cambridge, 1955], p. 101) says, "The theory of soul as attunement (*harmonia*) which Simmias now puts forward is a thoroughly rationalist theory, utterly opposed to the mystical and religious conceptions characteristic of Orphics and Pythagoreans. What its origin is it is impossible to say with certainty." The utter opposition of which Hackforth speaks was convincingly explained more than a generation ago as a revision of Pythagorean doctrine. See A. E. Taylor, *Plato* (London, 1926), p. 194, and John Burnet, *Early Greek Philosophy* (London, 1945; first published 1892), pp. 295-96; see also n. 7. For the scholiast's interpretation of *Eq.* 531-33, see Edmonds, *Fragments*, I, 18, n. a.

60. *Nub.* 1357, *Vesp.* 989, *Thesm.* 137-38 (cf. *Ran.* 1304-6, an attack on Euripides), *Fg.* 221 K. (*ap.* Athen. 184e).

61. In *New Chapters in the History of Greek Literature, Second Series* (J. U. Powell and E. A. Barber, eds.; Oxford, 1929), pp. 164-65, J. F. Mountford suggests that this accusation is hardly supported by the ancient evidence. In the *New Oxford History of Music* (I, 337-38) Mrs. M. I. Henderson has recently pointed out that Dionysius was quoting from or recalling a faulty text, since one of the lines has been transposed. The reference here is to his claim (*De Comp. Verb.* 19) that strophe and antistrophe must correspond melodically, a view which has been widely rejected. It cannot be assumed that he offers reliable testimony concerning the nature of Euripides' original setting. "Dionysius," says Amy M. Dale (*The Lyric Metres of Greek Drama* [Cambridge, 1948], p. 195), "is not an author whose evidence can be pressed in detail on a technical question of this kind." Her discussion of the *Orestes* fragment and the vexed question of strophic responsion (pp. 194-96) sums up the issues most judiciously. The reader may be put off, however, by her opening statement that the fragment "is probably the music which Euripides himself composed" because Dionysius does not question its authenticity. The arguments of D. D. Feaver ("The Musical Setting of Euripides' *Orestes*," *AJP*, 81 [1960]: 1-15) appear unconvincing. See also nn. 2 and 4 to ch. i. In "Relazione melodica di strofe e antistrofe nel coro greco" (*Rivista di filologia*, N.S. 9 [1931]: 185-206) Romualdo Giani and Carlo del Grande maintain that probably Dionysius cited Euripides from memory, and that the choral ode "era tutta un ricorrere lirico d'inflessioni sonore su una o più basi tematiche, ed ogni antistrofe non ripetizione ma variazione di un' unità." Pöhlmann has attacked their views in his discussion of this passage (pp. 19-23), dismissing Dionysius' claim of melodic correspondence between strophes as sheer anachronism and reaction. The point that the text here goes on to mention nothing but modulation among the three genera is not mentioned. He rather unconvincingly rejects (p. 19, n. 1) several dissenting views. See most recently Hermann Koller (*Musik und Dichtung*, pp. 146-47), who cites Dionysius' comments as clear evidence of the victory of *Taktprinzip* over speech rhythm.

62. The charges against Euripides: *Ran.* 849, 944, 1281-82, 1301-3. Aeschylus: *Ran.* 1298-1300, 1252-56 (lyric choruses); *Pax* 748-49.

63. "In many of the choral songs of Euripides," says Thomson (pp. 2-3), "we feel that the author is writing for an audience which is more intent on following his music than his poetry . . . The words are weak and sometimes repeated without regard to

the sense for the sake of the musical accompaniment." He cites *Or.* 1414-17. Still another way of maltreating the text may underlie the description of a certain Artemon as "too fast at music" (*Ach.* 850-51); see n. 21 to ch. iii.

64. The verb *enteinesthai* is used here with *harmonian* in a figurative sense, not in the supposed technical sense of "raise to a higher pitch" given in *LSJ.* (This is properly *epiteinein:* see Burnet, n. on Pl. *Phaedo* 86c3. The various figurative terms applied to the soul as *harmonia* in this dialogue may profitably be compared with Aristophanes' use of language.) Mrs. Henderson has seen the correct meaning (*New Oxford History of Music,* I, 347). Düring, p. 181, follows the scholiast in believing that the passage refers to keeping the Dorian high pitched, not in the low register like the melodies of Aristophanes' own day; see n. 54. It has been evident, however, that Aristophanes avoids baldly technical terms of a theoretical kind. Chailley ("Le mythe," p. 149) feels that in the present passage *harmonia* means simply "arrangement." *Diachaskein,* used of the modes in *Eq.* 533, may well represent an approach to the theoretical; in its primary intention, however, it is boldly figurative (the gaping, toothless old man), part of an extended metaphor already discussed on p. 57; see also n. 59. E. K. Borthwick ("ΚΑΤΑΛΗΨΙΣ—A Neglected Term in Greek Music," *CQ,* 11 [1959]: 23-29) makes a strong case for a similar interpretation of *krousis* and *katalêpsis* in *Nub.* 318.

65. It was learning to sing these which proved difficult, not learning to play them. If the ability to tune without an aulos or pitch pipe (*tonarion*) was considered a basic accomplishment, this might admittedly have caused problems; yet it does not seem necessary to postulate tuning cycles such as the familiar pattern of fourths and fifths. A person who had learned to distinguish the modes in singing should have been able to voice his lyre accordingly, though with less precision than the set pitches would afford. Experiments with replicas of the kithara show that the instrument does not take kindly to a complete revoicing; nor do the *kollopes* seem at all adapted to rapid or frequent changes. See pp. 5-6 and n. 5 to ch. i. The whole problem of lyre tuning is a vexing one; it remains almost entirely a mystery. Wegner's tentative suggestion of a tuning key (*Musikleben,* p. 34) does not make the matter less puzzling. Concerning the role of the rotating crossbar—if it did in fact rotate—two possibilities might be considered. It may have made available the transposition scales, or it may have enabled the player to slacken his strings when the kithara was not to be used for a time. Such deliberate untuning is today a recognized part of the care of certain stringed instruments; Plutarch knew of it in his

day (see *De Educ. Puer.* 13, p. 10 Didot). Gombosi (*Tonarten und Stimmungen der antiken Musik* [repr.; Copenhagen, 1939], p. 37, n. 7), whom Reese follows (p. 16, n. 17), points out that only the kithara is shown with grips at the ends of the yoke: lyres and barbitons are not. Simultaneous tuning of all the strings up or down would be meaningless and impracticable, he maintains, and the strings would in fact have gotten out of tune. These objections have some weight; they do not, however, rule out the possibility (which Gombosi does not consider) of a deliberate slackening of the strings.

66. Aristophanes' attitude is that of a practicing poet-composer, not that of a philosopher; see n. 64. He did not deal with theory, either his own or that of the opposition, but with the respects in which he felt his art to be endangered. It is not likely that he knew Damon personally: the two men were of different generations. On the other hand, it would be strange if he had not become acquainted with Damon's ideas.

67. The emphasis on rhythms in passages of the *Laws* dealing with musical paideia (such as 798d7-e8, 802d8-e11, 812b9-e6) shows how lasting was Plato's sense of their importance.

68. C. H. Whitman (*Aristophanes and the Comic Hero* [Cambridge, Mass., 1964], p. 13 and n. 35) maintains that Aristophanes was not so hostile as has been supposed in his reactions to the new developments in music, and that he was very much aware of them. The second of these two points we can readily accept (see n. 66); not so the first. The article Whitman cites (G. Pianko, "La musica nelle commedie di Aristofane," *Eos*, 47 [1954]: 23-34) has little value.

III. PLATO

1. At the close of his final statement of belief in the dialogue, Socrates (*Crito* 54d2-5) tells Crito that considerations of justice and the obligation to preserve the laws are wholly filling his mind: "Just as persons in a Corybantic frenzy imagine they hear auloi, so the . . . reverberation of these words buzzes in my ears and prevents me from hearing any others." A buzzing, droning sound is several times mentioned as characteristic of auloi. Aristophanes (*Ach.* 866) also speaks in this way, and his *bombaulioi*—perhaps "buzzpipers" in a variation on *askaulioi*, "bagpipers"—parallels Plato's use of *bombeô* in the present passage. The drone of the bagpipes is well known; and only this instrument, with its untempered scale, can give Occidental hearers any idea of the penetrating and rousing powers of Greek auloi (see Jeanmaire, p. 134, on the passage in the *Crito*); in their quieter moods they may have

sounded rather like oboes. The analogy with bagpipes would seem particularly close if one could believe that the ubiquitous double aulos used one pipe for a drone bass as does the corresponding double reed pipe in Oriental music today. There is no firm evidence, however, to support this belief. Because of its strident and penetrating aspects of tone, the aulos has been compared by Karl Geiringer (*Musical Instruments* [New York, 1945], p. 42) to the medieval shawm. Reinach (Daremberg-Saglio, V, 300) takes the shawm to be a direct descendant of the Greco-Roman *monaulos*, a rare instrument in antiquity. Since the choice of material for the body of the pipe cannot have affected tone quality in any great degree, we may suppose that cutting the reed in different fashions produced varied timbres, then as now. See p. 8 and n. 11 to ch. i.

2. Evanghélos Moutsopoulos, *La musique dans l'oeuvre de Platon* (Paris, 1959), p. 88, sec. 57, speaks of this passage as recalling the historical connection between the new forms of stringed instruments and the developed forms of the aulos; but on pp. 95-96, sec. 63, he recognizes that the former developed before the latter and therefore suggests that Plato was referring not to the instruments themselves but to the way the virtuosi used them. Thus *heterophônia* supposedly was an imitating first of the double and then of the single aulos on the kithara. (Moutsopoulos does not note that in a passage of the *Laws* (700d7-8) Plato refers to the imitation of singing to aulos accompaniment by singing to the kithara; see Schönewolf, p. 18.) This explanation is inadmissible; see n. 62.

3. Probably this was the Theban aulos, although one cannot be certain. On the resources and techniques of the Theban aulete see the detailed account given by Francisque Greif in "Etudes sur la musique antique (cont.)" (*REG*, 23 [1910]: 33-41). Pollux, 4.80, says Diodorus of Thebes introduced this fashion of spacing the finger holes; Diodorus' date is not given. It would seem that in the present passage Plato "lags far behind the professional theory of his time," as Mrs. Henderson says ("The Growth of the Greek 'APMONIAI,'" p. 100). This is more probable than the view held by J. D. Denniston ("Some Recent Theories of the Greek Modes," *CQ*, 7 [1913]: 95, n. 1), who took Plato's criticisms here and Pausanias' account (9.12.5) of the Theban aulete Pronomus as proof that a modal complex fitted to a single instrument or scale was still a new idea. In "The Growth of Ancient Greek Music," p. 12, Mrs. Henderson describes an anachronistic Plato who "talked of the innovations of thirty years ago and called them modern." Laloy, p. 105, is even more outspoken about both Plato and Aris-

totle: "Neither . . . seems to have been aware of the profound changes that music was undergoing in their time . . . They remained faithful, their whole life long, to the 'classics of the lyre' and the 'masters of the dithyramb' whose beauties had been revealed to them at school when they were fifteen." We may agree with the same writer's claim (p. 106) that Plato seems to have gone no farther in his musical knowledge than the average well-educated Greek youth; but we must also recognize that in his thinking on music he went a good deal farther than others. H. I. Marrou (*Saint Augustin et la fin du monde antique* [Paris, 1937], p. 207) presents the same view as Laloy.

4. Plutarch (*Quaest. Conviv.* 3.8.2) notes that "the threnody and the 'mourning aulos' at first stir up the emotions and make the tears flow, but then they gradually calm sorrow." Elsewhere, however, he says that the frenzied motion of the Bacchantes and Corybants is quieted and checked "by changing from a trochaic rhythm and Phrygian melody" (*Amat.* 16).

5. This seems to have been a distinctively Athenian view: see above, pp. 45-46.

6. He does speak of playing the lyre with the fingers alone (*Lys.* 209b7); nowhere else does he use *psallein,* as opposed to *krouein,* of playing on stringed instruments (Lukas Richter, *Zur Wissenschaftlehre von der Musik bei Platon und Aristoteles* [Berlin, 1961], p. 82). According to the evidence assembled by Moutsopoulos (pp. 181-82; secs. 135-36, esp. n. 4 to sec. 136), playing without a plectrum would have been very old-fashioned by Plato's time. The *Protagoras* (326d6-327c4, esp. 327a8-b1) indicates that the secrets of auletics were kept jealously guarded. This unique claim, if true, would help to explain why Greek literature in the fifth and fourth centuries affords so incomplete an account of the aulos and its use.

7. Common terms do occur: *Rep.* 349e11-12 (cf. 412a1-2), *epitasis* and *anesis* for tuning the lyre up or down respectively; *Legg.* 669e6, *aptaisia,* for glibness of technique. Moreover, one passage of the *Laws* (812d1-e6) brandishes a whole array of terms mainly technical and descriptive of the contemporary musical styles which Plato so deeply detested. Suspicious in general when encountering specialists' jargon, he has no patience with the technical cant of chorus masters who say that a piece of music is *euchrôs,* meaning that it has "a good color"; terms such as "rhythmic" he will allow, but not this misuse of metaphor (*Legg.* 655a4-8). The fourth-century historian Philochorus (*Fg.* 66) uses *euchrôs* in speaking of the "colors (*chrômata*)" of music. Of Plato and the theoreticians Laloy says (p. 133): "On conçoit, devant

leur science, toute de détail et de mésure, le dédain superbe et la sereine ignorance de Platon."

8. On his reference in *Rep.* 443d6-7 to the "fixed" and "movable" notes of the tetrachord as model elements, see below, p. 71. It shows no unusual knowledge of music; from a technical point of view it is interesting only because it suggests that Plato had octave-species in mind.

9. Moutsopoulos (p. 366, sec. 256 and n. 2) suggests that Plato is perhaps indicating an even closer relationship—almost an identity—when he employs both quanta and intervals in the numerology of the *Timaeus.* It is of course a belief in the "harmony of the spheres" that unites the two sciences, according to the Pythagoreans. On the use of *mousikê* with a specialized meaning in this and other passages, see Richter, *Zur Wissenschaftlehre*, p. 43.

10. Richter (*Zur Wissenschaftlehre*, p. 68) holds that *Rep.* 531c3-4 shows numbers treated as transcendent substances existing separately. By referring the *sumphônoi arithmoi* to the *Timaeus* scale, he finds in this passage an indication that the conception of music as "einer philosophisch oder theologisch gedeuteten Zahlenwissenschaft" occurs in early antiquity. It is not clear that he is warranted in going beyond John Adam's interpretation (n. *ad loc.*) of ratios such as 4:3 or 3:2 rather than 9:8 or 256:243. The use of *anametrountes* (531a2) seems puzzling in connection with the Pythagoreans. As B. L. van der Waerden has suggested, however, the reference may simply be to the representation of notes and intervals through numbers and ratios, and in any case it does not constitute evidence for the exact measurement of string lengths. See "Die Harmonielehre der Pythagoreer" (*Hermes*, 78 [1943]: 176-77), an important article; also Lukas Richter, "Platons Stellung zur praktischen und spekulativen Musiktheorie seiner Zeit" (*Bericht über den internationalen Musikwissenschaftlichen Kongress: Hamburg 1956* [Kassel and Basel, 1957], pp. 199-200. R. L. Crocker has given a pleasing account of the theoretical background in a two-part article, "Pythagorean Mathematics and Music" (*Journal of Aesthetics and Art Criticism*, 22 [1963-64]: 189-98, 325-35).

11. Bacchic and similar dances: *Legg.* 815c2-d3. Private rites (*teletai idiai*): *ibid.* 908d6. According to E. R. Dodds (*Euripides: Bacchae* [Oxford, 1944], p. 73, n. on *Bacch.* 72), *teletê* originally applied to many kinds of ritual but was used chiefly of the mystery-cult rites from the later fifth century onwards. The old liturgical airs were variously attributed to Olympus, Marsyas, and Hyagnis; the important point is that they had a Phrygian origin (so Bellermann's *Anonymus* 28; see ps.-Plut. *Mus.* 7, p. 114.8-28 L., pp. 6.10-7.7 Z.).

12. In *Oxford History of Music*, ed. W. H. Hadow, Introductory Volume (Oxford, 1929), p. 89. Glenn R. Morrow (*Plato's Cretan City* [Princeton, 1960], p. 342, n. 158) comments on the strange ambivalence of Plato's references to the aulos and auletics. It is doubtful, however, whether the association of this instrument with orgiastic rites should be taken as the explanation.

13. *Rep.* 395d1-3, 400d1-3, 522a3-b1; *Legg.* 655a4-b6.

14. Jules Combarieu, *La musique et la magie* (Paris, 1909), p. 121. One passage from this work (p. 11) might almost be a commentary on the present excerpt from the *Laws:* "In magic everything necessarily takes place independently of the agent's mind, and by virtue of laws against which no one can do anything unless he . . . puts into effect a counter-charm." On Plato's and Aristotle's attitude towards the magical efficacy of music see Combarieu, *Histoire*, I, 62, 153. His view as a whole seems extreme. An effective counterbalance is provided by Morrow (pp. 309-11, esp. p. 310), who discusses at some length this use of ἐπῳδή as it occurs in 659e1. Of the so-called chants he says, "If there is magic in them, it is the magic of meaningful words . . . when accompanied by rhythm and melody." This particular statement shows an overly rationalistic approach. See E. R. Dodds, *The Greeks and the Irrational* (Boston, 1957), p. 154 and n. 119, on "the incantatory power of music, as in the catharsis attributed to the Pythagoreans, which seems to have developed from primitive charms (ἐπῳδαί)." He fails to cite the *Laws* but does mention the use of *epôidai* to heal the soul by Thracian followers of Zalmoxis (*Charm.* 156d8-157a6, esp. 157a3-5).

15. Chailley, "Le mythe," p. 157.

16. Aristoxenus, *Fg.* 28, mentions that his father boasted of having known Socrates; see Laloy, p. 4. It will be noted that Aristides' scales are given in the enharmonic, while Aristoxenus (*Harm.* 1, p. 2 M.) takes the harmonicists to task for showing only the enharmonic octave systems in their *diagrammata* (divided-line representations of the *harmoniai*). This fact makes less likely the possibility that the scales in Aristides' treatise come from a work by Aristoxenus, but the off chance remains.

17. Athen. 624c-625d. For the fragments of Heraclides' *De Musica* in three books, see *Fgs.* 156-63 in Fritz Wehrli, ed., *Die Schule des Aristoteles: Texte und Kommentar*, 10 vols. (Basel, 1944-59), vol. VII: *Herakleides Pontikos* (Basel, 1953), pp. 46-50, with commentary on pp. 112-17. Wehrli has clearly pointed out the specific instances in which he parts company with his teacher Plato and with Damon. In almost every respect this edition supersedes Otto Voss, *De Heraclidis Pontici vita et scriptis* (diss.

Rostock, 1896); but with regard to modality at least (see n. 2 to ch. ii) it is Voss, p. 81, who has noted that Heraclides sharply distinguishes the Harmoniai from the Tonoi, the former as Dorian, Aeolian, and Ionian and the latter as Dorian, Phrygian, and Lydian. This differentiation is that of a man accustomed to thinking in terms of octave-species where modality was concerned. His standards of race and culture are taken, as Wehrli notes (p. 116), from the fixed world of Homer and Pindar; the world of Damon and Plato was a different one. There is nothing more than conjecture in the claim of Walther Vetter (*Antike Musik* [Munich, 1935], p. 35) that the predilection for Dorian in tragedy must have been a conscious emphasizing of the racial factor. This factor received considerable attention from German musicologists between the two World Wars.

18. *Lach.* 188d2-8; so also 193d11-e2. There is no striking idea here; it has been rightly observed that any educated Athenian might have said this (Burnet, n. on *Phaedo* 61a3). Richter (*Zur Wissenschaftlehre*, p. 33) renders the adverb *atechnôs* ("simply [*sc.* in Dorian]") as *kunstlos;* this seems unduly narrow. As he himself points out, Plato here shifts the meaning of the term *mousikos* from the professional specialist to the ethical prototype, the model for sound paideia. Gerhard Müller (*Studien an den platonischen Nomoi* [Munich, 1951], p. 170) notes the occurrence of Δωριστὶ ζῆν in *Ep.* VII, 336c6. This, he maintains, is offensive as being given without the qualification of simile. It is certainly unusual, if not unique, in Plato's writings. Combarieu (*Histoire*, I, 86) holds that the Greeks were to some extent taken in by an association of ideas which connected Dorian modality with the civic genius of the people who used it (see n. 17); but, like the dialogue which takes its name from him, Plato's Laches is concerned with bravery, a martial and not a civic virtue. Moreover, this view does not take into account the role expressly assigned to Phrygian in the *Republic.*

19. There has been much disagreement over the precise meaning of lines 9-10; see n. 36 to ch. ii, and cf. n. 35 on the larger aspects of the problem. To sum up once more, the essential question is whether *chalarai* designates specific types of Lydian and Iastian Harmoniai, as Westphal and Gevaert supposed. For the references see Svoboda, p. 188, n. 5. Here the decisive point would seem to be the use of τινες; see Adam's note *ad loc.* The choice in translation between "slack Lydian" and "Chalaro-Lydian," and so on, is unimportant.

20. The Pythagoreans reportedly saw under a triple aspect what they called the concord, or rule of the best, in all things: in the

universe this was *harmonia*, in the state *eunomia*, and in the home *sôphrosunê* (Theo Sm. *De Arithm.* 1.15). As for the hypothesis of modal variety, R. C. Lodge (*Plato's Theory of Art* [London, 1953], p. 221) holds this same view; he lists a number of circumstances in which modes other than Dorian and Phrygian would presumably be used. Not all his conjectures are likely. [The name "Eunomopolis" does not pretend to any authority: it is my own coinage, used simply for convenience. Its formation approximately parallels that of "Kallipolis."]

21. On the "naturalistic mimesis" of this passage see Richter, *Zur Wissenschaftlehre*, p. 84. As for rapidity being a fault, the *Charmides* (159c8-9) contains the statement that the lyre is better played swiftly than slowly, but the other relevant passages one and all condemn rapid playing; see n. 63 to ch. ii. According to Marcus Meibom (in C. F. Abdy Williams, *The Aristoxenian Theory of Musical Rhythm* [Cambridge, 1911], p. 95), the seventeenth-century editor of classical writers on Greek musical theory, all antiquity believed that hymns and sacred songs should be sung very slowly; the statement is at any rate still a difficult one to disprove. Plato's brief discussion of rhythms and rhythmic ethos (*Rep.* 400b1-c5) makes clear the importance, in Damonian theory at least, of tempo as well as rhythm. The clear distinction between the two indicates a high degree of sophistication in musical theory, as Louis Harap claims in "Some Hellenic Ideas on Music and Character" (*Musical Quarterly*, 24 [1938]: 158); the article is almost entirely a reproduction of Abert's views. His appraisal may be exaggerated. Johannes Quasten (*Musik und Gesang in den Kulten der heidnischen Antike und christlichen Frühzeit* [Münster-Westph., 1930], pp. 69-70) strangely claims that Plato's contemptuous dismissal of music that lacked words (*Legg.* 669e2-4) can only be understood if one remembers the inferior place of music in cult practices. Further, Quasten sees in this passage signs of an attitude that sought to eliminate instrumental music from the service of the gods. Although the latter point may have some validity, both his assertions show thinking too narrowly channeled by a given topic and approach.

22. This portion of the chapter presents in shortened form the arguments of my article, "The Importance of Damonian Theory in Plato's Thought," *TAPA*, 86 (1955): 88-102. In the work of Evanghélos Moutsopoulos and of the immediate predecessors on whom he draws so heavily (Hermann Koller and François Lasserre above all), a distinction is drawn once or twice between Damonian and Platonic theory to indicate Plato's special stress on the ethical as all-important. The general portrait of Damon nevertheless is

that of a towering figure who almost completely overshadows Plato where music and paideia are concerned. On A. J. Janssens see n. 11 to ch. v.

23. *Lach.* 180d2-3, 197d1-5, 200a2; *Rep.* 400b1-c5, 424c5-6.

24. Agathocles as a Sophist: *Prot.* 316e1-3. Damon's skill at definition: *Lach.* 197d1-5. His *sophia*: *Lach.* 194e3-7. On the significance of the title *mousikos* see n. 29 to ch. v.

25. Plut. *Per.* 4.1-2, *Arist.* 1.7, *Nic.* 6.1. The latter two are probably echoes of Isocrates, 15.235.

26. The following passages seem relevant: pp. 90, 101-2, 110, 122 W. I find nothing in any of these that is clearly and demonstrably Damonian. A mere reference to *hoi palaioi* does not constitute sufficient proof. In pp. 101-2, moreover, this phrase can only refer to the Pythagoreans, whose connection with Damon has never been clearly defined. A number of other passages cited as cosmological do not seem to be so: see pp. 10, 40, 80-81, 105 W. The only mention of Damon by name occurs on p. 80 W., in a passage which does not deal with cosmology. See G. F. Else's long note (n. 53 to p. 85) on the use of Aristides as a source for Damonian theory. Morrow (p. 307, n. 36) is clearly correct in pointing out that Pierre Boyancé (*Le culte des Muses chez les philosophes grecs* [Paris, 1937], pp. 129-30) errs when he apparently supposes that Damon could not have had a part in formulating the fifth-century theory of modal ethos because these beliefs originally were grounded in magic and religion—or so Boyancé claims.

27. Richter, *Zur Wissenschaftlehre*, p. 33 and n. 3, briefly discusses the problem of determining what is Damonian in the dialogues. For his general treatment, especially in relation to Plato, see pp. 22-24 of his work. Throughout it he draws upon the theorizing of Ryffel, Lasserre, and Hermann Koller, all of whom have given extreme estimates of Damon's importance.

28. All references in this section are to the *Laws* unless otherwise identified. Morrow (pp. 302-18) gives an excellent summary of the place of *mousikê* and *choreia* in the *Laws*.

29. In a private criticism of this statement the late Werner Jaeger noted that the common basis of the two works is the belief that "to change the music in a *polis* is to destroy its *politeia*." His *Paideia* (III, 250-51) sets the distinction in the following terms: in the *Republic* Plato's chief purpose was "to test the content and form of 'music' by the new ethical and metaphysical standards set up by his philosophy," while the *Laws* shows him "chiefly interested in the psychological basis of education." Combarieu (*Histoire*, I, 144) argues that music was in a certain degree one of the bases of

the city-state because of its close connection with the religious beliefs that were basic to the state. Concerning Plato's theory of "the birth of culture from the spirit of music" in the *Laws*, Hermann Koller (*Musik und Dichtung*, p. 157) says, "It contains the deepest interpretation of *mousikê* in Greek literature and indicates above all the significance of music for wholeness in man's nature." On the relationship between culture in the *polis* and the cultured individual—the *pepaideumenos anêr*—see Jaeger's *Humanistische Reden und Vorträge* (Berlin, 1960), *passim.*

30. In actual fact the music of Egypt by Plato's time had already gone through at least as sweeping a change, under foreign influence, as was then taking place in Greece; Curt Sachs' study of Egyptian art has made this clear. Also, Plato shows himself less inflexible than Egyptian conservatism seems to have been.

31. 656d3-657a8, cf. 660c1; 799a1-2. Herodotus (2.79.3) says that the Egyptians claim the Linus song as their "first and only melody."

32. In 800c5-d6 Plato cites an actual example of shocking behavior during public sacrifice. This profanation was not only tolerated but, so it would seem, generally accepted. Plato's attack did not banish it: in the next generation Xenocrates (*ap.* Plut. *De Is. et Osir.* 26) details its offensive features.

33. Plato's remarks immediately following show that he believed *nomos* to have been taken over into music from law; compare the statement (722e1-2) that political *nomoi* are really and truly laws. He nowhere speaks of the notion of selectivity (root *NEM-*), which is especially important and revealing in connection with the musical usage. See F. A. Wright, "The Technical Vocabulary of Dance and Song," *CR*, 30 (1916): 9-10, for a useful analysis. Wright, however, defines the musical nome as "a rhythmical measure which gives to sounds instead of motions their allotted place"; in fact the nome is primarily a melodic "measure," not a rhythmic one. It has striking parallels with the *raga* of Indian music (see above, n. 4 to ch. ii); H. A. Popley, *The Music of India* (Calcutta, 1921), pp. 153-68, gives many examples of the *raga*, showing the respective styles of melodic development as well. On Laroche see n. 69.

34. In stages of culture prior to that which conceives of the prelude strictly as an art form, actual musical preluding always represents a tentative exploration of the shape and (more especially in vocal music) the range of what is to be essayed. The *alapa* of Indian music has just such a function, though formalized to a considerable extent; see Sachs' description of ensemble playing in India (*Rhythm*, pp. 113-14). Such is the conception that Plato adapts and refines to suit his comments on legislation. The effectiveness of his

analogy can perhaps be conjectured when one reads Lachmann's words (p. 59): "The Oriental musician by his preluding . . . addresses his entire being to the performance before him. Furthermore, he prepares not only himself but his hearers as well for what is to come." The importance of the audience in Greek music is stressed by Abert, "Die Stellung der Musik in der antiken Kultur" (*Die Antike*, 2 [1926]: 139), who avowedly has Oriental music in mind as a parallel.

35. It is taken seriously by Moutsopoulos, p. 177, sec. 132.

36. *Ion* 534a1-4, c7-d1; cf. *Apol.* 22b8-c3. Here Plato transfers the notion of Dionysiac ecstasy to the sphere of poetical inspiration. When he says elsewhere (*Symp.* 196e2-3) that possession by Eros makes every man a poet, Plato is partly quoting and partly paraphrasing Euripides (*Fg.* 663 Nauck). See Richter (*Zur Wissenschaftlehre*, pp. 29-30) on the aspects of irrationality and inspiration (*enthousiasmos*), which he traces to Democritus and Gorgias respectively, and the essay "Musischer Enthusiasmus" in Hermann Koller's *Musik und Dichtung*, pp. 28-35. See also n. 37.

37. *Rep.* 601a7-b2. In *Principium Sapientiae* (Cambridge, 1952) F. M. Cornford argues at length for the view that Plato has an overwhelming respect for poetic inspiration; he does not take into account the many passages which show a view diametrically opposed. The final truth in this matter would appear to incorporate both extremes. I find my view on Plato's indecisiveness in this matter (see also the text, below) paralleled by a remark in Hermann Koller's *Musik und Dichtung*, p. 34: "Platon nimmt verschiedentlich, aber keineswegs eindeutig Stellung zu dieser Frage." See also n. 36.

38. The unimportance of technical excellence: *Symp.* 215c2-6, *Legg.* 654c3-e1. The real purpose of technical knowledge: *Legg.* 812b9-c7. Johannes Regner (*Platons Musiktheorie* . . . [diss. Halle, 1924]) stresses the fact that when Plato deals with *kinêsis* and *harmonia* his interest is not in acoustical relationships, but in the psychological and physiological effect of musical tones. According to Regner he transfers the whole treatment of music to the province of the soul; in actual fact, however, the body is not forgotten. A generation later Richter ("Platons Stellung," p. 201) portrays a thinker who held in very low esteem the harmonicists' preoccupation with structural elements and subjective tuning experiments, counting only Pythagorean harmonic theory as truly scientific. This is likely to mislead. Van der Waerden, p. 190, furnishes a needed word of caution: "Man soll nie vergessen, dass Platon sich nicht nur auf Zahlenspekulation, sondern auch auf wirkliche Musik versteht."

39. Moutsopoulos (p. 213, sec. 158) raises the point that in

thus making a cult of virtue Plato parts company with Damon, whose theory never ceased to be musical, whatever stress it might have placed on the role of morality. The national anthem (947c8 *patrion melos*) which will be sung at state funerals would presumably be the work of the civic poet. "The song leader has the dominant role in any sacred performance. This person is selected by seniority in age and knowledge, but not necessarily musicianship": thus Catherine J. Ellis ("Pre-Instrumental Scales," p. 127), of the aborigines of Central Australia. This is not the only instance in which Plato displays an almost atavistic tribal sense.

40. The inference seemingly would be that the average member of a Greek theater audience did not readily recognize them, except perhaps by association. See the next note.

41. Lucian (*Harm.* 2, p. 853 Jacobitz) makes the celebrated musical performer "Harmonides" say that most of the audience are vulgarians who approve whatever they perceive to win the approval of the experts. They themselves know only how to clap and whistle, and the actual judgment is passed by a scant half dozen among the listeners. Pickard-Cambridge, *Festivals*, p. 99, has collected references to the influence of the audience or of powerful individuals (Alcibiades, Philemon); his sixth chapter (pp. 268-85) is the best available treatment of the subject. To cite one startling example, Aeschines (*In Ctes.* 232) states that judges of the cyclic choruses are publicly tried if they do not judge rightly. To Plato this would have been, or perhaps actually was, intolerable in the last extreme. On 658e see Morrow, p. 308 and n. 40.

42. The provision for new settings possibly is not so radical as it might seem. Protagoras is made to speak of music teachers setting lyric poetry (*Prot.* 326a7-b1 *eis ta kitharismata enteinontes*), as if this were the most normal thing imaginable. Mrs. Henderson (*New Oxford History of Music*, I, 339) maintains on the basis of *Legg.* 812d that "the composer's legacy was simply the sung poem: the instrumental part is conceived as a free accompaniment at the executant's pleasure." This, of course, is not at all what Plato personally advocates. We have seen (above, p. 60) that when Aristophanes speaks of "old-fashioned education" he describes schoolboys of an earlier time as using the Harmonia which their fathers had handed down to them (*Nub.* 968-69, cf. 961). There is a discrepancy here; apparently reverence for modal tradition in the earlier fifth century was at times accompanied by a somewhat different attitude toward traditional melodies. An inscription found at Isthmia (see Oscar Broneer, "Isthmia Excavations, 1952," *Hesperia*, 22 [1953]: 192-93) states that one Themison, a musician of the late Empire, was the "first and only" person to compose new

musical settings (*melopoiein*) (?) for the lyrics of the tragedians and Timotheus. This claim is hardly likely to reflect anything more than ignorance and local pride, although Chailley thinks it highly important ("La musique de la tragédie grecque devant une découverture épigraphique," *Revue de Musicologie*, 39 [1957]: 6-9). Also, it is possible that *meta*, "after," should be read before the names of the dramatists, and this would alter the sense completely. In "A propos de Thémison," [Part 1] *ibid.*, 40 (1958): 3-14, Armand Machabey replies to Chailley, whose rebuttal is contained in the same article [Part 2], pp. 15-26. More heat than light is produced. Pöhlmann, p. 15, gives the text of the Themison inscription, with brief comments, as part of a valuable section, "Die musikalische Überlieferung," pp. 11-16.

43. Achieving the aims of the lawgiver: 802a5-c4. The approved types of composition: 829e1-3. Variety of sentiment maintained: 665c5-7. We are told that one must have knowledge of the comic, even though it is concerned with unsightly bodies and unseemly thoughts, because serious things are comprehended through their opposites (816d5-e2). But this knowledge must not be translated into action (816e2); nor may any comic, iambic, or lyric poet use ridicule either in jest or in earnest (935e3-6). It is evident from these passages that Plato did not wish to forbid absolutely the performance of comedy.

44. Walther Vetter (*RE*, XVI, 878) is not exaggerating to any serious degree when he declares that Plato's remarks on music always start from the assumption that the musical arts are the property of the whole populace. The secret of Platonic paideia is that one learns *aretê* dynamically, by singing and by exercising in well-coordinated movements. Lodge (p. 5) has well said, "The influence of the community or choric dance spreads itself over the whole of educative behavior, and provides each and every medium of artistic activity, not merely with a general principle of value (an idea of 'good'), but with concrete structural patternings, whose detailed analogies in song, dance, and sentiments can be recognized as arising from an identity of underlying rhythm peculiar to the species." Abert ("Die Musik der Griechen," in *Gesammelte Schriften und Vorträge*, ed. Friedrich Blume [Halle, 1929], p. 30) surmises that the concept of ethos is connected with the view of the political or communizing (*gemeinschaftbildenden*) power of music. As he points out, it was precisely during the classical period that this view was in favor. Laloy (*La musique chinoise* [Paris, 1909], p. 14) compares ancient China with the Greek city-states in this regard. [References to Laloy without book title are to his *Aristoxène de Tarente* throughout these notes.]

45. 665c2-5. E. B. England (*The Laws of Plato* [Manchester, 1921], I, 311, *ad loc.*) has pointed out that ἐπῳδή and ἐπᾴδειν are stock terms (cf. 666c6) of "soul-therapeutics" with Plato, and that his use of the verb here indicates that the *choreia* spoken of is often a mental process rather than a bodily performance. The aged choristers of Dionysus are not meant to function as actual performers, except with small groups of acquaintances on an easy private basis (665e5-10, 666c4-6). Through superior insight and training they constitute the repository of correct taste: "Their function is to be the *mind* of the state in the matter of *choreia*" (England, I, 313-15). Morrow, pp. 312-18, has a fine discussion of the chorus of elders with many points not to be found elsewhere. (Although one which seems a bit unexpected is the comment in n. 62, p. 316, that the forms of diversion at Athenian symposia included "the singing of scholia [*sic*]"!)

46. A calendar to be strictly observed: 799a1-b8. The sacred bounds ordained for song and the dance: 800a4-7. (It will be noted that at this point the two senses of *nomos* have achieved complete unity.) Choice of songs suitable for each sex: 802d8-e11.

47. *Mus.* 2.14, pp. 80.23-81.6 W. Thus Moutsopoulos (p. 219, sec. 163, n. 16) says, "L'esprit de ce passage tout entier est manifestement damonien."

48. *Legg.* 653a5-c4, esp. b6-c1. On this and other uses of the term *paideia* in the *Laws*, see Morrow, p. 302. The words of the ancient Chinese writer Sse-ma-ts'ien (in Combarieu, *La musique et la magie*, p. 346) furnish a striking parallel: "When the kings of old time made their ordinances regarding ceremonial and music, they did not seek to satisfy the desires of ear and eye, but wished to teach the people to bestow aright their love and their hatred."

49. 654a9-b1. The Syrtos Kalamatianos, a popular round dance of modern Greece, affects the dancers in a way which shows vividly the end that Plato had in mind. Thrasybulos Georgiades describes it thus: while watching the dancing or taking part in it "one feels the ancient tradition in the attitude of the dancers. They exhibit a dignity otherwise foreign to them; their faces become mask-like . . . The dancers convey a primeval tradition . . . their reverence for their forefathers and their unity with them become manifest" (*Greek Music, Verse and Dance*, tr. Erwin Benedikt and Marie L. Martinez [New York, n.d.], pp. 139-40). See p. 57 of *Musik und Rhythmus*, the same work translated into German. This later version has been enlarged, particularly through an invaluable appendix on sources for Greek musical theory, and is in every way to be preferred to the amateurish English translation. Speaking of the brilliant musical life of Sparta in the seventh and sixth centuries, Morrow

(p. 304) notes that "the thought of this early bloom of choral art among the Dorians, and the charm of the archaic forms preserved in their purity at Sparta, must have been in Plato's mind when his Athenian praises choreia to his Cretan and Spartan companions."

50. 654b9-d3. On 654c3-d3 see England, I, 278. Abert (see n. 44) comments on the interrelation of ethical and musical factors. During the classical period itself, he maintains, strict control of music was a necessity; and here the theory of ethos did music a service. "In stating that Dorian was suited to the highest seriousness and Mixolydian to passionate lamentation, it effected the result that choice of mode alone sufficed to bring the emotion to the level of expression, so that corroboration of it in the form of unrestrained subjective stresses was superfluous. Thus when the ancient musician chose his mode with regard to the expression of feeling he was already bound *ipso facto* to follow a fixed line of march, one which guarded him . . . from falling into the danger of civically destructive (*staatsgefährlicher*) innovations through side ventures of a subjective sort." Besides assuming what we cannot actually know with certainty this gives the impression that modal ethos, though very real, was at bottom an arbitrary affair; nevertheless it forces attention on an aspect seldom considered.

51. Delight in the best music: 658e6-659a1. The need to hear what is above one's own standards: 659c3-4. See nn. 57 and 70 to ch. iv.

52. 659d1-e5. Plutarch (*De Virt. Mor.* 3) says that Pythagoras, "knowing well that the soul is not entirely rational, advised that music be used as temptress and handmaiden of philosophy." This may have been the germinal idea from which Plato developed his views on music as a propaideutic working irrationally. Vetter ("Die Musik im Erziehungsplane der griechischen Antike," *Deutsche Musikkultur*, 7 [1942]: 39) contends that the introduction of the concept of "play" witnesses to Plato's awareness of the artistic field of vision beyond the ethical, a field first truly revealed by Aristotle. It might be more correct to say that the two thinkers worked towards different ends which are discernible in their last works. Aristotle laid the foundations of musical aesthetics, as Vetter and many others have pointed out again and again; Plato came at length to the belief that man is the plaything of the gods and should spend his time in "the noblest of play," the singing and dancing and sacrificing which go to make up "the life of peace" (803c4-e4). There is a profound difference in orientation here. Max Pohlenz ("Τὸ πρέπον: Ein Beitrag zur Geschichte des griechischen Geistes," *Göttingen Gelehrten Nachrichten* [Berlin, 1933], pp. 54-55) has taken a different view, arguing that Plato's use of such terms as *to*

prepon and *prepei* witnesses to an aesthetic theory of literature in existence as early as about the year 400. He notes that Plato, unlike Xenophon, Isocrates, and Aristotle, does not make *prepon* a synonym of *kalon*; for *prepontôs* used of music, *Rep.* 399a(7) is cited.

53. Moral paideia as a means of implanting a love of reason: *Rep.* 401e1-402a4. On the relation of *paidia* to paideia in Plato's view see below, n. 55. Vetter (*RE*, XVI, 878) holds that ancient pedagogy, taken as a whole, started from the assumption that any training carried out under compulsion of whatever sort is absolutely worthless. This should not be taken to mean that painless learning was the ideal. On the contrary, Aristotle said that pain attends the learning process (*Pol.* 1339a28-29). With his words in mind H. I. Marrou (*A History of Education in Antiquity*, tr. George Lamb [London and New York, 1956], p. 159), probably the foremost contemporary authority on ancient education, is wholly forthright: "None of the schools of antiquity ever shared our illusions about 'teaching without tears.' They had their own motto: 'No progress without painful effort.'" Except perhaps for *Crito* 50d6-e4, there is no clear indication that schooling was compulsory at Athens; see Paul Girard, *L'Education athénienne* (Paris, 1891), pp. 33-35, and Marrou, p. 382. It is possible that, as the latter believes, the passage in the *Crito* refers to unwritten laws of custom.

54. This statement also occurs in 644d7-9, as one of two possibilities, and it lies implicit in 804b1-3. In 716c4-5 God is said to be the measure of all things. England (I, 6) argues that in the present passage Plato's aim is constructive, that he means to foster humbleness toward the supreme Intelligence. A similar note is sounded by Jaeger (III, 253): "If humanity is not seen in that divine perspective, it loses its own independent value." We must ask how much this independent value mattered to Plato. There can be no doubt, at any rate, that Plato here is deeply concerned to controvert that subjective kind of valuation which has become forever associated with the teaching of the Sophist Protagoras; 716c5-6 directly attacks the Protagorean position. In "Theory of Education in Plato's 'Laws'" (*REG*, 50 [1937]: 318), R. G. Bury explains the reference to man as *paignion* of the gods: "men in their play (which is worship) are dependent on, and imitate, the Divine play (the Choric dances of the Star-gods)." (But was this ever made clear?) Similarly, when Plato in 644d suggests the hypothesis that each of us is a puppet (*thauma*) of the gods we should see the Divine hand, Bury maintains, only in Plato's claim that we ought properly to be led by "the holy and golden cord of reason (*logismos*), termed the common law of the state (*tês poleôs*

koinon nomon)." H. D. Rankin ("Plato and Man the Puppet," *Eranos*, 60 [1962]: 127-31), who does not mention Bury's article, concedes the role of *logismos* in 644d but finds 803c to be stamped with something of the pessimism that had been avoided in the *Republic*. See also above, n. 52.

55. 803c4-e6; see above, nn. 52, 54. No further motive will underlie these pastimes; they are to be ends in themselves. England (II, 272) believes Plato is hinting here that play, "which includes all *Art* . . . is the true paideia, because it develops our highest possibilities." Probably a better statement of this point is the one given by R. G. Bury (p. 312): Plato "delights in establishing the paradox that *paidia* is the only true *spoudê*" or serious pursuit; he combines these two apparent opposites under "the wider unity of *paideia*."

56. The verb *paizein* regularly occurs as "sing, dance, play"; only when used of religious sacrifice would it have seemed unusual and possibly incongrous to Plato's contemporaries.

57. *Theaet.* 145a7-8. Musical paideia as vocal: *Legg.* 673a3-5. For references to the teachers of music, in the *Protagoras* alone see 312b2, 312d9-e2, 325e1, 326a4-b4.

58. *Rep.* 410b5-8; *Legg.* 813b2-4.

59. Balance vital in the system of education: *Rep.* 401d3-402a2. Innovations forbidden: *ibid.*, 424b5-6. Mere drill disparaged: *Legg.* 670b8-c2. If the *Clitophon* is to be accepted as Plato's work, 407b8-d2 show much the same attitude; see Hermann Koller, *Musik und Dichtung*, pp. 87-88. Morrow (p. 331, n. 117) points out that *Rep.* 410c5-6 explicitly revises 376e3-4. He believes that the present contradictory passage in the *Laws* is likewise countered, although implicitly, by the division of gymnastic into dancing (partly a musical activity) and wrestling (which does not cover all the rest of gymnastic). Plato's treatment of the question nevertheless leaves an impression of irregularity, at the very least.

60. 653a8-9; so also Aristotle, *Pol.* 1342b27-29. Marrou (*History*, pp. 98-99) speaks of such an attitude towards paideia as distinctively Hellenistic rather than Hellenic.

61. The general plan of education: 804c2-e1. Lyre study: 809e7-810a4. That foreigners should be allowed to teach in such a city-state surprises us, but it must have seemed only natural to Plato. The Greeks generally showed a quite uncharacteristic lack of chauvinism in their readiness to assign a foreign origin to their musical instruments and forms. On occasion their zeal took them quite beyond what the facts warranted, but in most instances it was rightly directed. Foreign experts on the kithara and aulos regularly won the great competitions; Plato's readiness to avail himself of the musical experience of Sparta, Crete, and Egypt has

already been shown; and even Sparta had once welcomed foreign musicians such as Terpander and Alcman. See n. 33 to ch. i.

62. *Heterophônia* is a general term; Frédéric Montargis (*De Platone musico* [diss. Paris, 1886], p. 56) narrows it without warrant; see Reese, p. 50. On Moutsopoulos see n. 2. We shall find that Plato is looking back to the ideal of deliberate simplicity which the pseudo-Plutarchian *De Musica* (18, pp. 118.35-119.1 L., p. 14.7-11 Z.) says was realized by the school of Olympus and Terpander, from whose music *poluchordia* and *poikilia* were absent. Abert (*Lehre*, p. 54) takes *poikilia* to be the antonym of *orthotês* in Plato.

63. The literal meanings of *sumphônos* and *antiphônos* are to be understood here: "sounding together" and "sounding in answer," not "concordant" and "concordant at the octave," as *LSJ* renders them for this passage. The latter meanings, common elsewhere, make no sense with the words to which they must be attached here. See Husmann, p. 18. H. J. Scheltema ("De antiphonia," *Mnemosyne*, 60 [1932]: 239-53) convincingly shows that Plato is forbidding "symphonic" and antiphonal melodic treatment as displays of heterophony and ornamentation respectively. The distinctive feature of antiphony is taken as rhythmic variety in the higher of the two roughly parallel melodic lines. Sachs (*Rise of Music*, p. 257) misunderstands the text and consequently supposes it to refer to the impropriety of playing contrapuntally. When performing lyric poetry a young pupil might very likely have found it necessary to sing the melody *ottava:* at thirteen, the age set by Plato and by tradition for the beginning of lyre study, the childish treble has not often been replaced by the deep adult male voice. Since Hippocrates (*Coac.* 1, p. 321 Kühn) appears to set puberty as occurring at fourteen, it may be that the actual singing was not intended to come for another year. Protagoras (*Prot.* 326a6) implies that the first part of lyre study as he knew it was devoted to learning how to handle the instrument. A noteworthy interpretation of the regular methods of musical instruction implied in this passage of the *Laws* is offered by Vetter (*RE*, XVI, 880-81), who reproduces Westphal's view for the most part. Wegner's remarks (p. 104) on the relation between teacher and pupil stress ethical values; his approach resembles that of Plato himself.

64. The term for microtone, *puknôma*, is misinterpreted in *LSJ* and by Adam (*The Republic of Plato* [Cambridge, 1929], II, 133). Vetter (*RE*, XVI, 828) and Adolf Ahlvers (*Zahl und Klang bei Platon* [Bern, 1952], p. 51) correctly interpret it as the attempted subdivision of the quarter tone, and this is Richter's tentative rendering ("Platons Stellung," p. 199).

65. *Mus.* 18, p. 119.2 L., p. 14.13 Z. Commentators do not

appear to have grasped the import of ἀποδιδόντας πρόσχορδα τὰ φθέγματα τοῖς φθέγμασι; yet Plato could hardly have made his meaning more emphatically clear. The normal phrase for unison accompaniment was πρόσχορδα κρούειν; but Plato's suggestion came as a surprise in an age which had forgotten what such accompaniment was like. Aware of this, he added an explanatory phrase to the adverb.

66. This may underlie Aristotle's brief comment (*Pol.* 1340b33-34) that it will not be difficult to find suitable material for children to learn. Sachs (*Rise of Music*, pp. 254-55) is the authority for the statement that Herodotus tells us of the strict priestly control over education in Egypt which permitted only good music to be taught. "In the same order of thought," he continues, "Greek boys started from the oldest hymns and eventually arrived at contemporary music." Herodotus, who had no great interest in music at any time, never says any such thing; it is Plato who does (*Legg.* 656d5-657a8). Of the order of thought we know little. Sachs' claim is true of the training given in Arcadia, as Polybius (4.20.8) described it, but Arcadia preserved old ways where most of the rest of Greece did not; the Arcadian conservatism in music suggests an origin in the neighboring territory of Sparta. Nevertheless, it is reasonable to suppose that teachers did proceed from the older music to the newer.

67. The effort to prevent a desire for novelty and varied pleasure: 798e4-7. The *Laws* itself as paradigm: 810e6-811d5. Contemporary musical composition indicted: *Gorg.* 501d10-502c4. As for tragic poetry being mere flattery of the audience, Phrynichus' tragedy on the fall of Miletus and Euripides' *Troiades* partially disprove Plato's statement.

68. *Legg.* 817a2-d8. Only the last sentence is closely rendered.

69. "Our songs are our laws": 799e10-11, cf. 700b5-6. As for the corollary idea that "our laws are our songs," the use of ἐπᾴδειν in 665c4 strongly supports this; see n. 45. In his extremely detailed study of the *NEM*- words Laroche has paid almost no attention to Plato's paradoxical joining of the two main fourth-century uses of *nomos*. He does make clear that the idea of fixity and obligation does not appear earlier than the sixth century under the general concept of *nomos* (see p. 170 and n. 51, where *Legg.* 799e is cited). Philosophy as *hê megistê mousikê: Phaedo* 60e2-61b7. Strabo (10.3.10, p. 468 Meineke) says *mousikê* was called "the philosophy" by Plato and earlier still by the Pythagoreans. For Plato the true Muse speaks through the rational discourse of philosophy (*Rep.* 548b8-c1). F. M. Cornford (*Principium Sapientiae*, pp. 68, 87) views the admonition *mousikên poiei kai ergazou* with the greatest

seriousness, taking the *Phaedo* and *Phaedrus* to signalize a great change in Plato's beliefs. Hackforth, on the other hand, denies (pp. 33-34, 37) that *Phaedo* 59-61 anywhere refers to music in our sense of the word. This sense is proposed for *mousikê* in *Symp.* 187a-b, *Phileb.* 17b-c, and *Legg.* 655a by Hugo Perls ("Μοῦσα: Etude sur l'esthétique de Platon," *Revue Philosophique,* 117 [1934]: 264, n. 1). Arthur Darack ("Aesthetics of Music: Early Greek Views" [unpubl. diss. Bloomington, 1951], p. 32) attempts to distinguish three meanings of *mousikê* in Plato: the pattern of elementary schooling, the Pythagorean scheme of supersensible ratios, and the modern concept of "music as composed, studied, and performed by skilled specialists." According to Darack, Plato makes no effort to realize these three distinctions. Relying on translations evidently proved misleading: the second category is that of harmonics, and for the third there were available various specialized terms such as *kitharistikê* which Plato did not fail to use.

70. The types of song: 800e11-801b1, 801e1-802a5. The "song of praise": *euphêmia,* rendered here as "peace" by Jowett. *LSJ* does not note the present passage but does define this usage as "prayer and praise," and in equating it with *euchê* cites first of all Eur. *I.A.* 1469. In the latter passage Iphigeneia speaks with repressed sorrow, as 1466 shows; the word refers to a somber prayer. It is plain from Plato's division immediately following that he means *euphêmia* as "song of praise"—a literal "speaking well" of the gods; thus he looks in usage not to his contemporary Euripides but (as one would expect) backward to Pindar, prototype of his ideal civic bard. *Pythian* 10 has exactly the joyful meaning wanted: "Apollo rejoices exceedingly in songs of praise" (35-36). Moutsopoulos (p. 312, sec. 227 and n. 6) sees the reference in the *Laws* as being merely to optimism.

71. Vetter (*RE,* XVI, 837) says eloquently of the nomes, "These melodies were the nation made flesh and blood; the Hellene experienced in them a type of himself (*Art von seiner Art*)." See also above, n. 33. In an important study (*Nomos: Ein Beitrag zur griechischen Musikgeschichte* [diss. Heidelberg, 1937]) Heinz Grieser argues that *nomos* always expresses what is customary, what specifically characterizes god or man whether in usage or in song. Marrou (p. 140) seems to confuse *nomos* and mode in his attempt to explain the validity of the Hellenic theory of ethos for its own time. Laloy, p. 86, defines the nome as "neither a melody nor a scale, but something halfway between the two: a motif, a formula, a unique but clearly defined inflection, a short phrase made up, as Aristoxenus says, of a few notes . . . such was the primitive nome, a kind of musical germ which had not yet taken root." He claims

that only three notes were in fact used; this is a misunderstanding of the figurative *trichorda* in ps.-Plut. *Mus.* 18, p. 119.2 L., p. 14.3 Z. (see *app. crit.*). Lasserre, p. 173, has fallen into the same error. The chief source is now undoubtedly ch. vi of Laroche's study (pp. 163-219, esp. pp. 166-71 on the musical nome). He demonstrates at length the derivation of *nomos* from *nemô* in the sense of "arrange, distribute, set in order." In music, he says (p. 170), the term designates the sequence and interrelationships of the notes in a given scale, the melody. It refers to the arrangement which is proper to a given musical theme; "cet ordre est l'âme du chant" (p. 170). In *La houlette et la lyre . . .* (Paris, 1960), I, 238-53, Jacqueline Duchemin argues that the familiar νόμος (paroxytone accent) comes originally from the pastoral νομός (oxytone); that the moral-political sense of the word is not a secondary, later appendage but goes back to the idea of pasturing and the pastoral life. It would seem that Laroche (esp. pp. 176-77 and 187) had already disposed of this theory. Reese (pp. 10-11) wrongly equates the musical nome with "law" but quite rightly speaks of it as a fundamental melodic and rhythmic type. Laroche, who does not seem to have been concerned with comparative musicology, ignores the important factor of rhythm.

72. The choice of music for the civic chorus: 670c8-e4. The "beneficial pleasure" of learning melodies: 813a1-3. The moral affirmation of happiness and unhappiness: 660e2-6. The choice of modes and rhythms: 661c5-8.

73. England (I, 281) supposes the direct expression to be that of actual virtue, the indirect that of an artist's purely imaginative conception of any given virtue or excellence, such as one might see in drama.

74. See Pickard-Cambridge, *Festivals*, pp. 251-57.

75. Like the former (the *emmeleia* of tragedy) it is taken from drama, and Plato here applies to it the normal critical standards of the expert theatergoer. Athenaeus says that it originated in Sparta and also—less credibly—that there was a comic dance called the "pyrrhic" (630e, 629f). The Spartan background of the serious pyrrhic is discussed in some detail by K. M. T. Chrimes, *Ancient Sparta* (New York, 1952), p. 126. See also Adolf Kleingünther ("ΠΡΩΤΟΣ 'ΕΥΡΕΤΗΣ, Untersuchungen zur Geschichte einer Fragestellung," *Philologus*, Supplementband XXVI, Heft 1 [Leipzig, 1933], p. 32, n. 51) and n. 19 to ch. ii, above. Plato's pyrrhic is quite frankly a war dance (815a1-7). The Xenophontic Socrates (*Mem.* 3.3.14) proposes that the discipline of the chorus be adopted as a pattern for the discipline of the army; this connection is brought out strongly by Vetter (*RE*, XVI, 824-25). Athenaeus

(628f) quotes a poem, attributed to Socrates, which holds that those who are the finest dancers in honoring the gods prove best in war. Lucian (*Salt.* 8-10, pp. 273-74 Jacobitz) stresses the close relationship between dancing and armed combat among the Spartans, and says of Meriones that his training in dancing made him nimble enough to avoid the darts thrown at him by the enemy. (Aeneas calls him a "dancer" when he dodges a spear, *Il.* 16.617; see Leaf on *Il.* 7.241.) An extensive discussion of the pyrrhic dance has been undertaken by Moutsopoulos (pp. 138-47, secs. 99-106) and also by Roos (p. 128, n. 3; cf. pp. 226-27). In a curious work (*Sociologie de la musique* [Paris, 1951], p. 175) Marcel Belvianes quotes a detailed description of this dance from the *Encyclopédie française*. The tempi are said to have simulated those of actual combat. There were advances, feints, retreats, with the feet beating the ground in a rapid cadence. Then came the "manual of arms" section (for the young warriors carried sword, spear, and shield), and after this a sequence of leaps, as if clearing walls or trenches. A slower, calmer section followed: muscular activity had reached its height in the leaping phase of the dance. This latter point indicates a common area with the "dance of peace."

76. This was the euphemism employed to justify the repression of cultural freedom in Sparta during the fifth and fourth centuries, and we know that Plato emphatically approved of the principle underlying that repression. He may, therefore, have had actual Spartan dances in mind. On this point and on the "dance of peace" see n. 19 to ch. ii and Roos, esp. p. 155, n. 3. Also relevant is Moutsopoulos, pp. 149-50, sec. 108; on the parallel with modal ethos see p. 147, n. 14 to sec. 105.

77. Technical questions referred to Damon: *Rep.* 400c4. The dangers of wrong procedure in dealing with music: *Legg.* 669b8-670a3. The question of meaning and mimesis in solo playing: *ibid.* Imitations of types of character: 798d8-9. Hindus still draw and paint actual pictures of the *ragas* used in their music (see above, n. 4 to ch. ii). These are normally anthropomorphic and executed with the greatest realism. Lachmann (p. 62) describes one of them and reproduces the picture itself (p. 134, fig. 9).

78. Music as mimetic: 668a6-b7. In the passage which precedes this, Plato declares that equality (*isotês*) and not pleasure gives imitative works of art rightness (667d5-7); thus mimesis ought on no account to be judged according to pleasure and untrue opinion, since the fact of equality or symmetry is not a subjective, but an absolute, truth (667e10-668a4).

79. *Rep.* 399a3-c4, e8-11. As Vetter (*RE*, XVI, 826) points out, the Platonic enoplius and heroic measure are not merely to

be understood in a comparative sense or metaphorically; real effects and impressions correspond to them. See W. J. W. Koster, *Rhythme en metrum bij de Grieken van Damon tot Aristoxenus* (Groningen, 1940).

80. On the terms for various kinds of sound see Moutsopoulos, pp. 24-25, secs. 15-16 and nn. Nothing could be further from the truth than Husmann's claim, p. 5, that the Greeks considered music to be the natural antithesis of language; see n. 88. Pöhlmann, p. 24, holds that the respective musical equivalents of the "tones" and "accents" are choice of mode and naturalistic declamation of the text; these he sees as concessions to the "new school" in music. Plato, however, nowhere conciliatory toward musical innovators. Pöhlmann's selection of equivalents reflects his general thesis (see p. 23) that even in strophic composition there was no attempt to shape the melody to the tonemic pattern of the text. Hermann Koller (*Musik und Dichtung*, p. 175) rightly points out that in the old *mousikê* rhythm derived from the words of the text and formed an indissoluble unity with it. This unity had already been largely destroyed by the close of the fourth century, as music and speech had come to be almost wholly independent of each other. "From that time on," says Koller (p. 177), "music and poetry develop independently . . . and follow their own laws."

81. We do not know whether the statement on rhythm and harmony in man's life represents the thought of Protagoras himself. Richter, following Ryffel's lead, considers it more probable that the common element between this statement and the passage in the *Republic* on rhythmic ethos was originally Damonian (*Zur Wissenschaftlehre*, p. 34). See Lasserre, pp. 66-73, for extensive conjectures concerning Damon's contributions to ethical doctrine as it applied to the rhythms.

82. Similarly Lachmann (p. 83) says of Oriental rhythmic types that the imaginative names given to them in India and the Near East show that they are thought of "not as dry schemes of time relationships but rather as living movement-forms." On the process of development and abstraction see Combarieu, *La musique et la magie*, p. 236. Reconstructing the various stages in the evolution of rhythm, Bela Bartók (*Hungarian Folk Music*, tr. M. D. Calvocoressi [London, 1931], p. 9) postulates first a *tempo giusto* (strict) rhythm and then a *parlando-rubato* form in which the melody gradually became independent of bodily motions and its rhythm began to adapt itself to that of the words. (There is a third division, which need not be given here.) Max Schoen (*The Psychology of Music* [New York, 1940], p. 21) notes that practically

all of the hundreds of modern investigations into the nature of the rhythmic experience find a motor or muscular factor.

83. 673c9-d5. This and other passages show how unfounded is Vetter's claim ("Die antike Musik in der Beleuchtung durch Aristoteles," *Archiv für Musikforschung*, 1 [1936]: 15-16) that Plato, unlike Aristotle, knew nothing of the spontaneous feeling for rhythm and mode as an innate and basic human motive. His thesis as stated here certainly does not appear to merit the charge of confusion that Moutsopoulos brings against it (p. 303, sec. 222). For the counter thesis that the dance originated in imitation of words through gesture, see 816a5-6.

84. *Rep.* 398c11-d2. Georgiades' *Der griechische Rhythmus* heavily stresses the completeness with which these two aspects were fused into one. On Plato's conviction that the true Muse is rational and philosophic, see above, n. 69.

85. 669a7-b3. In the reference to the three criteria the text may be corrupt, since nature, rightness, and excellence (surely the *tauta tria* of 669a9) do not conclude the listing. As for the addendum on their applicability, England (I, 325) holds that it makes the paragraph hopelessly illogical. Coming after a generalizing particle it is certainly awkward. Edith W. Schipper ("*Mimesis* in the Arts in Plato's *Laws*," *Journal of Aesthetics and Art Criticism*, 32 [1963]: 199-202) is well beyond her depth in attempting to deal with this problem. For a careful survey of many different interpretations of ὡς εὖ (whether, for example, it is technical or ethical excellence here), see Morrow, p. 314, n. 55. He does not consider possible textual difficulties. For Plato's objections to solo instrumental music, see 669e1-4 and *Rep.* 396b5-9, 397a1-7.

86. *Rep.* 600e4-6; *Legg.* 889d1-2.

87. For a comparable view of this passage as an exception see Moutsopoulos, pp. 263-64, secs. 194-95. He claims that Pythagorean influence "reappears" in the view that music, which combines art and science, succeeds as nothing else can in raising the spirit to that harmony which prevails in the universe. Strict chronology cannot be intended here, but one does find this view in the *Republic* and *Timaeus*. See Abert's criticisms of the passage (*Lehre*, pp. 12-13). Mario Untersteiner (*The Sophists*, tr. Kathleen Freeman [New York, 1954], p. 244) believes that Plato is voicing a doctrine of Antiphon here. Walther Vetter (art. "Ethos" in *Die Musik in Geschichte und Gegenwart*, vol. III [Kassel, 1954], p. 1583) has attempted to answer Abert by interpreting Plato's position as follows: like any other art, music may have its childish, negative side in which mere *eidôla* are dealt with, but in Greek music the theory of ethos served to guard against this by introducing concepts

of what was real and ethically profitable. If this interpretation is correct, Plato was notably careless. Elfriede Huber-Abrahamowicz (*Das Problem der Kunst bei Platon* [diss. Basel, 1954], p. 35) presents a more convincing thesis: it is through harmony and rhythm that every kind of art influences the human soul, which is related through its motions to the world-soul (*Tim.* 47b-e, 90c-d); and when the soul which is represented in art constitutes a true *harmonia*, a unity attuned to the cosmos, then these two factors are no longer mere "images of images" at a third remove from reality.

88. When Plutarch (*Quaest. Conviv.* 7.8.4) says that playing the aulos or kithara without either singing or words is not to be tolerated, one seems to hear an echo of the Platonic view. In the case of the aulos it should be particularly noted that this instrument cannot demonstrate the regularity and clarity which Plato thinks essential to proper rhythms. "Breath, as the medium of singers and pipers," says Curt Sachs (*Rhythm and Tempo*, p. 39), "is a continuum almost independent of actual respiration and directly under the impact of emotive, melodic inspiration." In *Musik und Rhythmus*, p. 21, Georgiades states emphatic views on the expressive power of the aulos: the tone of such a wind instrument is in many respects closely similar to that of the human voice, since both have their being by means of the breath, through an impulse of air. The voice can express feelings without using words ("Der Schrei ist hörbares Leben"); wind instruments have this same capacity, bringing to expression something which is akin to it. "Die Musik auf dem Aulos," Georgiades concludes, "kann eine dem Affektausdruck verwandte Haltung verwirklichen." See n. 80.

89. In *Primitive Song* (New York, 1963), pp. 243-45, C. M. Bowra makes it clear that the process of adapting words to song must have been a very slow one, requiring perhaps thousands of years. Svoboda, p. 187, considers important the fact that Plato (= Socrates) does not formally identify the Harmoniai of war and peace with Dorian and Phrygian (it is Glaucon who does so), nor does he agree with the identification once it has been made, possibly because he realized that his antithesis did not precisely correspond to the modes in actual use. But the true reason—the one that is valid within the dramatic context of the dialogue—has been accurately stated by John Adam (n. on *Rep.* 399c1-4), to whom Svoboda gives insufficient credit. Socrates is not a *mousikos* or even equipped, as Glaucon would have been, with the full standard training in *mousikê;* therefore he must be made to say, "Let us have two Harmoniai expressive of the following traits (etc.)," and the specific choices can then be named by his interlocutor. There is still a discrepancy, to be sure: one is led to ask why Glaucon should

have chosen as he did, and with so little hesitation. For artistic credibility, however, it is much more important that the characterization of Socrates should remain consistent. Also, Plato was writing about his own brother: one would not expect an inept portrait. On dramatic realism in the dialogues see p. 78 and Burnet, *Plato's Phaedo*, p. xxxiii (Introduction).

90. Abert, *Lehre*, p. 86. On Plato's alleged inconsistency see Vetter, *RE*, XVI, 882-83. Pseudo-Plutarch surprisingly omits all mention of Phrygian when dealing with Plato's views on modal ethos. Reinach (n. on *Mus.* 17, p. 118.20-33 L., pp. 13.14-14.5 Z.) conjectures a lacuna or careless compilation, or perhaps use of an incomplete source. It seems at least as likely that neither the writer nor his sources could explain why Plato chose Phrygian.

91. R. P. Winnington-Ingram, *Euripides and Dionysus* (Cambridge, 1948), p. 151. The same conclusion is reached by Dodds in his rather more extensive treatment of this point (*Euripides: Bacchae*, pp. xviii-xx). Plato was twenty-one when the *Bacchae* was performed. We may also note that the absence of the thyrsi could have provided a precedent for banning the aulos: both were primitively regarded as phallic symbols and therefore associated with ideas of fertility and rebirth. See Sachs, *History of Musical Instruments* (New York, 1940), p. 44.

92. Proclus, on *Rep.* 399a, says Phrygian suits "rites and occasions of divine infilling, as being an ecstatic mode." Boeckh (p. 239) claimed that Proclus has reconciled the clashing views of Plato and Aristotle; this is wishful thinking. Lucian (*Harm.* 1, p. 851 Jacobitz) calls this mode *entheon*, and Apuleius (*Flor.* 1.4, p. 5 Helm) speaks of the *Phrygium religiosum* in clear contrast to the *Dorium bellicosum.*

93. *Rep.* 427b2-c4. See M. P. Nilsson, *A History of Greek Religion*, pp. 208-9. His whole account shows that the absorption of Dionysiac frenzy into Apolline calm was historical reality. Once again the realistic basis of Plato's thought is impressed upon us. Walter Spiegel (*Die Bedeutung der Musik für die griechische Erziehung im klassischen Altertum* [diss. Erlangen; Berlin, 1910], pp. 67-68) stresses the affinities between the two gods. Both, for example, embody inspiration, and both inspire. Wegner (*Musikleben*, p. 19) has said of the relationship that "Dionysus himself . . . is notably less wild than his throng of followers, and it is not without significance for the understanding of his nature that he could rule in Delphi while Apollo was away among the Hyperboreans." As Wegner notes, Dionysus is never pictured playing an aulos; only in a few vase paintings does he have any instrument at all, and it is invariably one of the stringed variety. This con-

ception of the god may have been encouraged by the authorities at Delphi.

94. Hermann Koller (*Musik und Dichtung*, p. 22) claims that Plato has taken over the basic division into Dorian and Phrygian from Damon and brought it into careless conjunction with the ethical requirements of his own theory, in order to suit his needs of the moment. One would like some proof before accepting this unflattering estimate of Plato's abilities.

95. The practice is not confined to Plato. J. D. Denniston ("Some Recent Theories," p. 99) says, "The rich, sensuous softness of Mixolydian, the stern resolve of Aeolian and the salt sea smack of Dorian are all unmistakeable." Pratinas in particular would have felt the liveliest interest in this description of Aeolian, the mode which he said "becomes all braggarts in song."

IV. ARISTOTLE

1. Characteristic reciprocity of contrary qualities: *De Gen. et Corr.* 324a7-8. Change of patient into agent: *ibid.*, 12-14. Example of this: *De An.* 425b22-23. Form but not matter acquired in perception: *ibid.* 424a18-19, 425b23-24. Undifferentiated perception: *De Somno* 465a12-26; *De Mem.* 450a10-15. "The soul never thinks without an image": *De An.* 431a16-17; cf. 432a7-10. *De Mem.* 449b31. Undifferentiated perception as the means of distinguishing among impressions from the various senses: *De An.* 426b8-427a16. The case concerning what a thing may become is variously stated; to judge from the actual examples, it may be best to adopt a qualified view. Sense perception as a developing of potential into actual: *De An.* 417b2-7. W. D. Ross (*Aristotle* [London, 1945], p. 135) criticizes this approach as being under the lingering influences of earlier, materialistic theories and therefore not recognizing adequately the "distinctively mental, non-corporeal nature" of the act of sensation. In "Aristotle's Account of Aesthesis in the *De Anima*" (*CQ*, 9 [1959]: 6-16) D. W. Hamlyn has characterized Aristotle's treatment as transitional and involved in difficulties; his interpretation differs at several points from that of Ross, whom I have followed.

2. *De An.* 420b5-7, 29-32. See 420a27-b4, the passage immediately preceding, for a discussion of the metaphor involved in calling sounds "grave (*baru*)" and "acute (*oxu*)." Both Plato and Aristotle contend that music is the great medium of ethos; neither considers the possibility of ethos in nonmusical sound. One view is that such sound in itself has no ethos. If we grant this, however, Plato's annoyed concern over animal imitations and the like in

music would seem to be baseless. The explanation may be that anything at all may take on potential ethical force, once it has been transmuted into musical terms, for in music the two types of sound often are very closely intermingled. We know that a musical sound, i.e., a tone, has a regular pattern of vibration frequencies, while a nonmusical sound is identifiable as such because its pattern lacks regularity. Though Aristotle could not have known this, Alexis Kahl (*Die Philosophie der Musik nach Aristoteles* [diss. Leipzig, 1902], pp. 52-53) believes that his exceptionally keen aesthetic sense nevertheless brought him some presentiment of it: witness *Probl.* 19.27, p. 93.1-12 Jan, which speaks of the kinesis that is consequent upon a tone and is perceived by the listener. According to Kahl, Aristotle means that there are tones of a certain class which not only please the ear but also rouse in us a consciously experienced emotion, and that it is just these which are musical notes. This interpretation stresses the importance of the listener; it is supported to some extent by *Probl.* 19.40, p. 102.5-11 Jan. On the role of the audience in Greek music, see above, n. 34 to ch. iii.

3. Interplay of body and soul: *De An.* 403a16-19. The soul's affections inseparable from the material substratum: *ibid.*, 403b17-18. The soul as unmoved: *De Motu An.* 700b34-701a2; *De An.* 405b31-406a2. How the soul initiates action: *De Motu An.* 700b17-19, 23-29, 33-701a2. A syllogistic presentation of purposive action thus based on desire is given in 701a28-32.

4. Attitude as an ethical disposition: *Met.* 1022b4-14. Attitude distinguished from disposition: *Cat.* 8b25-9a13. Aristotle's terms are *diathesis* and *hexis*, respectively. For the attitudes as differentiae see *Met.* 1020b18-21.

5. The origins of intellectual and moral virtue: 1103a14-18. (References in the notes to this section of ch. iv designate the *Nicomachean Ethics* unless otherwise specified.) Plato puts the matter with greater caution and accuracy (*Legg.* 792e2): it is particularly true of infancy, he says, that character (ἦθος) is the result of habit (ἔθος). A needed qualifying comment is added by J. A. Stewart (*Notes on the Nicomachean Ethics of Aristotle* [Oxford, 1892], I, 169, on 1103a17): moral virtue as such comes from habit, but habit requires a certain amount of innate excellence to work upon. "The children of a civilized community," he says, "inherit tendencies to virtue which make habituation easy." Receptiveness and habituation: 1103a19-20, 24-26; cf. *Met.* 1021b20-21, "Virtue is a kind of bringing to perfection."

6. Action as the moral determinant: 1103b7-12. The origin of

attitudes in activities, and the supreme importance of habituation: 1103b21-25.

7. Observing due measure in the virtues: 1104a11-13, 17-18. The principle of the mean: 1104a26-27. Temperateness and abstinence: 1104a33-35. Plato's view on moral conditioning commended as right education: 1104b11-13 (see Pl. *Legg.* 653a5-c4; cf. *Rep.* 401e3-402a4). The question of justness and wisdom, and the possibility of acting accidentally or through prompting: 1105a17-23. Meaningful action defined: 1105a23-26.

8. H. H. Joachim (*Aristotle: The Nicomachean Ethics*, ed. D. A. Rees [Oxford, 1951], p. 69) has realized the implications of this point. "The moral virtues," he says, are to Aristotle "excellences of ἦθος (character). They are formed states, disciplined habits, of that element or side of the self which Aristotle conceives as not itself intelligent—i.e. originative of thought—but as capable of listening to, obeying, intelligence . . . The agent who had, by imitation, by practice under authority, etc., developed such moral virtues, would do as a matter of habit what a healthy public opinion surrounding him would approve . . . Whether the rules of his action—the ideals which it expressed—were really right or not would depend not upon him but upon the authority under whose control he had developed his habit."

9. Plato on ethical training as unsuited to early adolescence: *Legg.* 659e3-4. Aristotle on the restlessness of children: *Phys.* 247b18-248a2.

10. The criteria of a just or wise act: 1105a26-33. Their importance, and the role of repetition: 1105b3-5.

11. Virtue and the individual virtues categorized: 1105b19-1106a13. Virtue as a particular kind of attitude: 1106a15-24.

12. *Phys.* 245b3-247a8, *passim.* The Oxford translation by R. P. Hardie and R. K. Gaye is used.

13. The Pythagorean theory of the heaven as Harmonia and number: *Met.* 985b32-986a2. The "harmony of the spheres": *De Caelo* 290b21-23, cf. b12-15. Here the Pythagoreans, not Plato, are attacked. Handschin (p. 122) cites this as evidence for his view that Plato never meant his description of the harmony of the spheres to be taken with strict literalness. It is noteworthy that Aristotle describes the sound which the planets make as *enarmonios.* This has nothing to do, of course, with the enharmonic genus. It means simply "harmonized," "in a harmony," or "in tune"; the equivalent term in Plato is *emmelês* (see n. 41 to ch. ii). The astronomer Kepler actually worked out all the scales which he supposed could be played by the planets, whose course he had discovered to be elliptical. The Pythagorean belief in things as

numbers: *Met.* 1090a20-23. W. K. C. Guthrie (*The Greek Philosophers from Thales to Aristotle* [New York, 1960], pp. 37-40) briefly summarizes the vital place of music in Pythagorean cosmology. See also his *History of Greek Philosophy*, vol. I (Cambridge, 1962), pp. 220-28.

14. Plato's alleged doctrine of numbers identified with Forms: *De An.* 404b24-25. Popular numerology: *Met.* 1093a28-b4.

15. The Harmonia illustrating the ruling principle: *Pol.* 1254a32-33. In *Met.* 1018b29, a difficult reference to interpret, Aristotle states that in the lyre this principle is the Mese. The constitution of the Harmonia (from the aspect of *sumphônia*): *Top.* 139b37-38. Its definition and its relation to the soul: *De An.* 408a5-10.

16. Dorian and Phrygian termed the chief modal categories: *Pol.* 1290a19-22. With reference to this passage Laloy, p. 123, says: "The question of modes continued to be raised, but the modes themselves were suffering a gradual effacement. This is why some of those who opposed the false precision of the mensural approach were trying to reduce still further the number of modes by classifying them, for example, under two headings only: Hellenic (*nationaux*) and barbarian." Chailley ("Le mythe," p. 160) believes that the name *iasti* is undoubtedly a late one. The threnodic nature of the Lydian system: Pl. *Rep.* 398e1-2.

17. The negative power of pleasure and pain: *E.N.* 1104b8-13. Moral excellence in one's likes and dislikes: *Pol.* 1340a15. Paideia as the training of the *sôphrôn anêr: E.N.* 1104b5-6.

18. *E.N.* 1170a6-11. In the former case the actions are probably, as Stewart suggests, those not only of the man himself but of his friends as well—the passage comes from Book 9 of the *Ethics,* the great study of *philia.* The musical analogy confirms this interpretation, for such a person is interested in, and concerned with, the melodies of other men at least as much as with his own. In the *Poetics* (1448b4-9) Aristotle defines the two deeply rooted natural causes of poetry as the instinct of imitation (or representation, *mimêsis*) and the universal pleasure men feel in what is so treated. "The melodies of other men" constitute an example of what is referred to in the latter instance.

19. See Burnet on *E.N.* 1113b14.

20. The need for laws governing the education and activities of children: *E.N.* 1179b20-26, 29-32, 34-35. Skill required in legislation as in *mousikê: ibid.*, 1181a15-23. The advantages of experience and of theoretical study: 1181a23-b2, b6-12.

21. As stated earlier, the alliance was an uneasy one. Laches appears to speak for Plato (though not, of course, in matters of specific doctrine) when he claims that the true *mousikos* is the man

who has made word and deed concordant, the noblest Harmonia of all (*Lach.* 188c6-d8). Here one finds the spirit, at least, of the Platonic view.

22. Aristotle's theory of aggregate excellence: *Pol.* 1281a42-b10. (The remaining references in this chapter are to the *Politics* unless otherwise indicated.) Its restatement: 1286a30-35. Conditions added: 1286a36-37.

23. Pl. *Legg.* 701a3-5. Aristotle does not speak out with the same degree of partisan conviction, so that the reader of Book 3 of the *Politics* is led to wonder what the author's attitudes really are. W. L. Newman (ed., *The Politics of Aristotle*, 4 vols. [Oxford, 1887-1902], III, 213) suggests that his aim "is in the main a negative and critical one—to overthrow the exclusive claims of the Few Best" in whose hands Plato had placed the governing of Kallipolis.

24. The translation is that of Newman (III, 515-16). Jowett and Rackham mistranslate the passage, most of all by supposing *mousikê* to be a *diagôgê*. Such a usage is possible (see Rackham on 1339a25), but it is very unlikely here.

25. 1339a14-21. Among many other references, Newman cites here without comment Pl. *Symp.* 181a2-3 (of drinking, singing, and conversing: "None of these things is excellent in itself, but rather turns out to be so in practice according to the way it is done"). Aristotle may well have had this statement in mind when he wrote. If so, he certainly was aware of its central point, not expressed here, which connects closely with the injunction of the *Ethics* (1103b22) that "we must qualify our activities." The symposium, then, may have a real place in the scheme of paideia; see also p. 143. The paideutic role of the symposium from the earliest times is vividly described by Jaeger (II, 176-77) and treated more briefly by J. M. Edmonds (*Lyra Graeca*, III, 583-84). The latter, clearly with the evidence of Aristophanes in mind, points out that when a young man came to take part in the symposia "his choice was not always the latest thing . . . but often what he had learnt at school." That skolia were at times regarded with a keen awareness of religious and moral purpose is clear from the remarks of Theognis and especially of Xenophanes; see C. M. Bowra, *Problems in Greek Poetry* (Oxford, 1953), pp. 1-14.

26. Music's possible contributions to paideia through ethos or to leisure and intellectual culture: 1339a21-26. The aulos indicted: 1341b6-7.

27. Aristotle's denial that "play" is the end of paideia: 1339a26-29, countering Pl. *Rep.* 401e4-402a4. In *E.N.* 1176b32-35 Aris-

totle does seem to understand and approve of Anacharsis' view that to "play" for serious ends is right and proper.

28. Intellectual recreation unsuited to the formative years: 1339a29-31. An argument considered and refuted: 1339a31-36. There is no need to change the text in the passage which refers to learning music by attending professional performances. Of course one does not "learn" music merely by hearing it—Aristotle is stating a position with which he in fact disagrees. The pseudo-philosophers of the *Ethics* (1105b11-18), who delight in contemplating virtue but carefully avoid putting it into practice, constitute a striking parallel. In their case Aristotle uses outright condemnation. The present handling proves more difficult to follow, not only because it is subtler but because our modern Western approach to music constantly suggests preconceptions which cannot be applied to the Greek idea of training in music and literature. On this question Aristotle points out in lines 39-40 that if personal participation is necessary for enjoyment, one might with equally good reason undertake to learn cookery. Here again he presents not his own belief but an argument advanced by those who did not believe in musical ethos (see Richter, *Zur Wissenschaftlehre*, p. 124). This same argument will be encountered again in Philodemus, three centuries later; see pp. 164-65 and n. 37 to ch. v. For comparable references elsewhere in Aristotle and also in Aristophanes and Plato, see n. 35 to ch. v.

29. Here again Jowett ("as they say") is right, and Rackham ("so it is said") wrong. The parenthetical phrase is important because it refers to the Spartans themselves, identifying the claim as coming from Sparta's ministry of propaganda. Richter (*Zur Wissenschaftlehre*, p. 124) takes it seriously, again following Ernst Koller ("Musse und musische Paideia," *MH*, 13 [1956]: 1-37, 95-124), and sees the attitude championed by Damon and Plato. This Spartan theory of the amateur critic was enthusiastically adopted by Plato in the *Laws* (659a6): his judge, we recall, is not to be deterred by mere lack of musical education.

30. 1339a41-b10.

31. 1339b10-42. The cardinal importance of leisure is not stressed in this discussion because Aristotle has previously (1333a33-36) stated very clearly his view that it is the noblest end in human life, and the justification for work and recreation. As Newman points out in his excellent note, the hearing of noble music would be a part of leisure, as "employment in work desirable for its own sake"; cf. 1338a1-13.

32. 1339b42-1340a12. On the effect of Olympus' melodies see Pl. *Symp.* 215c5-6.

33. Pl. *Legg.* 801b10-c1; cf. a8-b2. Also, the writer of the *Magna Moralia* says that those who are in this state act irrationally (1207b4).

34. The effect of listening to musical mimesis: 1340a12-14. In *Poet.* 1447a14-16 *aulêtikê* and *kitharistikê* are said to be "for the most part forms of mimesis in their general conception." S. H. Butcher (*Aristotle's Theory of Poetry and Fine Art* [London, 1898], p. 7) translates them as "the music of the flute and of the lyre." This is inadequate; the Greek terms specifically denote solo instrumental playing. W. Hamilton Fyfe (*Aristotle: The Poetics* [London, 1939], p. 5), Ingram Bywater (*Aristotle on the Art of Poetry* [Oxford, 1909], p. 3), and Karl Svoboda (p. 190) make the same mistake. For a correct interpretation see G. F. Else, *Aristotle's Poetics: The Argument* (Cambridge, Mass., 1963), p. 34. Svoboda follows A. Doering, *Die Kunstlehre des Aristoteles* (Jena, 1876), which I have not used. On this work see Janssens, "Aristoteles," p. 119. The use of *aulêsis* and *kitharisis* in 1448a9-10 is difficult to explain, however, particularly since none of these terms occurs after section 1448. We tend to regard the expressiveness of purely instrumental music as imprecise, although real. Among primitive peoples the case is quite otherwise: melody may be used by them as an actual language, a medium of communication in the strictest sense. Adolf Busse ("Zur Musikästhetik des Aristoteles," *RhM*, 77 [1928]: 45, n. 1) cities the explorer Leo Frobenius on the use of flutes to communicate between native villages in Africa: "Auf kleinen Flöten erzählen sie sich von Dorf zu Dorf das neueste. Die Leute können auf diese Weise jeden mit Namen anrufen, jede Zeit und Stunde angeben, jeden Gegenstand, jede Pflanze, jedes Tier benennen, auf ihren Flöten alles so gut ausdrücken wie mit der Sprache." K. L. Pike (*Tone Languages* [Ann Arbor, 1948], p. 36) explains this seeming miracle: "Communication by drum signals or by horns, and so on, in Africa, seems to involve a mimicry of the linguistic tonemes. The instruments are usually (but not always) formed so as to have just enough pitches to correspond to the number of registers (levels) in the language. Rhythm and quantity are reproduced in addition to relative pitch contrasts."

35. With regard to the first point above concerning rhythmic and melodic representations, one should bear in mind Aristotle's theory of the mimetic origin of poetry (*Poet.* 1448b4-9; see n. 18). Emotional change through music and "imitations" of character in melodies: 1340a18-39. On the *mimêmata tôn êthôn* J. G. Warry (*Greek Aesthetic Theory* [New York, 1962], p. 109) suggests that the difference between this and pictorial mimesis is the difference between a rational and irrational faculty: music produces a nervous

or muscular reaction reproducing the experience of life, while painting creates a mood. The varied affective nature of the Harmoniai: 1340a40-b10. The need for educating the young in music, its natural pleasurableness, and our apparent affinity with modes and rhythms: 1340b10-18.

36. The soul as actually existent only when thinking: *De An.* 429a15-24. The "likenesses" are discussed by Kahl (p. 7), who stresses their importance for Aristotle's theory of art and their difference from mere symbols. In a significant study (*Die Bewertung der Musik bei Stoikern und Epikureern: Eine Analyse von Philodems Schrift De Musica* [diss. Berlin, 1956], pp. 78-79, 92) Annemarie Neubecker holds that *homoiôma* in the present passage is a synonym for *mimêsis* and derives originally from Damonian theory. Her treatment of Damon may have been too much influenced by the great play which Hermann Koller has made with Damon in *Die Mimesis in der Antike*, although she devotes an appendix to refuting one of the main theses of this controversial work. G. F. Else cites the present instance of *homoiôma* as Pythagorean and finds similar ideas to be associated with Damon in the *Republic* (pp. 85, 87 and n. 62; see n. 13 to ch. ii and n. 36 to ch. v.

37. Abert (*Lehre*, pp. 84) believes a similar change in the ethos ascribed to this mode took place during earlier centuries.

38. Heraclides Ponticus: *ap.* Athen. 624c-625f. The infallibility of individual perception: *De An.* 427b11-12. cf. *Met.* 1011a28-b1. Newman, on 1340b6-7 ("for these men take the proofs of their theories from actual experience"), holds that the best method of inquiry is thereby adopted and compares Aristotle's remarks on the generation of bees, *De Gen. An.* 760b30-34. ("The facts have not been sufficiently ascertained; if they are ever to be ascertained we must trust perception rather than theorizing, and believe theories only when the conclusions they indicate agree with observed facts.") This passage does not suffice to show that inquiry based on *ta phainomena* is in general the best method. It is a specific conclusion with regard to particular circumstances, and to raise it to the status of a general truth would involve any exposition of Aristotle's doctrines in the most acute difficulties. Nonetheless, his approach to modal ethos is undeniably empirical. In "Die Beziehung zwischen Theorie und Praxis der Musik im aristotelischen Protreptikos" (*Hermes,* 88 [1960]: 177-88) Lukas Richter has shown how Aristotle, like Plato, recognized only Pythagorean harmonic theory as a legitimate branch of science. As Richter notes, Book 8 of the *Politics* deals with the actual practice of music; thus we can better understand the acceptance of empirical data.

39. On rhythm in Aristotle as a rational element (though not a purely rational one) and its equation with form, see Warry, pp. 109-18.

40. 1340b23-1341a5.

41. This point, seldom sufficiently recognized, is well brought out by Morrow, pp. 311-12. See also above, p. 66.

42. Rackham takes *ta kala* as "what is beautiful." It may be noted also that *melôn* in 1341a1 is given the impossible meaning of "times," while *tropous tinas tês mousikês* in a4-5 becomes "modes of music." The latter is a possible translation, but it becomes misleading in the present case, where *tropos* does not have a technical musical meaning. On the charge of vulgarity, see 1339b9-10.

43. In Oriental music intensive vocal training has brought about a partial reversal of this natural division of capacities: the singer occasionally displays an astonishingly supple technique in duplicating the flourishes of the accompanying instrument. Such treatment of the voice was unthinkable during the great period of Hellenic music.

44. A connection between paideia and *aretê* (moral excellence) clearly exists in the argument of the *Politics*, although it is not so obvious as in Plato's dialogues. Aristotle approves the contention that both have as their end the "good life" (1283a24-25), which is the standard of achievement (1256b31-32) and the lawgiver's goal (1325a7-10). "Paideia and *aretê* are here conjoined," Newman remarks (*ad loc.*), "as in Plato, *Laws* 757c, and in 1291b29 and 1295a26 sqq."

45. The need for simplicity in musical studies and the goal of appreciating ethically profitable music: 1341a6-14. Reasons for rejecting the aulos: 1341a18-b7. Grieser (pp. 63-64), who mentions the tradition that Athena played the aulos to accompany the *enoplios nomos* of the Dioscuri (Epicharmus, *Fg.* 75 Kaibel; cf. above, n. 25 to ch. ii), denies that the goddess originally had any musical attributes.

46. Ar. *Fg.* 221 Kock, *Thesm.* 137-38. Pl. *Rep.* 411a5-b4, *Symp.* 179d4-5.

47. William Barclay (*Educational Ideals in the Ancient World* [London, 1959], p. 130) notes, "It is told that the Earl of Kinnoull came to Handel after the first performance of his *Messiah*, and thanked him for the magnificent entertainment which he had given the audience. 'My Lord,' said Handel, 'I did not mean to entertain them, I meant to make them better men and women'; and that would be no inaccurate description of the aim of Athenian *mousikê*." The anecdote also suggests, however, the vital difference in

attitude between Plato and Aristotle regarding the use of concert music; see p. 138 and n. 51 to ch. iii.

48. When he mentions slaves and children together, Aristotle may have in mind *Laws* 700, esp. c6: there Plato recalls the strict control once exercised over boys and their slave escorts in the audience. Aelian (*N. A.* 12.45; cf. Sext. Empir. *Contra Math.* 6.32) speaks of dolphins swimming toward oarsmen because the sound of the aulos has charmed them.

49. Heinrich Sanden (*Antike Polyphonie* [Heidelberg, 1957]) misuses critical sources in an unsuccessful attempt to show that the Greeks used a highly developed polyphony. Curt Sachs tended to hold the same belief but never committed himself. In *The Wellsprings of Music* (ed. Jaap Kunst; The Hague, 1962) he came to a more cautious position than in his better-known earlier works. Pointing out that the Greeks themselves never clearly defined *heterophônia,* he suggests that they, as well as the Romans, "were to a certain degree prepared for vertical hearing" (pp. 185, 190; cf. p. 189 on Pl. *Legg:* 812d-e). On *heterophônia* see n. 62 to ch. iii. The sharply drawn contrast between Oriental and Occidental music with which Lachmann (p. 103) concludes his *Musik des Orients* deserves quotation: "The West continually seeks new technical possibilities, the East holds fast to the old, unassuming ways of expression; in the West one sees a perpetually renewed struggle for personal expression, in the East retention of a heritage which is strictly guarded and kept safe by fixed patterns of musical form."

50. Its counterpart in India and its actual descendants in the Arab countries are a farrago of superstition and magic by comparison. One finds a highly educated Indian gentleman of our own time writing as follows: "Many of us have heard that mad elephants could be controlled by drumming *Gaj Paran* and even brought down upon their knees by the magnetising influence of the dance of Lord Shiva!" (Rai Bahadur R. L. Batra, *The Science and Art of Indian Music* [Lahore, n.d.], p. 9.) The facts are not completely impossible, perhaps; but the attitude is interesting.

51. Intellectual well-being as one of the ends of music: 1339a25-26. Reason and intelligence as the end of our being: 1334b15-17. Training in the aulos as nonintellectual: 1341b6-7. Paideia, play, and recreation as possible functions of music: 1339b14-15. Though Aristotle does not speak of intellectual well-being in his conclusion, in 1334a23 he uses still another term, *philosophia.* Bonitz (821a6) renders it for this passage as *virtus intellectualis.* The terms "pastime" and "amusement," which I had first used in this passage of the text to render *diagôgê,* were justly criticized as belittling the

high function Aristotle assigns this sphere of activity in the life of a freeborn man. *Diagôgê* is indeed literally "a way of passing time," but not in the trivial sense which English usage would tend to make us assume: it is much closer to what we mean by "a way of life." What makes this latter phrase somewhat misleading is its failure to suggest vital concern with leisure. A rare commodity today, leisure was the central fact of existence for a fourth-century Greek *eleutherios:* he literally had no more important continuing problem than the proper handling of *diagôgê.* Again following Ernst Koller, Richter (*Zur Wissenschaftlehre*, p. 110; "Die Beziehung," p. 183) gives the two aspects of the musical-ethical as *diagôgê*, "musikästhetisch: rechte Freude an schöner Musik," and *paideia*, "rein musikalisch: ethische Formung durch wertvolle Musik." For Koller's theory that in Book 8 of the *Politics* Aristotle adapted the thought of his lost *Protrepticus*, see Richter's comments (*Zur Wissenschaftlehre*, p. 110; also part II, section 1 generally [pp. 98-112, "Das Verhältnis zwischen Theorie und Praxis der Musik im Protreptikos"]). As Svoboda says, p. 176, *diagôgê* is not always clearly distinguished from other kinds of amusement in Aristotle's works, but its proper meaning of "spending time" or "life" occurs quite frequently. When it bears this meaning it designates in particular an agreeable life like that of a god (*Met.* 1072b13-14) or wise man (*E.N.* 1177a25-27), or life with one's friends (*E.N.* 1171b12-14); cf. Pl. *Rep.* 557e2-558a2. On *diagôgê* see further n. 54.

52. These involve one instance of usage which has aroused some debate, namely the occurrence of *theôria* in 1341a23. Bonitz (329a43), with some others, seems to give it the meaning of *spectaculum* here. Newman, preferring Susemihl's identification of the word with *akroasis*, points out that the aulete not only played but went through a series of bodily movements. This was sometimes true, as Newman's many examples show (n. on 1341b18). The examples also show, however, that these instances are concerned with auletic nomes, solo pieces which pleased audiences by their vividness and usually by their humorousness as well. It must be clear that Aristotle does not mean to refer to these exhibitions in connection with katharsis; in the *Poetics* (1461b29-31) he says that such pantomiming is resorted to by incompetent performers. Further, if we ask whether *theôria* here means "public spectacle" or "being an auditor," the first alternative does not prove attractive: *theôria* would then repeat *kairous* (22), and *dunatai* (23) seems odd on such an interpretation. Newman's choice is far more preferable, even though it may have been made on a mistaken hypothesis.

53. This conclusion seems implicit in the fact that when Aristotle dismisses the subject of katharsis he promises a fuller treatment in the *Poetics*. See Jeanmaire, pp. 316-21 (ch. vii, sec. 5: "Mimésis et Catharsis").

54. Butcher (p. 115) remarks that we owe to Aristotle "the first clear conception of fine art as a free and independent activity of the mind . . . having an end distinct from that of education or moral improvement." Pages 230-35 of his commentary show Aristotle's attitude toward the relationship between morals and aesthetics, and also the significant shift in the use of *spoudaios*. According to Vetter (*RE*, XVI, 839), in ranking *diagôgê* above paideia and play alike Aristotle takes the step from musical ethic to musical aesthetic. With this generally accepted interpretation Ernst Koller partially disagrees: he sees leisure and paideia as closely related, the one being the intelligent continuation of the other. See n. 51. Richter, who is very much Koller's disciple in these matters, states that Aristotle's concept of musical *diagôgê* has its essential affinities with the ethical valuation championed by Damon and Plato. See Winnington-Ingram in *Lustrum*, 3 (1958): 55.

55. According to Bywater (p. 156), Aristotle realized that "the dramatic performances in the theatre were not sufficiently frequent or continuous to generate a moral habit, or make a lasting impression for good or evil on character." While this is a legitimate interpretation of Aristotle's view, considerable evidence from Hellenic literature witnesses in one way or another to the high paideutic role of the dramatist. There is the added fact that the plays were in a sense continually remounted throughout the year, in public or private recitations or indeed in the memory and creative imagination of the individual Athenian, whose attention was not incessantly commanded by media of mass communication.

56. Pl. *Gorg.* 502b1-c1, *Legg.* 817a2-d8. Plato's attribution may be apparent rather than real. As Abert (p. 15) emphatically points out, the use of music for katharsis has nothing whatever to do with its use for ethical ends; Aristotle's explicit statement of the case (*Pol.* 1341b38) keeps paideia and katharsis quite separate. Aristoxenus several times mentions the view of the Pythagoreans that katharsis was a useful part of *mousikê;* for the references see Wehrli, *Die Schule des Aristoteles,* vol. II: *Aristoxenos* (Basel, 1945), pp. 11, 15, 55. It would appear that their approach did not distinguish consistently between physical healing and ethical correction, but fused the two ideas.

57. The need to expose audiences to a higher ethic: Pl. *Legg.* 659c3-4. Aristotle's proposal to suit the music to the audience: 1342a18-28.

58. On the weakness of Aristotle's historical sense see Laloy, p. 281. The aulos rejected on ethical grounds: 1341a37-39.

59. On this reading, *kai pros paideian* (20) in the first heading is bracketed as contradictory in view of the broad discussion that follows; see Newman's critical note. In the second heading I have adopted Susemihl's *tina heteran* ("some other"), *triton de*. The text as it stands, for example in the Loeb edition, does not seem to yield any acceptable sense.

60. Details to be settled by specialists and philosophers: 1341b27-32. Laloy, p. 138, notes that it was left to his pupil Theophrastus to abandon Aristotle's pointless distinctions of old-fashioned modal doctrine and to develop a theory more in keeping with the spirit of the *Poetics:* Theophrastus (*Fg.* 90) reduced music to *enthousiasmos*, *hêdonê*, and *lupê*.

61. 1341b32-41. The explanation of the term katharsis is promised for the *Poetics;* see also n. 53. On the "practical" *melê* see n. 74.

62. 1342a1-4. At this point there occurs an excursus (lines 4-16) on the psychic effects of katharsis.

63. 1342a16-28. In the *Poetics* Aristotle maintains that poetry, after its initial formative period, "broke up into two kinds according to the differing types of character in the individual poets; for the graver among them would represent noble actions, and those of noble personages; and the meaner sort the actions of the ignoble. The latter class produced invectives at first, just as others did hymns and panegyrics" (1448b24-27, tr. Bywater, slightly emended).

64. 1342a28-b17. Svoboda, p. 187, suggests that Aristotle considers Dorian a mean not only because of its character, which was midway between the threnodic and the slack Harmoniai, but also because of its middle position among "the seven ancient modes"—meaning apparently the octave-species, which certainly were not ancient.

65. 1342b17-20. The text is difficult to interpret; Jowett omits the greater part of it.

66. The criticism of Socrates' ban on the relaxed modes in paideia: 1342b23-27. See n. 73. Most MSS have *paideian* here, the reading followed by Jowett and Newman. Immisch suggested *paidian*, Rackham's reading (perhaps accidental, since it is wrongly accented) in the Loeb text. There are in fact no grounds for supposing that Plato had Socrates reject these or any other modes as unfitted for "amusement." *Paidia* is seriously discussed only in the *Laws:* there Plato holds that children, whose minds cannot yet grasp serious material, must be educated through "play and songs" (659e4-5). In the *Republic* he deals with paideia by that name;

the word must not be removed from Aristotle's reference. The approval of any suitable mode and the final statement of principles: 1342b27-34. With reference to *Poet.* 1447a28 Butcher (p. 132, n. 1) points out that the present triple classification of melodies matches "the three objects of imitative art: *êthê*, *pathê*, *praxeis*." The presence of these three mimetic objects brings with it certain difficulties, however; see Else (*Aristotle's Poetics*, pp. 35, 37), who claims that in *Poet.* 1447a22-b9 Aristotle "has established for the first time in classical Greece a partial distinction between poetry and music." See Hermann Koller, *Musik und Dichtung*, p. 163, for an attempt to schematize Aristotle's views.

67. So Newman, n. on 1341b32. His inference presumably is that "ethical" tragedy, meaning the tragedy of character, would employ *êthika melê*. This cannot be admitted, since it flatly contradicts Aristotle's assignment of the three varieties of mode in 1342a1-4. We must accept the paradox that tragedy, while sometimes ethical in the sense of dealing critically with problems of character, is not ethical within the paideutic frame of reference. In this connection it must be noted that the earlier Pythagorean and the later Aristotelian concepts of katharsis are not one and the same. The former is in this context an ethical force signifying the improvement of character, and may be termed allopathic. The latter is aesthetic, consisting in the rousing of an emotion, and may be termed homoiopathic. This distinction is made by Busse, pp. 49-50; his antithesis and terminology are taken without acknowledgment from Kahl, pp. 22-23. See also Jeanmaire, p. 319; Boyancé and Croissant (see next note) hold this same view, which he strongly endorses.

68. Jeanne Croissant (*Aristote et les mystères* [Liège and Paris, 1932], p. 61) suggests that the definition of Phrygian as having an "enthusiastic" ethos belongs to a period in which art has freed itself from its cultic origins and in which aesthetic criticism, as a corollary, has extended its investigations to include religious ceremonies.

69. Pl. *Prot.* 347c3-e1. The demoralizing influence of professional aulos music at such a party is described with great vividness by Plutarch, *Symp.* 7.5.1: "Finally the company leaped up and began to go through motions unworthy of freeborn men."

70. The benefits of choric song: Pl. *Legg.* 670d7, 813a2-3. As Harap says (p. 161), Aristotle "saw all orders of life on their own terms and dealt with them accordingly, while for Plato every aspect of life was subordinated to the transcendent ideal of philosophic vision." For the common man, and indeed for every man, this ideal was to be realized through a correct application of paideia.

71. Aristotle's correction does not accept the theory of Dorian-Phrygian with composite variants, as Newman assumes (n. on 1342a23). If it did, the acceptance would make the present chapter sweepingly contradictory and also (what is less easily tolerated) would place Aristotle in near agreement with Plato on modal ethos. By the same token, his statement makes no commitment concerning the nature and extent of musical deviations; rather it utilizes musical terms to clarify constitutional theory, which is quite another matter. One does, however, receive the impression that Aristotle himself thought of the "highly-strung" and "relaxed" modes as deviations.

72. 1342b22-23, 27-29. It is difficult to explain the *kai* of line 27 unless these modes are approved for earlier life as well.

73. The canon of feasibility: Pl. *Legg.* 785b8. It is also anticipated in the *Politics*, 1329a30-34, with phrasing that is echoed here. Sung music in old age: Pl. *Legg.* 670d5-6. Two relaxed modes banned: *Rep.* 398e10-399a3; see also n. 66. Laloy, p. 103 and n. 3, maintains that up to the time of Aristotle the nature of the intervals was implicitly determined by that of the mode; hence Aristotle can speak here and in 1290a27-28 of *suntonoi* and *aneimenai* modes with easier intonations that suit the voices of old men. For the larger presentation of Laloy's views see pp. 100-3 of his work; see also n. 35 to ch. ii.

74. Busse, p. 44, thinks it obvious that Aristotle's acceptance of Lydian and his defence of the "relaxed" modes represent doctrines of the experts mentioned earlier (1342a1). These experts, according to Busse, are almost certainly to be identified as Aristoxenus (so Bergk), Theophrastus, and Heraclides. But we are dealing here with something more than a mere "acceptance" of Lydian. The time at which Lydian came to prevail remains unknown, but its central status may be seen in Bellermann's *Anonymus*, Alypius, and Boethius: thus the first technical facts Alypius states in his *Isagoge* (3, p. 367.20-21 Jan) are that the "Tropoi and Tonoi" number fifteen and "the first of these is the Lydian." Laloy, p. 106, makes no mention of Aristoxenian influence as a possible factor in Aristotle's acceptance of Lydian; he supposes it to be a unique demonstration of his breadth of taste and cultivated nature in musical matters. Hermann Koller (*Musik und Dichtung*, pp. 162-63) so prizes symmetrical patterns that he ascribes to the *praktika melê* of 1341b34 (see n. 61) not only Lydian as the modality but also—though tentatively—the pektis as characteristic instrument.

V. THE HIBEH MUSICAL PAPYRUS; PHILODEMUS

1. The text is edited by B. P. Grenfell and A. S. Hunt, *The Hibeh Papyri* (London, 1906), pt. 1, no. 13, pp. 45-58 and fig. V. The dating is that proposed by Wilhelm Crönert, whose article "Die Hibehrede über die Musik" (*Hermes*, 44 [1909]: 503-21) has remained the principal study of this work; Untersteiner (*Sofisti*, pp. 208-11) contributes nothing new.

2. Crönert, p. 503, believes that these are the Amphictyons; the point is uncertain.

3. Aristox. *Harm.* p. 23 Mb. Crönert, p. 508, explains the reference in Plutarch, *De Audiendo* 15 (Euripides derided by a chorus member for singing an air in Mixolydian), with the conjecture that the poet used an enharmonic Mixolydian, no longer generally familiar. For the passage see Henri Weil and Théodore Reinach, eds., *Plutarque: De la musique* (Paris, 1900), p. lix. Reinach, pp. xvi-xvii, attributes the fourth-century reaction against enharmonic to the intrusion of microtones in the fifth century, and rightly states that this altered form had scarcely more than a nominal identity with the primitive enharmonic of the old libation melodies, which had large intervals. On the quarter tones as a relatively new feature, see Pl. *Rep.* 531a1-b8. Reinach in a later article ("Euripides und der Choreut," *Hermes*, 45 [1910]: 151-55) reconsiders Plutarch's story and finds the text impossible as it stands, since it equates genus with mode. His emendation changes the reference from "enharmonic" to "a mode (Harmonia)." If correct, this does away with the relevance of Aristoxenus' comment that ignorant men "vomit bile when they hear the enharmonic" (*Fg.* 74; *ap.* Plut. *Quaest. Conviv.* 7.8.1). A. J. Janssens ("De muziekaesthetische papyrus van Hibeh," *Philologische Studien*, 11 [1939-1940]: 100, n. 30) finds special significance in the fact that the Hibeh writer, contrary to traditional practice, mentions genus rather than mode.

4. One might add that the opening words call to mind those of the *Panegyricus.* Janssens (pp. 110-11) argues at some length that Crönert's stylometric findings are inconclusive and have led to premature conclusions. Although he rightly joins Crönert in denying that Hippias can have been the Hibeh writer, he believes that "the unusual talent of the writer, like the self-satisfaction with which he indicts the clumsiness of his opponents," suggests Sophistic circles or influence. His respect for the anonymous author's literary abilities is rather difficult to share: "More than the witty criticism (which is in the popular manner)," he says (p. 96), "the calculated sentence structure and the careful choice of

language allow one to surmise that this is an extraordinary talent."

5. Olympiod. *Vit. Plat.* 1. Grenfell and Hunt (pp. 45-46) tentatively assign the Hibeh discourse to Hippias of Elis, Socrates' contemporary and the opponent of Damon. This suggestion, which had originated with Friedrich Blass, found acceptance with Abert, Ruelle, Reinach, and others; see Abert, "Ein neuer musikalischer Papyrusfund," *Zeitschrift der Internationalen Musikgesellschaft,* 8 (1906): 79-83, and C.-E. Ruelle, "Le papyrus musical de Hibeh," *RPh,* 31 (1907): 235-40. Setting aside Crönert's arguments for a date around 390, we must acknowledge that Plato shows Hippias to have been interested in music and also represents him as about to speak at the Olympic games; this is the sum of the evidence. The countering arguments seem too weighty to be withstood. Hippias was not argumentative by nature, and his competitive appearances (cf. Pl. *Hipp. Min.* 364a8) consisted in using his ability and knowledge to strive continually for novelty (Xen. *Mem.* 4.4.6). It may also be suggested—a point not made by Crönert—that Hippias' versatility and insistence on being self-sufficient hardly accord with a violent attack on persons who go "outside their proper fields."

6. A detailed defense of this interpretation will be found in Appendix C, which also deals with *psaltêriou* in line 31.

7. This is the Sophistic and Isocratean σύγκρισις: see Richter, *Zur Wissenschaftlehre,* p. 41 and n. 2, and on the Hibeh diatribe generally pp. 40-42. In "Die Beziehung," p. 183, he finds the basis for the opposition between theory and practice in Plato's Theory of Ideas, which led to the rejection of experimental tuning methods along with all other kinds of practical empirical activity. (The parallel with Plato's well-known passage in the *Republic* [531] is striking, as Professor Reese has pointed out to me.) This division, however, is Pythagorean and pre-Platonic. The two schools of harmonicists are well distinguished by Richter elsewhere ("Platons Stellung," p. 198). His division separates the members of the technically oriented group, busying themselves with tonal structure, from those with musical-ethical interests, pursuing stylistic criticism and hermeneutics; the latter belonged to the Damonian school. Rudolf Schäfke has presented Damon as a founder of aesthetic doctrine in a work which I have not been able to consult, *Geschichte der Musikästhetik* (Berlin, 1934), pp. 93ff. See Richter, "Platons Stellung," p. 198, n. 13.

8. Philod. *Mus.* 3.77.13-17, p. 55 Kemke; cf. 1.13.10-12, p. 7 K., 4.24.9-35, pp. 92-93 K.

9. Theon Sm., pp. 54-56 Hiller. So late an opinion as that of Theon cannot be accepted without question as valid for any part of the Hellenic period. Laloy, p. 277, reasonably contends that

the two very closely related *pukna* or mobile inner notes of the enharmonic tetrachord exerted a strong pull toward the tonic. It is difficult, on the other hand, to see any grounds for his attendant claim that "enharmonic music had a clear-cut, sinewy quality of motion (*une allure décidée, nerveuse*) that was to a Hellene's liking." Nevertheless, the primacy of the enharmonic genus and the late acceptance of diatonic, at least by the specialists (and this distinction could have importance), is well established.

10. Had mere programmatic musical association been the fact underlying the reference to laurel and ivy, one would not find the division of melodies generally into two categories. Janssens, p. 95, sees not only an Apolline-Dionysiac contrast as probable here, but an added contrast between traditional Greek and contemporary Oriental art. This would seem to be a case of reading too much into the text. As for the aptness and importance of what is symbolized, we shall find sufficient warrant in the words of Curt Sachs (*Vergleichende Musikwissenschaft: Musik der Fremdkulturen*, p. 51): "Physiologisch betrachtet, gibt es zwei Arten musikalischer Wirkung: Erregung, Aufpeitschung die eine, Beruhigung, Bändigung die andere. Jene atemraubend, pulsbeschleunigend und die motorischen Nerven reizend, diese herabsetzend und ausgleichend." In the classical frame of reference, he goes on to point out, this is the Dionysiac-Apolline antithesis. See also n. 11 to ch. i. On the mimetic excellence of music as its "rightness" see Pl. *Legg.* 670c2-671a1, 667d5-668b7; cf. 655c8-d3, 700d4-e4.

11. The mention of incoherence seems to prove this sufficiently. Janssens, however, is convinced that the harmonicists themselves are attacked: "the presentation obviously is caricaturized, and ridicule forms its chief weapon" (p. 96). It is true at least that such crudeness could and did characterize Sophistic rhetoric at times. Janssens ably presents an extended treatment (esp. pp. 96-97) of the harmonicist school, although he interweaves conjecture closely with fact. He had intended (p. 102) to develop in subsequent articles the view that musical-ethical doctrines in the *Republic* were meant partly as a reply (*repliek*) to Damon's theories, which he believes met with opposition. It is greatly to be regretted that these articles never were written. Richter (*Zur Wissenschaftlehre*, p. 42) holds that the persons addressed in the Hibeh diatribe cannot be termed *harmonikoi* in the accepted sense of that term, and that they are treated as thoroughgoing dilettantes. While the main view here is sound, dilettantism may be too weak an indictment, considering the tone of the speech. Pöhlmann, p. 2, takes lines 7ff as showing how slight was the connection, even as early as the fourth century, between the classicism of music theory and

the actual practice of music; but the circumstances here do not offer a basis solid enough to bear the weight of generalizations. In the same way, Richter ("Platons Stellung," p. 198) is not persuasive when he argues that Damon's followers may be under attack here for inquiries thought to be outside the proper province of the harmonicist. Carlo del Grande (*Filologia minore*, p. 353) suggests that the Hibeh diatribe is the work of a writer "che respira nell' aura etica di Damone" but not of Damon himself. With the last point, at any rate, there certainly can be no quarrel. According to Wilhelm Nestle (*Vom Mythos zum Logos* [Stuttgart, 1940], p. 437) the Hibeh writer is obviously a professional musician who here takes exception to Sophistic discourses on his art; and these discourses must have touched upon the Damonian theory of ethos that this writer so decisively rejects. I have not seen the study by Ernst Graf, *Der Kampf um die Musik im klassischen Altertum* (Gymnasium-Programm, Quedlinburg, 1907).

12. The whole tone is that of a speech intended for delivery: it is not that of a literary production in the guise of an oration or dialogue, such as many suppose Damon's lost speech to have been. See Appendix D. Busse (p. 38, n. 2) suggests that the form of address "O men of Hellas" shows the speech to be a dig at Damon himself: its author appeals not merely to the Areopagites but to all the Greeks. Whatever may lie behind the opening words, it seems clear for reasons already stated that the Hibeh diatribe as a whole cannot be directed against Damon. According to Busse, Damon in his Areopagitic address systematized Pythagorean musical theory and set forth the influences of the various genera on the soul; this is fantasy.

13. The text is that of Johannes Kemke's Teubner edition, *Philodemus de musica librorum quae exstant* (Leipzig, 1884). This is supplemented by the readings of Theodor Gomperz, *Zu Philodem's Büchern von der Musik: ein kritischer Beitrag* (Vienna, 1885), and of D. A. van Krevelen, *Philodemus—De Muziek: Met Vertaling en Commentaar* (diss. Amsterdam; Hilversum, 1939). Readings other than those of Kemke are identified. No English translation of the *De Musica* has been published; all versions given here are mine. A brief general outline, almost devoid of any discussion, is provided by Abert (*Lehre*, pp. 28-32); my own treatment is wholly independent. See also Otto Luschnat, *Zum Text von Philodems Schrift De Musica* (Berlin, 1953). Heinrich von Arnim, ed., *Stoicorum Veterum Fragmenta* (Leipzig, 1905), I, 221-35, reprints from Kemke the passages which he takes as coming from the lost treatise on music by Philodemus' opponent, the Stoic Diogenes Babylonius.

14. 1.19.1-9, p. 10 Kemke. Pseudo-Plutarch (*Mus.* 32, p. 126.28-33 L., p. 26.21-27 Z.) speaks of the ancient musical paideia of these same three peoples. In their systems of instruction, he says, one mode, or a few at most, served "to correct manners." Both references probably derive from the lost treatise of Heraclides Ponticus; Laloy, p. 166, for no evident reason attributes the material in pseudo-Plutarch to Aristoxenus.

15. Other items are more commonplace, such as the note on Argive wrestling to the sound of the aulos (1.26.3-5, p. 14 K.). Disappearance of the chorus from comedy and tragedy alike is reflected in the opinion that "we are none the worse off for dancing being taken out of dramatic performances" (4.7.3-6, p. 70 K.). The process was gradual: its end cannot be marked with certainty but is probably to be placed in the third century. Plato Comicus (*Fg.* 130 Kock [Edmonds, *Fragments*, I, 530-31]; *ap.* Athen. 628e), writing probably around the end of the fifth century, already laments the passing from the stage of any dancing worth looking at. Of all the extant comedies of Plautus only the *Rudens* has a chorus, and this appears very briefly. By Horace's time singers performed arias from tragedy; the plays were no longer presented in full. See the discussion of Hor. *Serm.* 1.3.7-8 by Friedrich Marx ("Musik aus der griechischen Tragödie," *RhM*, 82 [1933]: 230-46), who cites the present passage in Philodemus as expanded through Dio of Prusa (19.5.2, p. 258 Arn.).

16. Music first approved and then rejected: 4.11.14, p. 75 K. Aristotle on aulos playing: *Pol.* 1341a26-28; explained *ibid.*, 28-39.

17. Music as profitless: 4.11.24-25, p. 76 K. The parallel with divination: 4.10.27-43, p. 75 K.

18. Music a result of sound: 4.14.15-18, p. 79 K.; see Pöhlmann, p. 18. Enharmonic and chromatic as irrational: 4.2.15-19, pp. 63-64 K. Neubecker (pp. 18-19) believes that in a lost section of Book 1, between 1.21 and 1.22, Diogenes must have referred to the discrepancies in various characterizations of generic ethos, using these reactions as examples of the difference in the ethical effects of music. Philodemus now counters from the Epicurean point of view.

19. Democritus on the origins of music: 4.36.29-39, p. 108 K. (Diels 68B144). Polybius, 4.21.1, argues that this was not true of the ancient Arcadians. Democritus on musical paideia inculcating reverence: Diels 68B179. Neubecker (p. 81) justly observes that we must not simply assume Democritus rejected the possibility of music's ethical powers; had this been the case, Philodemus certainly would not have missed the chance to cite him as a supporting witness. She takes Democritus as seemingly the first to treat *ta*

mousika as a separate branch of study, and notes that one of his definitions of the soul's happiness is *harmonia* (p. 80 and n. 5; Diels 68A167). One wonders whether there is sufficient evidence to give Democritus this status. Plato's version: *Rep.* 373b2-c1, esp. b6 Richter (*Zur Wissenschaftlehre,* pp. 19, 109) believes that this Democritean thesis powerfully influenced both Plato and Aristotle. The influence is indeed clear, but there does not seem to be any evidence that it was extensive. On superfluity see *contra* Polyb. 4.21.1.

20. The text has τὰ λελεγμένα. Modal mimesis of tones and accents: Pl. *Rep.* 399a5-c4.

21. 4.38.19-25, p. 110 K. The Hibeh writer criticizes unfairly, but Aristotle's later comments seem without prejudice.

22. Philosophers and musical expertise: 3.48.2-4, p. 41 K. Arguments from celestial mechanics rejected: 4.30.9-19, p. 100 K. Lack of originality in the ancient theorists: 4.31.13-24, p. 101 K. To designate musical theory Plato uses *theôria,* seemingly with a play on the two senses of the word. Ethical meaning is even more vigorously denied to the "harmony of the spheres" by Sextus Empiricus (*Contra Math.* 6.37).

23. Intensification and moderation: 1.22.12-14, p. 12 K. The variety of terms in Plato and Aristotle suggests that usage had not yet become fixed in this regard. Verbal ambiguities: 3.8.1-6, p. 23 K. Instances of these: 3.22.7-20, p. 30 K.

24. Plato's attack on the poet-composers: *Legg.* 669b5-e6, reproduced in 1.1.2-37, p. 1 K. The Muse and order: 1.2.6-7, p. 3 K. The phrases, as restored, are *tês eutaktou mousês, tês de ataktou;* the corresponding nouns are *eutaxia* and *ataxia.*

25. Ethos in purely instrumental music: 4.26.14-27, p. 95 K. With regard to the final words, I follow van Krevelen (*machomenou*) in line 26; Kemke's reading will give no proper sense.

26. 3.23.1-12, p. 31 K.; 4.2.19-43, p. 64 K.

27. Protagoras' dictum: Pl. *Prot.* 326b5-6. Music as profiting the whole of life: 1.32.13-15, p. 19 K. Its powers to create a rhythmic and harmonious disposition: 1.13.2-4, p. 7 K. Diogenes' arguments and their rebuttal: 4.10.2-25, pp. 74-75 K.

28. 1.18.6-13, pp. 9-10 K. Edmonds (*Lyra Graeca,* III, 366-67) translates the passage as follows: "If we compare the dithyrambic styles of Pindar and Philoxenus we shall find a great difference in the characters presented but an identity of style." The relevant ancient evidence, which may be viewed most conveniently in Edmonds' own work, declares with one voice that the "styles" were anything but identical (see ps.-Plut. *Mus.* 31, p. 126.3-16 L., pp. 25.14-26.6 Z.). Actually Philodemus' context makes it quite clear that *tropos* has its technical musical sense here and indicates with

reasonable clearness that the *êthê* are not "characters" but types of ethos. The general problem of definition involved here is notably difficult. Plutarch (*De Ei apud Delphos* 10, p. 475 Didot; *An seni* 18, p. 968 Didot) speaks of Harmonia, Tropos, and Tonos as meaning the same thing. This identity is not easy to accept for the Hellenic period. Schäfke (pp. 82-83; cf. p. 173, n. 6, and p. 290, n. 6) makes a detailed distinction, taking Tropos as a medial concept between the ethical-musical phenomenon of the Harmonia and the purely musical phenomenon of the Tonos. It was after Damon, as he believes, that the latter became the important form; we have no reference to it from the early period. The confusion of terms is concisely discussed by Ingemar Düring in "Greek Music . . ." (*Journal of World History*, 3 [1956]: 311). Any statement on the whole matter contains some considerable element of conjecture.

29. 1.13.9-10, p. 7 K., as restored by Gomperz; cf. 1.13.4-8. Damon is here given the title of *mousikos;* so Aristoxenus, *Fg.* 69a-70 Wehrli, exalts the ideal of the *mousikos* as against the specialization of the *harmonikos* (Richter, *Zur Wissenschaftlehre*, p. 50 and n. 1).

30. 4.32.30-31, p. 103 K. Aristides discusses in detail the masculine and feminine characteristics of vowels and consonants, *Mus.* 2.13-14, pp. 78-80 W., pp. 92-95 Mb. There is a general reference in Plato (*Crat.* 424b8-c3) to specialists who work from individual letters through syllables to the rhythms; Schäfke takes Damon as an example of this school, but we must note that Plato mentions no one by name.

31. Damon quoted: 3.77.13-17, p. 55 K.; in partial form, 1.13.10-12, p. 7 K. Justice not related to music: 4.24.9-35, pp. 92-93 K. Lasserre (pp. 57-58, 73) conjectures references to Damon in several other passages.

32. Innovation forbidden: 1.18.1-6, p. 9 K.; 4-5 *suppl.* Gomperz. See Pl. *Legg.* 665, 669, 670, 700, 800, 803. Proper music as primarily honoring the gods: 1.23.8-13, p. 13 K. The true Platonic attitude can be seen in the way he introduces the subject of music in the *Laws.* His treatment comes near the beginning of Book 2 (653c9-d5), but after a detailed definition of paideia which contains many of his most important beliefs on the subject (653a5-c3). The discussion itself does not give the paideutic element a place of secondary importance for music: it has instead a synoptic quality that typifies Plato's whole approach to the whole subject.

33. The essential nature of music attacked: 4.25.3-12, pp. 93-94 K. "Things that one can see" is not a satisfactory rendering: as both Gomperz and van Krevelen have pointed out, *opseis* is meaningless here. The type of reference intended, however, is not difficult to

grasp. Cf. the distinction drawn between *opsis* and *mousikê* in 1.16.7-13, pp. 8-9 K., and see Lasserre, p. 87. Music as naturally unrestrained: 4.13.28-30, pp. 78-79 K. For *enamillos einai* van Krevelen gives *te wedijveren*, "rival, strive to outdo." This does not fit the present context. Threnodies as intensifying grief: 4.6.13-24, p. 69 K.

34. The theory of music's innate power: 1.27.7-9, p. 15 K. Its influence argued by analogy: 3.39.3-8, p. 38 K. Rebuttal: *ibid.*, 8-12. Plotinus, on the other hand, contends that "the effect of a melody on the soul is in some manner inevitable, precisely because of—not in spite of—the fact that music works upon the soul when it is in a state of nature and uninfluenced by reason" (in Combarieu, *La musique et la magie*, p. 140, n. 1). It should be remarked that when Philodemus calls music "irrational" he does not mean that it is vague. In his *Rhetoric* (35) he ranks music as an exact science characterized by a completely rigorous method and yielding precise results. The effect of music on the reason: 4.9.40-42, p. 74 K.

35. 4.3.2-42, pp. 64-66 K. "Artisans" is clearly the meaning in 4.5.26-27, p. 68 K. Van Krevelen (p. 139) restores 41-42 to give *di' harmoniôn estin dêmiourgein,* "it is (not) possible by means of the modes to produce the result that . . ."; he cites 41 as von Arnim's restoration. This meaning, however, does not seem to be attested for the verb. The comparison with cookery follows a long tradition. See Ar. *Ach.* 1015, Pl. *Rep.* 332c12, Arist. *Pol.* 1255b25-26, *E.N.* 1153a26; see also n. 37 and n. 28 to ch. iv.

36. Van Krevelen (p. xxiii) supposes Diogenes to have conceded that music cannot imitate anything. Neubecker does not directly acknowledge the difficulty, but in an attempt to get around it she argues (p. 93) that the present passage "obviously entails" a view of mimesis "in the narrow sense, somewhat as we now speak of program music." On the preceding page, however, she denies Hermann Koller's view of mimesis with the imitative element completely eliminated from the original concept. It is disproved, so she claims, by the occurrence of the terms for "likeness" in Aristotle (*Pol.* 1340a18), the Damonian school (*ap.* A.Q. 2.14, p. 80 W., 95 Mb.), and Philodemus (the present passage) with the same sense as mimesis. Her interpretation of the remarks under discussion is as follows (p. 20): "From 4.3.26-35 we conclude that Diogenes championed the view that music, while it does not imitatively express characteristics, is nevertheless thoroughly capable of making clear (?)whole ethical qualities as such." In the original the last phrase is *sämtliche sittlichen Qualitäten als solche zu verdeutlichen;* it seems to me that *als solche* misrepresents Philodemus' text. On the whole question of mimesis and assimila-

tion or "likeness" as divided between Plato and Damon respectively, see Else's article, especially pp. 85-87; see also n. 13 to ch. ii and n. 36 to ch. iv.

37. Neubecker (p. 21) very justly observes that this comparison between music and cookery shows what Philodemus thought of the former: "For him it stood on just the same level as the arts that minister to the other senses, e.g., cookery, which works upon our sense of taste." Here, as she remarks later (p. 32), he tacitly bases himself on the older Greek estimate of the artist, an attitude which had been generally overcome in the Hellenistic period. It will be noted that the attempt to ridicule musical ethos by means of this analogy is one which we have already seen (above, n. 28 to ch. iv) in Aristotle's acknowledgment of opposition views. See n. 35.

38. Melody as unrelated to impulse and choice: 4.7.36-41, p. 71 K. Music as affecting neither the mind nor the body: 4.8.36-9.15, pp. 72-73 K.

39. In 4.7.36-41, p. 71 K. (se n. 38), various expressions—37 *horman*, 38 *proaireisthai*, 41 *proairesin*—echo the *Nicomachean Ethics*.

40. On the opposition view see above, p. 159 and n. 27. Philodemus' counterarguments: 4.4.15-27, pp. 66-67 K. The Greeks' neglect of music explained: 4.11.18-22, p. 76 K.

41. 4.9.15-38, pp. 73-74 K.

42. Music as a thing for dinner parties: 4.11.1-5, p. 75 K. Music's only effect is to charm us, says Sextus Empiricus in a comparable view (*Contra Math.* 6.28; on melodic ethos see 6.49). Pindar cited: 4.12.3-4, p. 76 K. = *Fg.* 124c Schroeder, 111 Bowra. The evidence from Homer not cited: *Od.* 1.152, cf. 21.430. Philodemus' use of Homer: 4.16.16-21, p. 82 K.

43. The importance of liking the good: 3.53.11-15, p. 44 K. The claim that temperateness, not music, reveals propriety: 3.11.7-13, p. 25 K. Gentleness effected by reason and not by music: 3.27.8-14, p. 33 K.

44. Music as unrelated to reverence: 4.12.11-21, p. 77 K. The reference in "his" is perhaps to Diogenes. Gomperz' evidence: p. 15, on 3.16.9-15, p. 28 K. (Ar. *Ran.* 1021).

45. Bad habits appear because they actually exist: 1.9.1-8, p. 6 K. The causes of our habits are inward: 1.15.3-6, p. 8 K.

46. Psychic analysis and music: 3.23.1-6, p. 31 K. Symmetry in the soul: 3.26.9-12, p. 32 K.

47. Music as mere listening pleasure: see above, p. 160. Erotic poetry effective solely through the text: 4.5.42-6.5, pp. 68-69 K. The power of ideas in Ibycus and Anacreon: 4.14.4-13, p. 79 K. Dancing dismissed as not morally constructive: 4.7.3-8, p. 70 K.

48. Vetter (*RE*, XVI, 857), discussing the Sirens' song and the song of Circe in Homer, points out that they have nothing to do either with the ethically good or, in the strict sense, with the aesthetically beautiful. "They represent instead," he says, "something intellectually injurious (*etwas Sehrendes*, unless this is a misprint for *Sehnendes*), an entrancing marvel . . . This elemental naively felt music finds in Homer a pregnantly poetic issuance." Vetter maintains that Philodemus laid down many of his basic principles—notably that of the effect of music in virtue of the poetic text and its content of thought and feeling—in conscious opposition to musical ethic, and so in a one-sided and excessive manner.

49. Supposed musical analogies with celestial phenomena: 4.30.19-24, p. 100 K. The neo-Pythagorean approach to music: E. J. Dent, in *Oxford History of Music*, Introd. Vol., p. 185; also Werner, esp. pp. 393-97.

50. Philodemus on ethos in music: 3.21.1-3, p. 30 K., as tentatively restored by Gomperz, p. 16. In the *Meno* Plato states at some length his reasons for thus using *theios:* see 99b1-d9, esp. c3-9; d3 is relevant to the present passage.

51. Types of character: 1.32.4-5, p. 19 K. Change of emotion and character not possible through music: 3.54.6-9, p. 44 K.; see Gomperz, pp. 30-31. On the melodies of Olympus, cf. Arist. *Pol.* 1340a8-12.

52. Timotheus: 4.13.35-38, p. 79 K. Regarding modal shifts one notes a similar phenomenon in the case of Indian and Arab music. On the medieval Arab theorists' discussions of the actual procedures involved, see H. G. Farmer, *Sa'adyah Gaon on the Influence of Music* (London, 1948), pp. 87-89. Many references to ethos occur throughout this work.

53. Two statements on the effect of music: 1.22.4-6, p. 12 K.; 4.2.9-15, p. 63 K. Neubecker (pp. 18-19, 23, 86, 93) emphasizes this hitherto overlooked point concerning individualized ethos and presents a convincing case for it. She finds it confirmed by Hermann Koller's very different approach in *Die Mimesis in der Antike*, a work which she criticizes on many other points. This (as Professor Winnington-Ingram has reminded me) is the point of view adopted by Aristides Quintilianus, Book 2, in his musical psychotherapy: by trial and error you will find the right kind of music for treating your subject, and so on. See p. 41.

54. Gomperz, p. 28, on Arist. *Pol.* 1340b17-18 and Phld. *Po.* 2.47 (not in the *De Musica*). Perhaps Philodemus has in mind the lulling effect of music when he says (1.32.39-44, p. 20 K.): "The Carians, whenever a commotion arises in their public gatherings,

will start up some of the sweetest of their songs; then choral singing will follow, and finally an (?)untroubled calm." (I conjecture *ataraxias* for *a . . . . . . as*, 44-45.) Books 1 and 2 of the *De Musica* are so fragmentary that one cannot be certain the example of the Carians is taken seriously. Yet the portion immediately following, at least, gives one no reason to think otherwise, and the evidence certainly supplements Philodemus' belief that we are innately responsive to music.

55. Pl. *Legg.* 790d5-e4, esp. e1-2. On Philodemus' fondness for empirical proofs see P. H. and E. A. De Lacy, *Philodemus: On Methods of Inference* (Lancaster, 1941), p. vi.

56. See n. 32.

57. 4.33.34-35, p. 104 K.

58. 4.12.23-40, pp. 77-78 K.

59. 3.50.6-11, p. 43 K. Neubecker (pp. 23-24) believes there is a suggestion in 1.23.19 that Diogenes had referred to the connection of music with paideia. It is possible, even probable, that he did so; but an incomplete prepositional phrase is a rather fragmentary foot from which to reconstruct even so likely a Hercules.

60. See Abert, *Lehre*, p. vi, and Neubecker, p. 91, on the importance of Philodemus.

INDEX OF PASSAGES

INDEX OF SUBJECTS

INDEX OF PASSAGES

[For fragments of Greek lyric poetry, Oxford or Teubner texts have regularly been used; equivalents in other systems of numeration are given in the notes.]

INDEX OF PASSAGES

INDEX OF PASSAGES

INDEX OF PASSAGES

INDEX OF PASSAGES

INDEX OF SUBJECTS

INDEX OF SUBJECTS